Learning pandas

Get to grips with pandas—a versatile
and high-performance Python library for
data manipulation, analysis, and discovery

Michael Heydt

[PACKT] open source*
PUBLISHING   community experience distilled

BIRMINGHAM - MUMBAI

Learning pandas

First published: April 2015

Production reference: 1090415

Published by Packt Publishing Ltd.
Livery Place
35 Livery Street
Birmingham B3 2PB, UK.

ISBN 978-1-78398-512-8

www.packtpub.com

Credits

Author
Michael Heydt

Reviewers
Bill Chambers
S. Shelly Jang
Arun Karunagath Rajeevan
Daniel Velkov
Adrian Wan

Commissioning Editor
Kartikey Pandey

Acquisition Editor
Neha Nagwekar

Content Development Editor
Akshay Nair

Technical Editors
Shashank Desai
Chinmay Puranik

Copy Editors
Roshni Banerjee
Pranjali Chury
Stuti Srivastava

Project Coordinator
Mary Alex

Proofreaders
Simran Bhogal
Paul Hindle
Linda Morris
Christopher Smith

Indexer
Monica Ajmera Mehta

Graphics
Sheetal Aute

Production Coordinator
Arvindkumar Gupta

Cover Work
Arvindkumar Gupta

About the Author

Michael Heydt is an independent consultant, educator, and trainer with nearly 30 years of professional software development experience, during which he focused on agile software design and implementation using advanced technologies in multiple verticals, including media, finance, energy, and healthcare. He holds an MS degree in mathematics and computer science from Drexel University and an executive master's of technology management degree from the University of Pennsylvania's School of Engineering and Wharton Business School. His studies and research have focused on technology management, software engineering, entrepreneurship, information retrieval, data sciences, and computational finance. Since 2005, he has been specializing in building energy and financial trading systems for major investment banks on Wall Street and for several global energy trading companies, utilizing .NET, C#, WPF, TPL, DataFlow, Python, R, Mono, iOS, and Android. His current interests include creating seamless applications using desktop, mobile, and wearable technologies, which utilize high concurrency, high availability, real-time data analytics, augmented and virtual reality, cloud services, messaging, computer vision, natural user interfaces, and software-defined networks. He is the author of numerous technology articles, papers, and books (`Instant Lucene.NET`, `Learning pandas`). He is a frequent speaker at .NET users' groups and various mobile and cloud conferences, and he regularly delivers webinars on advanced technologies.

About the Reviewers

Bill Chambers is a Python developer and data scientist currently pursuing a master of information management and systems degree at the UC Berkeley School of Information. Previously, he focused on data architecture and systems using marketing, sales, and customer analytics data. Bill is passionate about delivering actionable insights and innovative solutions using data.

You can find more information about him at http://www.billchambers.me.

S. Shelly Jang received her PhD degree in electrical engineering from the University of Washington and a master's degree in chemical and biological engineering from the University of British Columbia in 2014 and 2009, respectively. She was an Insight Data Science fellow in 2014. During her tenure, she built a web app that recommends crowd-verified treatment options for various medical conditions. She is currently a senior data scientist at AT&T Big Data. Exploring complex, large-scale data sets to build models and derive insights is just a part of her job.

In her free time, she participates in the Quantified Self community, sharing her insights on personal analytics and self-hacking.

Arun Karunagath Rajeevan is a senior consultant (products) in an exciting start-up, working as an architect and coder, and is a polyglot. He is currently involved in developing the best quality management suite in the supply chain management category.

Apart from this, he has experience in healthcare and multimedia (embedded) domains. When he is not working, he loves to travel and listen to music.

Daniel Velkov is a software engineer based in San Francisco, who has more than 10 years of programming experience. His biggest professional accomplishment was designing and implementing the search stack for MyLife.com—one of the major social websites in the US. Nowadays, he works on making Google search better. Besides Python and search, he has worked on several machine learning and data analysis-oriented projects. When he is not coding, he enjoys skiing, riding motorcycles, and exploring the Californian outdoors.

Adrian Wan is a physics and computer science major at Swarthmore College. After he graduates, he will be working at Nest, a Google company, as a software engineer and data scientist. His passion lies at the intersection of his two disciplines, where elegant mathematical models and explanations of real-life phenomena are brought to life and probed deeply with efficient, clean, and powerful code. He greatly enjoyed contributing to this book and hopes that you will be able to appreciate the power that pandas brings to Python.

You can find out more about him at `http://awan1.github.io`.

www.PacktPub.com

Support files, eBooks, discount offers, and more

For support files and downloads related to your book, please visit www.PacktPub.com.

Did you know that Packt offers eBook versions of every book published, with PDF and ePub files available? You can upgrade to the eBook version at www.PacktPub.com and as a print book customer, you are entitled to a discount on the eBook copy. Get in touch with us at service@packtpub.com for more details.

At www.PacktPub.com, you can also read a collection of free technical articles, sign up for a range of free newsletters and receive exclusive discounts and offers on Packt books and eBooks.

https://www2.packtpub.com/books/subscription/packtlib

Do you need instant solutions to your IT questions? PacktLib is Packt's online digital book library. Here, you can search, access, and read Packt's entire library of books.

Why subscribe?

- Fully searchable across every book published by Packt
- Copy and paste, print, and bookmark content
- On demand and accessible via a web browser

Free access for Packt account holders

If you have an account with Packt at www.PacktPub.com, you can use this to access PacktLib today and view 9 entirely free books. Simply use your login credentials for immediate access.

Table of Contents

Preface

This book is about learning to use pandas, an open source library for Python, which was created to enable Python to easily manipulate and perform powerful statistical and mathematical analyses on tabular and multidimensional datasets. The design of pandas and its power combined with the familiarity of Python have created explosive growth in its usage over the last several years, particularly among financial firms as well as those simply looking for practical tools for statistical and data analysis.

While there exist many excellent examples of using pandas to solve many domain-specific problems, it can be difficult to find a cohesive set of examples in a form that allows one to effectively learn and apply the features of pandas. The information required to learn practical skills in using pandas is distributed across many websites, slide shares, and videos, and is generally not in a form that gives an integrated guide to all of the features with practical examples in an easy-to-understand and applicable fashion.

This book is therefore intended to be a go-to reference for learning pandas. It will take you all the way from installation, through to creating one- and two-dimensional indexed data structures, to grouping data and slicing-and-dicing them, with common analyses used to demonstrate derivation of useful results. This will include the loading and saving of data from resources that are local and Internet-based and creating effective data visualizations that provide instant ability to visually realize insights into the meaning previously hidden within complex data.

What this book covers

Chapter 1, A Tour of pandas, is a hands-on introduction to the key features of pandas. It will give you a broad overview of the types of data tasks that can be performed with pandas. This chapter will set the groundwork for learning as all concepts introduced in this chapter will be expanded upon in subsequent chapters.

Chapter 2, Installing pandas, will show you how to install Anaconda Python and pandas on Windows, OS X, and Linux. This chapter also covers using the conda package manager to upgrade pandas and its dependent libraries to the most recent version.

Chapter 3, NumPy for pandas, will introduce you to concepts in NumPy, particularly NumPy arrays, which are core for understanding the pandas Series and DataFrame objects.

Chapter 4, The pandas Series Object, covers the pandas Series object and how it expands upon the functionality of the NumPy array to provide richer representation and manipulation of sequences of data through the use of high-performance indexes.

Chapter 5, The pandas DataFrame Object, introduces the primary data structure of pandas, the DataFrame object, and how it forms a two-dimensional representation of tabular data by aligning multiple Series objects along a common index to provide seamless access and manipulation across elements in multiple series that are related by a common index label.

Chapter 6, Accessing Data, shows how data can be loaded and saved from external sources into both Series and DataFrame objects. You will learn how to access data from multiple sources such as files, HTTP servers, database systems, and web services, as well as how to process data in CSV, HTML, and JSON formats.

Chapter 7, Tidying Up Your Data, instructs you on how to use the various tools provided by pandas for managing dirty and missing data.

Chapter 8, Combining and Reshaping Data, covers various techniques for combining, splitting, joining, and merging data located in multiple pandas objects, and then demonstrates how to reshape data using concepts such as pivots, stacking, and melting.

Chapter 9, Grouping and Aggregating Data, focuses on how to use pandas to group data to enable you to perform aggregate operations on grouped data to assist in deriving analytic results.

Chapter 10, Time-series Data, will instruct you on how to use pandas to represent sequences of information that is indexed by the progression of time. This chapter will first cover how pandas represents dates and time, as well as concepts such as periods, frequencies, time zones, and calendars. The focus then shifts to time-series data and various operations such as shifting, lagging, resampling, and moving window operations.

Chapter 11, Visualization, dives into the integration of pandas with matplotlib to visualize pandas data. This chapter will demonstrate how to represent and present many common statistical and financial data visualizations, including bar charts, histograms, scatter plots, area plots, density plots, and heat maps.

Chapter 12, Applications to Finance, brings together everything learned through the previous chapters with practical examples of using pandas to obtain, manipulate, analyze, and visualize stock data.

What you need for this book

This book assumes some familiarity with programming concepts, but those without programming experience, or specifically Python programming experience, will be comfortable with the examples as they focus on pandas constructs more than Python or programming. The examples are based on Anaconda Python 2.7 and pandas 0.15.1. If you do not have either installed, guidance will be given in *Chapter 2, Installing pandas*, on installing both on Windows, OS X, and Ubuntu systems. For those not interested in installing any software, instructions are also given on using the Warkari.io online Python data analysis service.

Who this book is for

If you are looking to get into data science and want to learn how to use the Python programming language for data analysis instead of other domain-specific data science tools such as R, then this book is for you. If you have used other data science packages and want to learn how to apply that knowledge to Python, then this book is also for you. Alternately, if you want to learn an additional tool or start with data science to enhance your career, then this book is for you.

Conventions

In this book, you will find a number of styles of text that distinguish between different kinds of information. Here are some examples of these styles, and an explanation of their meaning.

Code words in text are shown as follows: "This information can be easily imported into `DataFrame` using the `pd.read_csv()` function as follows."

Any command-line / IPython input or output is written as follows:

```
In [1]:
    # import numpy and pandas, and DataFrame / Series
    import numpy as np
    import pandas as pd
    from pandas import DataFrame, Series
```

New terms and **important words** are shown in bold. Words that you see on the screen, in menus or dialog boxes for example, appear in the text like this: "Clicking on the **New Notebook** button will present you with a notebook where you can start entering your pandas code."

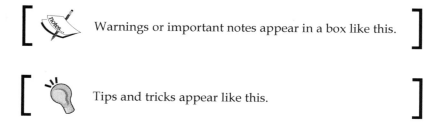

Warnings or important notes appear in a box like this.

Tips and tricks appear like this.

Reader feedback

Feedback from our readers is always welcome. Let us know what you think about this book—what you liked or may have disliked. Reader feedback is important for us to develop titles that you really get the most out of.

To send us general feedback, simply send an e-mail to feedback@packtpub.com, and mention the book title through the subject of your message.

If there is a topic that you have expertise in and you are interested in either writing or contributing to a book, see our author guide on www.packtpub.com/authors.

Customer support

Now that you are the proud owner of a Packt book, we have a number of things to help you to get the most from your purchase.

Downloading the example code

You can download the example code files for all Packt books you have purchased from your account at http://www.packtpub.com. If you purchased this book elsewhere, you can visit http://www.packtpub.com/support and register to have the files e-mailed directly to you. The code examples in the book are also publicly available on Wakari.io at https://wakari.io/sharing/bundle/LearningPandas/LearningPandas_Index.

 Although great efforts are taken to use data that will reproduce the same output when you execute the samples, there is a small set of code that uses current data and hence the result of running those samples may vary from what is published in this book. These include In [39]: and In [40]: in *Chapter 1, A Tour of pandas*, which uses the data of the last three months of Google stock, as well as a small number of samples used in the later chapters that demonstrate the usage of date offsets centered on the current date.

Downloading the color images of this book

We also provide you with a PDF file that has color images of the screenshots/diagrams used in this book. The color images will help you better understand the changes in the output. You can download this file from https://www.packtpub.com/sites/default/files/downloads/5128OS_ColoredImages.pdf.

Errata

Although we have taken every care to ensure the accuracy of our content, mistakes do happen. If you find a mistake in one of our books — maybe a mistake in the text or the code — we would be grateful if you would report this to us. By doing so, you can save other readers from frustration and help us improve subsequent versions of this book. If you find any errata, please report them by visiting http://www.packtpub.com/support, selecting your book, clicking on the **errata submission form** link, and entering the details of your errata. Once your errata are verified, your submission will be accepted and the errata will be uploaded to our website, or added to any list of existing errata, under the Errata section of that title.

Piracy

Piracy of copyright material on the Internet is an ongoing problem across all media. At Packt, we take the protection of our copyright and licenses very seriously. If you come across any illegal copies of our works, in any form, on the Internet, please provide us with the location address or website name immediately so that we can pursue a remedy.

Please contact us at copyright@packtpub.com with a link to the suspected pirated material.

We appreciate your help in protecting our authors, and our ability to bring you valuable content.

Questions

You can contact us at questions@packtpub.com if you are having a problem with any aspect of the book, and we will do our best to address it.

1
A Tour of pandas

In this chapter, we will take a look at **pandas**, which is an open source Python-based data analysis library. It provides high-performance and easy-to-use data structures and data analysis tools built with the Python programming language. The pandas library brings many of the good things from R, specifically the `DataFrame` objects and R packages such as plyr and reshape2, and places them in a single library that you can use in your Python applications.

The development of pandas was begun in 2008 by Wes McKinney when he worked at AQR Capital Management. It was opened sourced in 2009 and is currently supported and actively developed by various organizations and contributors. It was initially designed with finance in mind, specifically with its ability around time series data manipulation, but emphasizes the data manipulation part of the equation leaving statistical, financial, and other types of analyses to other Python libraries.

In this chapter, we will take a brief tour of pandas and some of the associated tools such as IPython notebooks. You will be introduced to a variety of concepts in pandas for data organization and manipulation in an effort to form both a base understanding and a frame of reference for deeper coverage in later sections of this book. By the end of this chapter, you will have a good understanding of the fundamentals of pandas and even be able to perform basic data manipulations. Also, you will be ready to continue with later portions of this book for more detailed understanding.

This chapter will introduce you to:

- pandas and why it is important
- IPython and IPython Notebooks
- Referencing pandas in your application
- The `Series` and `DataFrame` objects of pandas
- How to load data from files and the Web
- The simplicity of visualizing pandas data

pandas is always lowercase by convention in pandas documentation, and this will be a convention followed by this book.

pandas and why it is important

pandas is a library containing high-level data structures and tools that have been created to assist a Python programmer to perform powerful data manipulations, and discover information in that data in a simple and fast way.

The simple and effective data analysis requires the ability to index, retrieve, tidy, reshape, combine, slice, and perform various analyses on both single and multidimensional data, including heterogeneous typed data that is automatically aligned along index labels. To enable these capabilities, pandas provides the following features (and many more not explicitly mentioned here):

- High performance array and table structures for representation of homogenous and heterogeneous data sets: the `Series` and `DataFrame` objects
- Flexible reshaping of data structure, allowing the ability to insert and delete both rows and columns of tabular data
- Hierarchical indexing of data along multiple axes (both rows and columns), allowing multiple labels per data item
- Labeling of series and tabular data to facilitate indexing and automatic alignment of data
- Ability to easily identify and fix missing data, both in floating point and as non-floating point formats
- Powerful grouping capabilities and a functionality to perform split-apply-combine operations on series and tabular data
- Simple conversion from ragged and differently indexed data of both NumPy and Python data structures to pandas objects
- Smart label-based slicing and subsetting of data sets, including intuitive and flexible merging, and joining of data with SQL-like constructs
- Extensive I/O facilities to load and save data from multiple formats including CSV, Excel, relational and non-relational databases, HDF5 format, and JSON

- Explicit support for time series-specific functionality, providing functionality for date range generation, moving window statistics, time shifting, lagging, and so on

- Built-in support to retrieve and automatically parse data from various web-based data sources such as Yahoo!, Google Finance, the World Bank, and several others

For those desiring to get into data analysis and the emerging field of data science, pandas offers an excellent means for a Python programmer (or just an enthusiast) to learn data manipulation. For those just learning or coming from a statistical language like R, pandas can offer an excellent introduction to Python as a programming language.

pandas itself is not a data science toolkit. It does provide some statistical methods as a matter of convenience, but to draw conclusions from data, it leans upon other packages in the Python ecosystem, such as **SciPy**, **NumPy**, **scikit-learn**, and upon graphics libraries such as **matplotlib** and **ggvis** for data visualization. This is actually the strength of pandas over other languages such as R, as pandas applications are able to leverage an extensive network of robust Python frameworks already built and tested elsewhere.

In this book, we will look at how to use pandas for data manipulation, with a specific focus on gathering, cleaning, and manipulation of various forms of data using pandas. Detailed specifics of data science, finance, econometrics, social network analysis, Python, and IPython are left as reference. You can refer to some other excellent books on these topics already available at `https://www.packtpub.com/`.

pandas and IPython Notebooks

A popular means of using pandas is through the use of IPython Notebooks. IPython Notebooks provide a web-based interactive computational environment, allowing the combination of code, text, mathematics, plots, and right media into a web-based document. IPython Notebooks run in a browser and contain Python code that is run in a local or server-side Python session that the notebooks communicate with using WebSockets. Notebooks can also contain markup code and rich media content, and can be converted to other formats such as PDF, HTML, and slide shows.

The following is an example of an IPython Notebook from the IPython website (`http://ipython.org/notebook.html`) that demonstrates the rich capabilities of notebooks:

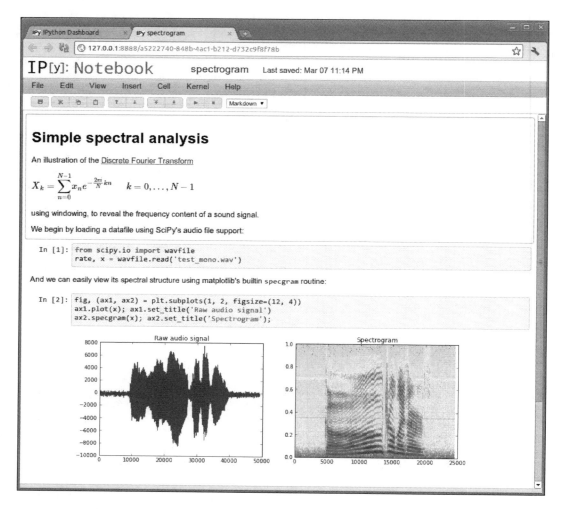

IPython Notebooks are not strictly required for using pandas and can be installed into your development environment independently or alongside of pandas. During the course of this this book, we will install pandas and an IPython Notebook server. You will be able to perform code examples in the text directly in an IPython console interpreter, and the examples will be packaged as notebooks that can be run with a local notebook server. Additionally, the workbooks will be available online for easy and immediate access at `https://wakari.io/sharing/bundle/LearningPandas/LearningPandas_Index`.

To learn more about IPython Notebooks, visit the notebooks site at `http://ipython.org/ipython-doc/dev/notebook/`, and for more in-depth coverage, refer to another book, *Learning IPython for Interactive Computing and Data Visualization, Cyrille Rossant, Packt Publishing.*

Referencing pandas in the application

All pandas programs and examples in this book will always start by importing pandas (and NumPy) into the Python environment. There is a common convention used in many publications (web and print) of importing pandas and NumPy, which will also be used throughout this book. All workbooks and examples for chapters will start with code similar to the following to initialize the pandas library within Python.

```
In [1]:
    # import numpy and pandas, and DataFrame / Series
    import numpy as np
    import pandas as pd
    from pandas import DataFrame, Series

    # Set some pandas options
    pd.set_option('display.notebook_repr_html', False)
    pd.set_option('display.max_columns', 10)
    pd.set_option('display.max_rows', 10)

    # And some items for matplotlib
    %matplotlib inline
    import matplotlib.pyplot as plt
    pd.options.display.mpl_style = 'default'
```

NumPy and pandas go hand-in-hand, as much of pandas is built on NumPy. It is, therefore, very convenient to import NumPy and put it in a np. namespace. Likewise, pandas is imported and referenced with a pd. prefix. Since DataFrame and Series objects of pandas are used so frequently, the third line then imports the Series and DataFrame objects into the global namespace so that we can use them without a pd. prefix.

The three `pd.set_options()` method calls set up some defaults for IPython Notebooks and console output from pandas. These specify how wide and high any output will be, and how many columns it will contain. They can be used to modify the output of IPython and pandas to fit your personal needs to display results. The options set here are convenient for formatting the output of the examples to the constraints of the text.

Primary pandas objects

A programmer of pandas will spend most of their time using two primary objects provided by the pandas framework: `Series` and `DataFrame`. The `DataFrame` objects will be the overall workhorse of pandas and the most frequently used as they provide the means to manipulate tabular and heterogeneous data.

The pandas Series object

The base data structure of pandas is the `Series` object, which is designed to operate similar to a NumPy array but also adds index capabilities. A simple way to create a `Series` object is by initializing a `Series` object with a Python array or Python list.

```
In [2]:
    # create a four item DataFrame
    s = Series([1, 2, 3, 4])
    s


Out [2]:
    0    1
    1    2
    2    3
    3    4
    dtype: int64
```

This has created a pandas `Series` from the list. Notice that printing the series resulted in what appears to be two columns of data. The first column in the output is not a column of the `Series` object, but the index labels. The second column is the values of the `Series` object. Each row represents the index label and the value for that label. This `Series` was created without specifying an index, so pandas automatically creates indexes starting at zero and increasing by one.

Elements of a `Series` object can be accessed through the index using `[]`. This informs the `Series` which value to return given one or more index values (referred to in pandas as labels). The following code retrieves the items in the series with labels 1 and 3.

```
In [3]:
    # return a Series with the rows with labels 1 and 3
    s[[1, 3]]
```

```
Out [3]:
    1    2
    3    4
    dtype: int64
```

It is important to note that the lookup here is not by zero-based positions 1 and 3 like an array, but by the values in the index.

A `Series` object can be created with a user-defined index by specifying the labels for the index using the `index` parameter.

```
In [4]:
    # create a series using an explicit index
    s = Series([1, 2, 3, 4],
              index = ['a', 'b', 'c', 'd'])

    s
```

```
Out [4]:
    a    1
    b    2
    c    3
    d    4
    dtype: int64
```

Notice that the index labels in the output now have the index values that were specified in the `Series` constructor.

Data in the `Series` object can now be accessed by alphanumeric index labels by passing a list of the desired labels, as the following demonstrates:

```
In [5]:
    # look up items the series having index 'a' and 'd'
    s[['a', 'd']]


Out [5]:
    a    1
    d    4
    dtype: int64
```

 This demonstrates the previous point that the lookup is by label value and not by zero-based position.

It is still possible to refer to the elements of the `Series` object by their numerical position.

```
In [6]:
    # passing a list of integers to a Series that has
    # non-integer index labels will look up based upon
    # 0-based index like an array
    s[[1, 2]]


Out [6]:
    b    2
    c    3
    dtype: int64
```

 A `Series` is still smart enough to determine that you passed a list of integers and, therefore, that you want to do value lookup by zero-based position.

The `s.index` property allows direct access to the index of the `Series` object.

```
In [7]:
    # get only the index of the Series
    s.index
```

```
Out [7]:
    Index([u'a', u'b', u'c', u'd'], dtype='object')
```

The index is itself actually a pandas object. This shows us the values of the index and that the data type of each label in the index is `object`.

A common usage of a `Series` in pandas is to represent a time series that associates date/time index labels with a value. A date range can be created using the pandas method `pd.date_range()`.

```
In [8]:
    # create a Series who's index is a series of dates
    # between the two specified dates (inclusive)
    dates = pd.date_range('2014-07-01', '2014-07-06')
    dates
```

```
Out [8]:
    <class 'pandas.tseries.index.DatetimeIndex'>
    [2014-07-01, ..., 2014-07-06]
    Length: 6, Freq: D, Timezone: None
```

 This has created a special index in pandas referred to as a `DatetimeIndex`, which is a pandas index that is optimized to index data with dates and times.

At this point, the index is not particularly useful without having values for each index. We can use this index to create a new `Series` object with values for each of the dates.

```
In [9]:
    # create a Series with values (representing temperatures)
    # for each date in the index
    temps1 = Series([80, 82, 85, 90, 83, 87],
                    index = dates)
```

```
temps1
```

Out [9]:

```
2014-07-01    80
2014-07-02    82
2014-07-03    85
2014-07-04    90
2014-07-05    83
2014-07-06    87
Freq: D, dtype: int64
```

Statistical methods provided by NumPy can be applied to a pandas Series. The following returns the mean of the values in the Series.

In [10]:

```
# calculate the mean of the values in the Series
temps1.mean()
```

Out [10]:

```
84.5
```

Two Series objects can be applied to each other with an arithmetic operation. The following code calculates the difference in temperature between two Series.

In [11]:

```
# create a second series of values using the same index
temps2 = Series([70, 75, 69, 83, 79, 77],
                index = dates)
# the following aligns the two by their index values
# and calculates the difference at those matching labels
temp_diffs = temps1 - temps2
temp_diffs
```

Out [11]:

```
2014-07-01    10
2014-07-02     7
2014-07-03    16
2014-07-04     7
2014-07-05     4
```

```
2014-07-06    10
Freq: D, dtype: int64
```

 The result of an arithmetic operation (+, -, /, *, ...) on two `Series` objects that are non-scalar values returns another `Series` object.

Time series data such as that shown here can also be accessed via the index or by an offset into the `Series` object.

```
In [12]:
    # lookup a value by date using the index
    temp_diffs['2014-07-03']

Out [12]:
    16

In [13]:
    # and also possible by integer position as if the
    # series was an array
    temp_diffs[2]

Out [13]:
    16
```

The pandas DataFrame object

A pandas `Series` represents a single array of values, with an index label for each value. If you want to have more than one `Series` of data that is aligned by a common index, then a pandas `DataFrame` is used.

 In a way a `DataFrame` is analogous to a database table in that it contains one or more columns of data of heterogeneous type (but a single type for all items in each respective column).

The following code creates a DataFrame object with two columns representing the temperatures from the Series objects used earlier.

```
In [14]:
    # create a DataFrame from the two series objects temp1 and temp2
    # and give them column names
    temps_df = DataFrame(
            {'Missoula': temps1,
             'Philadelphia': temps2})
    temps_df
```

```
Out [14]:
              Missoula   Philadelphia
    2014-07-01      80             70
    2014-07-02      82             75
    2014-07-03      85             69
    2014-07-04      90             83
    2014-07-05      83             79
    2014-07-06      87             77
```

 This has created a DataFrame object with two columns, named Missoula and Philadelphia, and using the values from the respective Series objects for each. These are new Series objects contained within the DataFrame, with the values copied from the original Series objects.

Columns in a DataFrame object can be accessed using an array indexer [] with the name of the column or a list of column names. The following code retrieves the Missoula column of the DataFrame object:

```
In [15]
    # get the column with the name Missoula
    temps_df['Missoula']
```

```
Out [15]:
    2014-07-01    80
    2014-07-02    82
    2014-07-03    85
    2014-07-04    90
```

```
2014-07-05      83
2014-07-06      87
Freq: D, Name: Missoula, dtype: int64
```

The following code retrieves the `Philadelphia` column:

```
In [16]:
    # likewise we can get just the Philadelphia column
    temps_df['Philadelphia']
```

```
Out [16]:
    2014-07-01      70
    2014-07-02      75
    2014-07-03      69
    2014-07-04      83
    2014-07-05      79
    2014-07-06      77
    Freq: D, Name: Philadelphia, dtype: int64
```

The following code returns both the columns, but reversed.

```
In [17]:
    # return both columns in a different order
    temps_df[['Philadelphia', 'Missoula']]
```

```
Out [17]:
                Philadelphia   Missoula
    2014-07-01            70         80
    2014-07-02            75         82
    2014-07-03            69         85
    2014-07-04            83         90
    2014-07-05            79         83
    2014-07-06            77         87
```

 Notice that there is a subtle difference in a `DataFrame` object as compared to a `Series` object. Passing a list to the `[]` operator of `DataFrame` retrieves the specified columns, whereas `Series` uses it as index labels to retrieve rows.

Very conveniently, if the name of a column does not have spaces, you can use property-style names to access the columns in a `DataFrame`.

In [18]:

```
# retrieve the Missoula column through property syntax
temps_df.Missoula
```

Out [18]:

```
2014-07-01    80
2014-07-02    82
2014-07-03    85
2014-07-04    90
2014-07-05    83
2014-07-06    87
Freq: D, Name: Missoula, dtype: int64
```

Arithmetic operations between columns within a `DataFrame` are identical in operation to those on multiple `Series` as each column in a `DataFrame` is a `Series`. To demonstrate, the following code calculates the difference between temperatures using property notation.

In [19]:

```
# calculate the temperature difference between the two cities
temps_df.Missoula - temps_df.Philadelphia
```

Out [19]:

```
2014-07-01    10
2014-07-02     7
2014-07-03    16
2014-07-04     7
2014-07-05     4
2014-07-06    10
Freq: D, dtype: int64
```

A new column can be added to `DataFrame` simply by assigning another `Series` to a column using the array indexer `[]` notation. The following code adds a new column in the `DataFrame`, which contains the difference in temperature on the respective dates.

```
In [20]:
    # add a column to temp_df that contains the difference in temps
    temps_df['Difference'] = temp_diffs
    temps_df
```

```
Out [20]:
```

	Missoula	Philadelphia	Difference
2014-07-01	80	70	10
2014-07-02	82	75	7
2014-07-03	85	69	16
2014-07-04	90	83	7
2014-07-05	83	79	4
2014-07-06	87	77	10

The names of the columns in a `DataFrame` are object accessible via the `DataFrame` object's `.columns` property, which itself is a pandas `Index` object.

```
In [21]:
    # get the columns, which is also an Index object
    temps_df.columns
```

```
Out [21]:
    Index([u'Missoula', u'Philadelphia', u'Difference'], dtype='object')
```

The `DataFrame` (and `Series`) objects can be sliced to retrieve specific rows. A simple example here shows how to select the second through fourth rows of temperature difference values.

```
In [22]:
    # slice the temp differences column for the rows at
    # location 1 through 4 (as though it is an array)
    temps_df.Difference[1:4]
```

```
Out [22]:
    2014-07-02      7
```

```
2014-07-03     16
2014-07-04      7
Freq: D, Name: Difference, dtype: int64
```

Entire rows from a `DataFrame` can be retrieved using its `.loc` and `.iloc` properties. The following code returns a `Series` object representing the second row of `temps_df` of the `DataFrame` object by zero-based position of the row using the `.iloc` property:

```
In [23]:
    # get the row at array position 1
    temps_df.iloc[1]
```

```
Out [23]:
    Missoula        82
    Philadelphia    75
    Difference       7
    Name: 2014-07-02 00:00:00, dtype: int64
```

This has converted the row into a `Series`, with the column names of the `DataFrame` pivoted into the index labels of the resulting `Series`.

```
In [24]:
    # the names of the columns have become the index
    # they have been 'pivoted'
    temps_df.ix[1].index
```

```
Out [24]:
    Index([u'Missoula', u'Philadelphia', u'Difference'], dtype='object')
```

Rows can be explicitly accessed via index label using the `.loc` property. The following code retrieves a row by the index label:

```
In [25]:
    # retrieve row by index label using .loc
    temps_df.loc['2014-07-03']
```

```
Out [25]:
    Missoula        85
    Philadelphia    69
    Difference      16
    Name: 2014-07-03 00:00:00, dtype: int64
```

Specific rows in a `DataFrame` object can be selected using a list of integer positions. The following code selects the values from the `Difference` column in rows at locations 1, 3, and 5.

```
In [26]:
    # get the values in the Differences column in rows 1, 3, and 5
    # using 0-based location
    temps_df.iloc[[1, 3, 5]].Difference
```

```
Out [26]:
    2014-07-02      7
    2014-07-04      7
    2014-07-06     10
    Name: Difference, dtype: int64
```

Rows of a `DataFrame` can be selected based upon a logical expression applied to the data in each row. The following code returns the evaluation of the value in the `Missoula` temperature column being greater than 82 degrees:

```
In [27]:
    # which values in the Missoula column are > 82?
    temps_df.Missoula > 82
```

```
Out [27]:
    2014-07-01     False
    2014-07-02     False
    2014-07-03      True
    2014-07-04      True
    2014-07-05      True
    2014-07-06      True
    Freq: D, Name: Missoula, dtype: bool
```

When using the result of an expression as the parameter to the `[]` operator of a `DataFrame`, the rows where the expression evaluated to `True` will be returned.

```
In [28]:
    # return the rows where the temps for Missoula > 82
    temps_df[temps_df.Missoula > 82]
```

```
Out [28]:
```

	Missoula	Philadelphia	Difference
2014-07-03	85	69	16
2014-07-04	90	83	7
2014-07-05	83	79	4
2014-07-06	87	77	10

This technique of selection in pandas terminology is referred to as a Boolean selection, and will form the basis of selecting data based upon its values.

Loading data from files and the Web

The data used in analyses is typically provided from other systems via files that are created and updated at various intervals, dynamically via access over the Web, or from various types of databases. The pandas library provides powerful facilities for easy retrieval of data from a variety of data sources and converting it into pandas objects. Here, we will briefly demonstrate this ease of use by loading data from files and from financial web services.

Loading CSV data from files

The pandas library provides built-in support for loading data in .csv format, a common means of storing structured data in text files. Provided with the code from this book is a file data/test1.csv in the CSV format, which represents some time series information. The specific content isn't important right now, as we just want to demonstrate the ease of loading data into a DataFrame.

The following statement in IPython uses the operating system to display the content of this file (the command to use is different based upon your operating system).

```
In [29]:
    # display the contents of test1.csv
    # which command to use depends on your OS
    !cat data/test1.csv # on non-windows systems
    #!type data\test1.csv # on windows systems

    date,0,1,2
    2000-01-01 00:00:00,1.10376250134,-1.90997889703,-0.808955536115
    2000-01-02 00:00:00,1.18891664768,0.581119740849,0.86159734949
    2000-01-03 00:00:00,-0.964200042412,0.779764393246,1.82906224532
    2000-01-04 00:00:00,0.782130444001,-1.72066965573,-1.10824167327
```

```
2000-01-05 00:00:00,-1.86701699823,-0.528368292754,-2.48830894087
2000-01-06 00:00:00,2.56928022646,-0.471901478927,-0.835033249865
2000-01-07 00:00:00,-0.39932258251,-0.676426550985,-0.0112559158931
2000-01-08 00:00:00,1.64299299394,1.01341997845,1.43566709724
2000-01-09 00:00:00,1.14730764657,2.13799951538,0.554171306191
2000-01-10 00:00:00,0.933765825769,1.38715526486,-0.560142729978
```

This information can be easily imported into `DataFrame` using the `pd.read_csv()` function.

In [30]:

```
# read the contents of the file into a DataFrame
df = pd.read_csv('data/test1.csv')
df
```

Out [30]:

	date	0	1	2
0	2000-01-01 00:00:00	1.103763	-1.909979	-0.808956
1	2000-01-02 00:00:00	1.188917	0.581120	0.861597
2	2000-01-03 00:00:00	-0.964200	0.779764	1.829062
3	2000-01-04 00:00:00	0.782130	-1.720670	-1.108242
4	2000-01-05 00:00:00	-1.867017	-0.528368	-2.488309
5	2000-01-06 00:00:00	2.569280	-0.471901	-0.835033
6	2000-01-07 00:00:00	-0.399323	-0.676427	-0.011256
7	2000-01-08 00:00:00	1.642993	1.013420	1.435667
8	2000-01-09 00:00:00	1.147308	2.138000	0.554171
9	2000-01-10 00:00:00	0.933766	1.387155	-0.560143

pandas has no idea that the first column is a date and has treated the contents of the date field as a string. This can be verified using the following Python statements:

In [31]:

```
# the contents of the date column
df.date
```

Out [31]:

```
0     2000-01-01 00:00:00
1     2000-01-02 00:00:00
2     2000-01-03 00:00:00
```

```
3        2000-01-04 00:00:00
4        2000-01-05 00:00:00
5        2000-01-06 00:00:00
6        2000-01-07 00:00:00
7        2000-01-08 00:00:00
8        2000-01-09 00:00:00
9        2000-01-10 00:00:00
Name: date, dtype: object
```

In [32]:

```
# we can get the first value in the date column
df.date[0]
```

Out [32]:

```
'2000-01-01 00:00:00'
```

In [33]:

```
# it is a string
type(df.date[0])
```

Out [33]:

```
str
```

To guide pandas on how to convert data directly into a Python/pandas date object, we can use the `parse_dates` parameter of the `pd.read_csv()` function. The following code informs pandas to convert the content of the 'date' column into actual `TimeStamp` objects.

In [34]:

```
# read the data and tell pandas the date column should be
# a date in the resulting DataFrame
df = pd.read_csv('data/test1.csv', parse_dates=['date'])
df
```

Out [34]:

```
         date          0          1          2
0  2000-01-01   1.103763  -1.909979  -0.808956
1  2000-01-02   1.188917   0.581120   0.861597
```

```
2  2000-01-03  -0.964200   0.779764   1.829062
3  2000-01-04   0.782130  -1.720670  -1.108242
4  2000-01-05  -1.867017  -0.528368  -2.488309
5  2000-01-06   2.569280  -0.471901  -0.835033
6  2000-01-07  -0.399323  -0.676427  -0.011256
7  2000-01-08   1.642993   1.013420   1.435667
8  2000-01-09   1.147308   2.138000   0.554171
9  2000-01-10   0.933766   1.387155  -0.560143
```

On checking whether it worked, we see it is indeed a `Timestamp` object now.

```
In [35]:
    # verify the type now is date
    # in pandas, this is actually a Timestamp
    type(df.date[0])
```

```
Out [35]:
    pandas.tslib.Timestamp
```

Unfortunately, this has not used the date field as the index for the `DataFrame`, instead it uses the default zero-based integer index labels.

```
In [36]:
    # unfortunately the index is numeric, which makes
    # accessing data by date more complicated
    df.index
```

```
Out [36]:
    Int64Index([0, 1, 2, 3, 4, 5, 6, 7, 8, 9], dtype='int64')
```

This can be rectified using the `index_col` parameter of the `pd.read_csv()` method to specify which column in the file should be used as the index.

```
In [37]:
    # read in again, now specify the data column as being the
    # index of the resulting DataFrame
    df = pd.read_csv('data/test1.csv',
                    parse_dates=['date'],
```

```
                     index_col='date')
    df
```

Out [37]:

```
                      0          1          2
    date
    2000-01-01   1.103763  -1.909979  -0.808956
    2000-01-02   1.188917   0.581120   0.861597
    2000-01-03  -0.964200   0.779764   1.829062
    2000-01-04   0.782130  -1.720670  -1.108242
    2000-01-05  -1.867017  -0.528368  -2.488309
    2000-01-06   2.569280  -0.471901  -0.835033
    2000-01-07  -0.399323  -0.676427  -0.011256
    2000-01-08   1.642993   1.013420   1.435667
    2000-01-09   1.147308   2.138000   0.554171
    2000-01-10   0.933766   1.387155  -0.560143
```

In [38]:

```
    df.index
```

Out [38]:

```
    <class 'pandas.tseries.index.DatetimeIndex'>
    [2000-01-01, ..., 2000-01-10]
    Length: 10, Freq: None, Timezone: None
```

Loading data from the Web

Data from the Web can also be easily read via pandas. To demonstrate this, we will perform a simple load of actual stock data. The example here uses the `pandas.io.data.DataReader` class, which is able to read data from various web sources, one of which is stock data from Yahoo! Finance.

The following reads the data of the previous three months for GOOG (based on the current date), and prints the five most recent days of stock data:

```
In [39]:
    # imports for reading data from Yahoo!
    from pandas.io.data import DataReader
    from datetime import date
    from dateutil.relativedelta import relativedelta


    # read the last three months of data for GOOG
    goog = DataReader("GOOG", "yahoo",
                    date.today() +
                    relativedelta(months=-3))


    # the result is a DataFrame
    #and this gives us the 5 most recent prices
    goog.tail()
```

```
Out [39]:
                Open     High     Low    Close    Volume    Adj Close
    Date
    2015-02-02  531.73   533.00   518.55  528.48   2826300     528.48
    2015-02-03  528.00   533.40   523.26  529.24   2029200     529.24
    2015-02-04  529.24   532.67   521.27  522.76   1656800     522.76
    2015-02-05  523.79   528.50   522.09  527.58   1840300     527.58
    2015-02-06  527.64   537.20   526.41  531.00   1744600     531.00
```

Downloading the example code

You can download the example code files for all Packt books you have purchased from your account at http://www.packtpub.com. If you purchased this book elsewhere, you can visit http://www.packtpub.com/support and register to have the files e-mailed directly to you. The code examples in the book are also publicly available on Wakari.io at https://wakari.io/sharing/bundle/LearningPandas/LearningPandas_Index.

This is actually performs quite a bit of work on your behalf. It makes the web requests retrieving the CSV data and converting it into a DataFrame with the proper conversion of types for the various series of data.

Simplicity of visualization of pandas data

Visualizing pandas data is incredibly simple as pandas is built with tight integration with the `matplotlib` framework. To demonstrate how simple it is to visualize data with pandas, the following code plots the stock data we just retrieved from Yahoo! Finance:

```
In [40]:
    # plot the Adj Close values we just read in
    goog.plot(y='Adj Close');
```

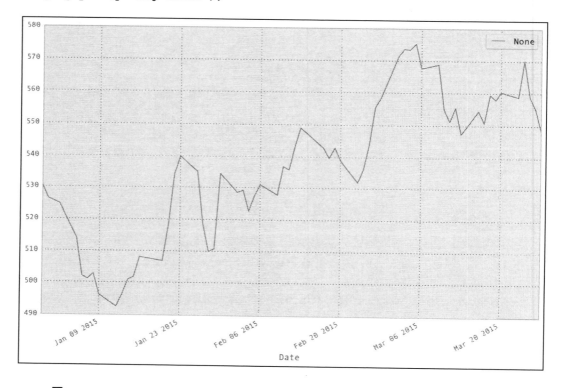

 We will dive deeper and broader into pandas data visualization in a section dedicated to it later in this book.

Summary

In this chapter we have taken a quick tour of the capabilities of pandas, and how easily you can use it to create, load, manipulate, and visualize data. Through the remainder of this book, we will dive into everything covered in this chapter in significant detail, fully demonstrating how to utilize the facilities of pandas for powerful data manipulation.

In the next chapter, we will look at how to get and install both Python and pandas. Following the installation, in *Chapter 3, NumPy for pandas*, we will dive into the NumPy framework as it applies to pandas, demonstrating how NumPy provides the core functionality to slice and dice array-based data in array-like manner, as the pandas `Series` and `DataFrame` objects extensively leverage the capabilities of NumPy.

2
Installing pandas

In this chapter, we will cover how to install pandas using the Anaconda Scientific Python distribution from Continuum Analytics. Anaconda is a popular Python distribution with both free and paid components, and it has cross-platform support—including Windows, Mac, and Linux. The base distribution installs pandas as part of the default installation, so it makes getting started with pandas simple.

The chapter will examine installing both pandas and Python through Anaconda, as this book assumes that you are new to both pandas and Python. This can include readers who are coming from an R environment to learn data manipulation skills using pandas. Those who already have more advanced Python skills can feel free to move onto later chapters or use alternative Python distributions and package managers, as well as virtualized development environments for multiple Python distributions.

In general, the remaining chapters of this book will focus on data manipulation with pandas. The examples can be run in any Python/pandas environment. Emphasis will not be towards learning Python programming. In fact, it is amazing how much you can do with just pandas statements in any Python / Ipython / IPython Notebook environment without performing much Python programming at all.

The default installation of Anaconda also installs an IPython Notebook server that can be used interactively to run the examples as well as the notebooks provided with the source of the book. IPython Notebooks are an excellent means of creating pandas applications, as well as sharing them with others on the Web. We will briefly cover starting this server and using IPython Notebooks.

An alternative to installing Python and pandas is through the use of an online Wakari account. Wakari is a web-based IPython Notebook service that has pandas installed by default and provides excellent capabilities for sharing Python applications online. Creating and getting started with Wakari will have its own brief exposition.

We will cover the following topics in this chapter:

- Getting Anaconda (and pandas)
- Installing Anaconda on Linux, Mac, and Windows
- Verifying the version of pandas
- Updating the pandas packages within Anaconda with `conda`
- Running a small pandas sample in IPython
- Starting the IPython Notebook server
- Installing and running the workbooks for the textbook
- Using Wakari for pandas

Getting Anaconda

We will focus on installing Anaconda Python and ensuring that pandas is up to date within that distribution. You are not limited to using pandas with Anaconda, as pandas is supported by *most* Python distributions — although the specific installation tasks on each distribution may differ from those covered in this chapter. If you use another Python distribution, feel free to use your package manager of choice or `pip` from PyPI.

 I would say *most* Python distributions because — being a Mac user — I've found it very difficult (if not impossible) to install pandas into the default Python provided in OS X by Apple.

At the time of writing, pandas is at Version 0.15.1. The current version of Anaconda is 2.1.9 that contains Python 2.7.8, but comes with pandas 0.14.1 by default. Therefore, we will update to v0.15.1 using the `conda` package manager provided by Anaconda.

Anaconda Python can be downloaded from the Continuum Analytics website at `http://continuum.io/downloads`. The web server will identify the browser's operating system and present you with an appropriate software download file for that platform. The following screenshot shows the download page when running on Ubuntu 13.10:

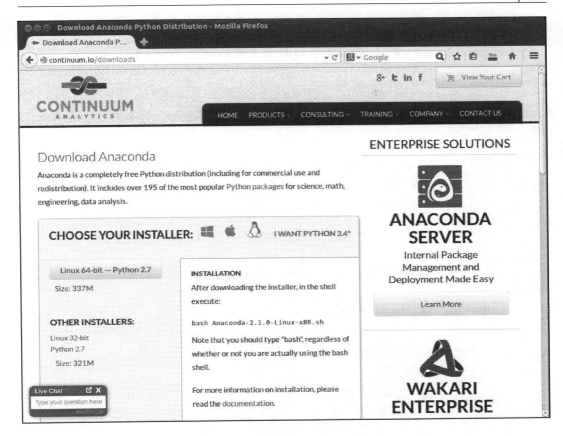

Linux users are presented with a download for a shell script to download and execute, and graphical installers are available for Windows and Mac platforms. Download the package for your platform, and then proceed to the appropriate section for installation details.

Installing Anaconda

The installation of Anaconda is straightforward, but varies slightly by platform. We will cover the installation of Anaconda on Linux, Mac, and Windows platforms. After this installation, pandas will likely need to be updated, which is an identical process across platforms using the conda package manager.

Installing Anaconda on Linux

The download will place a shell script/installer on your system (the following shell script/installer assumes to be downloaded to the ~/Download folder). The name of the file will differ depending upon the Anaconda version and the architecture of Linux selected. This example is using Ubuntu 13.10, AMD64 platform and Anaconda Version 2.1.0. The file downloaded in this scenario is Anaconda-2.1.0-Linux-x86_64.sh.

Once downloaded, make the script executable and run it with the following command:

```
mh@ubuntu:~/Downloads$ chmod +x Anaconda-2.1.0-Linux-x86_64.sh
mh@ubuntu:~/Downloads$ ./Anaconda-2.1.0-Linux-x86_64.sh
```

The script will execute and you will be requested to verify the installation by pressing *Enter*:

```
Welcome to Anaconda 2.1.0 (by Continuum Analytics, Inc.)


In order to continue the installation process, please review the license
agreement.
Please, press ENTER to continue
>>>
```

Then, verify the license terms:

```
Do you approve the license terms? [yes|no]
[no] >>> yes
```

Then, you will be requested to specify the installation location (here, the default value is accepted):

```
Anaconda will now be installed into this location:
/home/mh/anaconda

   - Press ENTER to confirm the location
   - Press CTRL-C to abort the installation
   - Or specify a different location below

[/home/mh/anaconda] >>>
```

Installation will proceed for a few minutes, and then you will be asked if you want to add Python to your shell path. Accepting the default will allow Anaconda to be run from the command line without you updating your path manually:

```
creating default environment...
installation finished.
Do you wish the installer to prepend the Anaconda install location
to PATH in your /home/mh/.bashrc ? [yes|no]
[no] >>> yes
```

Upon completion, the following messages will be displayed; at this point, Python can be run from the shell:

```
Prepending PATH=/home/mh/anaconda/bin to PATH in /home/mh/.bashrc
A backup will be made to: /home/mh/.bashrc-anaconda.bak


For this change to become active, you have to open a new terminal.


Thank you for installing Anaconda!
```

To ensure proper execution, close the current terminal session, open a new one, and issue the command. Successful installation of Anaconda should present the following information (or similar depending upon version):

```
mh@ubuntu:~$ python
Python 2.7.8 |Anaconda 2.1.0 (64-bit)| (default, Aug 21 2014, 18:22:21)
[GCC 4.4.7 20120313 (Red Hat 4.4.7-1)] on linux2
Type "help", "copyright", "credits" or "license" for more information.
Anaconda is brought to you by Continuum Analytics.
Please check out: http://continuum.io/thanks and https://binstar.org
>>>
```

Congratulations, you have installed Anaconda! Now proceed to the section on updating pandas.

Installing Anaconda on Mac OS X

On downloading Anaconda on a Mac, you will get an installation package, as shown in the following screenshot:

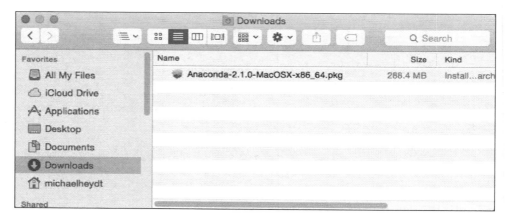

Open the package to start the installation. You will see an installation wizard:

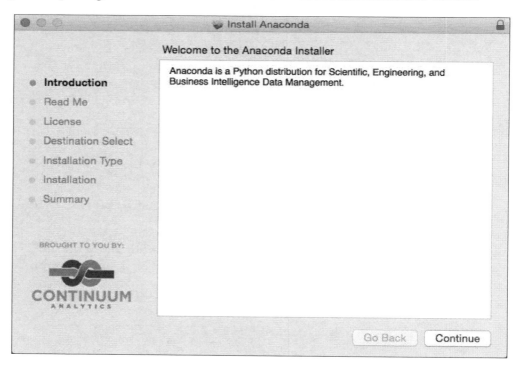

Continue through the wizard. When completed, open a terminal session and issue the `python` command. If all went well, you will see output similar to what is shown in the following screenshot:

```
MBPA:~ michaelheydt$ python
Python 2.7.9 |Anaconda 2.1.0 (x86_64)| (default, Dec 15 2014, 10:37:34)
[GCC 4.2.1 (Apple Inc. build 5577)] on darwin
Type "help", "copyright", "credits" or "license" for more information.
Anaconda is brought to you by Continuum Analytics.
Please check out: http://continuum.io/thanks and https://binstar.org
>>>
```

Anaconda is successfully installed, and you can continue to the section on updating pandas with `conda`.

Installing Anaconda on Windows

Downloading Anaconda on a Windows system will provide you with an installation executable similar to the one shown in the following screenshot:

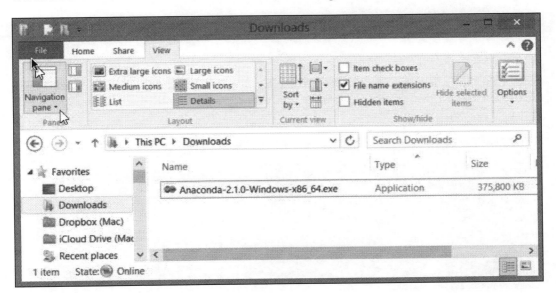

Run the installer, and you will see an installation wizard. It will be similar to the wizard shown in the next screenshot:

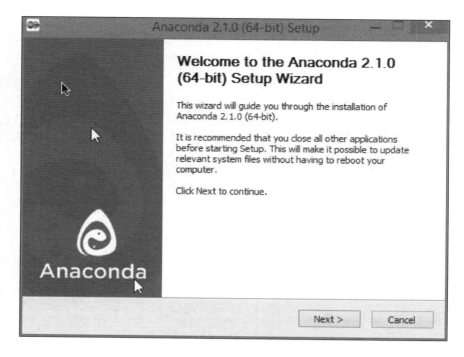

Continue through the wizard. When completed, open a command window and issue the `python` command. If all went well, you will see output similar to what is shown in the following screenshot:

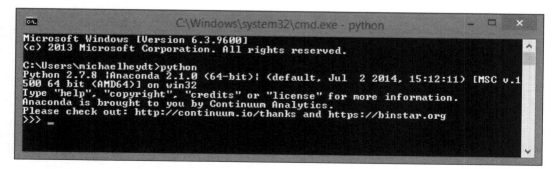

Anaconda is up and running and it is time to ensure pandas is up to date.

Ensuring pandas is up to date

Now that Anaconda is installed, we can check the version of pandas that is installed either from within the Python interpreter or from the command line. The means to perform both of these is the same on each platform, and this will be demonstrated from an OS X terminal.

From within the Anaconda Python interpreter, you can check the version of pandas on the system by importing pandas and then examining the version with the following two Python statements:

```
>>>import pandas as pd
>>>print (pd.__version__)
```

The preceding commands will then report the version of pandas. The following screenshot shows that v0.14.1 is the currently installed version:

```
● ● ●                    michaelheydt — python2.7 — 79×11
MBPA:~ michaelheydt$ python
Python 2.7.9 |Anaconda 2.1.0 (x86_64)| (default, Dec 15 2014, 10:37:34)
[GCC 4.2.1 (Apple Inc. build 5577)] on darwin
Type "help", "copyright", "credits" or "license" for more information.
Anaconda is brought to you by Continuum Analytics.
Please check out: http://continuum.io/thanks and https://binstar.org
>>> import pandas as pd
>>> print (pd.__version__)
0.14.1
>>>
```

This has reported that pandas version is 0.14.1, which is not the most recent, so we may want to update.

You can also check the pandas version using the `conda` package manager from the command line as follows (which also reports that version is 0.14.1):

```
Michaels-MacBook-Pro:~ michaelheydt$ conda list pandas
# packages in environment at //anaconda:
#
pandas                     0.14.1                    np19py27_0
Michaels-MacBook-Pro:~ michaelheydt$
```

To update pandas to the most recent version, use the following conda command:

```
Michaels-MacBook-Pro:~ michaelheydt$ conda update pandas
Fetching package metadata: ..
Solving package specifications: .
Package plan for installation in environment //anaconda:

The following packages will be downloaded:

    package                    |          build
    ---------------------------|-----------------
    conda-3.7.3                |          py27_0          156 KB
    numpy-1.9.1                |          py27_0          2.9 MB
    pandas-0.15.1              |      np19py27_0          4.6 MB
    pytz-2014.9                |          py27_0          175 KB
    requests-2.5.0             |          py27_0          586 KB
    setuptools-7.0             |          py27_0          436 KB
    ------------------------------------------------------------
                                          Total:          8.8 MB

The following packages will be UPDATED:

    conda:      3.7.0-py27_0         --> 3.7.3-py27_0
    numpy:      1.9.0-py27_0         --> 1.9.1-py27_0
    pandas:     0.14.1-np19py27_0 --> 0.15.1-np19py27_0
    pytz:       2014.7-py27_0        --> 2014.9-py27_0
    requests:   2.4.1-py27_0         --> 2.5.0-py27_0
    setuptools: 5.8-py27_0           --> 7.0-py27_0


Proceed ([y]/n)?
```

We can see that pandas can be updated to v0.15.1, along with all required dependent packages. Press *Enter* to proceed. The conda package manager will retrieve and install the required packages:

```
Fetching packages ...
conda-3.7.3-py 100% |############################| Time: 0:00:00 353.91
kB/s
numpy-1.9.1-py 100% |############################| Time: 0:00:04 711.95
kB/s
pandas-0.15.1- 100% |############################| Time: 0:00:06 733.99
kB/s
pytz-2014.9-py 100% |############################| Time: 0:00:00 373.63
kB/s
requests-2.5.0 100% |############################| Time: 0:00:01 336.99
kB/s
setuptools-7.0 100% |############################| Time: 0:00:00 571.84
kB/s
Extracting packages ...
[        COMPLETE       ] |#############################################
| 100%
Unlinking packages ...
[        COMPLETE       ] |#############################################
| 100%
Linking packages ...
[        COMPLETE       ] |#############################################
| 100%
Michaels-MacBook-Pro:~ michaelheydt$
```

You can check whether pandas v0.15.1 is installed with conda:

```
Michaels-MacBook-Pro:~ michaelheydt$ conda list pandas
# packages in environment at //anaconda:
#
pandas                    0.15.1                   np19py27_0
Michaels-MacBook-Pro:~ michaelheydt$
```

The pandas library is now updated. This can also be verified from within the Python interpreter as shown in the following screenshot:

```
MBPA:~ michaelheydt$ python
Python 2.7.9 |Anaconda 2.1.0 (x86_64)| (default, Dec 15 2014, 10:37:34)
[GCC 4.2.1 (Apple Inc. build 5577)] on darwin
Type "help", "copyright", "credits" or "license" for more information.
Anaconda is brought to you by Continuum Analytics.
Please check out: http://continuum.io/thanks and https://binstar.org
>>> import pandas as pd
>>> print (pd.__version__)
0.15.2
>>>
```

Running a small pandas sample in IPython

Now that Python and pandas is installed, let's write our first pandas application. We will write it in the IPython interpreter. IPython is an alternative shell for executing Python applications, and it conveniently provides numeric sequence numbers for thin input and output for example purposes. This is convenient for matching specific code examples in the book and will be used in all examples.

 IPython or IPython Notebooks will be the tools for all remaining examples in the book.

IPython is started using the `ipython` command from the shell or command line:

```
Michaels-MacBook-Pro:~ michaelheydt$ ipython
Python 2.7.8 |Anaconda 2.1.0 (x86_64)| (default, Aug 21 2014, 15:21:46)
Type "copyright", "credits" or "license" for more information.


IPython 2.2.0 -- An enhanced Interactive Python.
Anaconda is brought to you by Continuum Analytics.
Please check out: http://continuum.io/thanks and https://binstar.org
?         -> Introduction and overview of IPython's features.
%quickref -> Quick reference.
help      -> Python's own help system.
```

```
object?    -> Details about 'object', use 'object??' for extra details.
```

```
In [1]:
```

IPython is now ready to accept your programming statements. Enter the following three lines of code:

```
import pandas as pd
df = pd.DataFrame.from_items([('column1', [1, 2, 3])])
print (df)
```

When completed, you should have the following output in the IPython console:

```
In [1]: import pandas as pd


In [2]: df = pd.DataFrame.from_items([('column1', [1, 2, 3])])


In [3]: print (df)
   column1
0        1
1        2
2        3


In [4]:
```

Congratulations, you have created your first pandas application!

Starting the IPython Notebook server

IPython Notebooks are a web server-based interactive environment that combine Python code execution, text, mathematics, plots, and rich media into a single document, along with automatic persistence of code and an easy means of deploying code to the Web. You can find more details on the IPython Notebook site at http://ipython.org/notebook.html.

IPython Notebooks are an exceptional way to learn both Python and pandas. This book will neither assume the use of IPython Notebooks, nor teach their usage beyond the brief examples given in this section. However, the code provided with the book are IPython Notebook files, so demonstrating how to run the server provided by Anaconda is worth a few paragraphs of explanation.

The IPython Notebook server can be started with the following shell command (the same on all platforms):

```
ipython notebook
```

You will get a small amount of output on the console:

```
elheydt/.ipython/profile_default'
```

```
2014-12-06 21:36:11.547 [NotebookApp] Using MathJax from CDN: https://
cdn.mathjax.org/mathjax/latest/MathJax.js
```

```
2014-12-06 21:36:11.570 [NotebookApp] Serving notebooks from local
directory: /Users/michaelheydt
```

```
2014-12-06 21:36:11.570 [NotebookApp] 0 active kernels
```

```
2014-12-06 21:36:11.570 [NotebookApp] The IPython Notebook is running at:
http://localhost:8888/
```

```
2014-12-06 21:36:11.570 [NotebookApp] Use Control-C to stop this server
and shut down all kernels (twice to skip confirmation).
```

Then, a browser window that looks similar to the following screenshot will open:

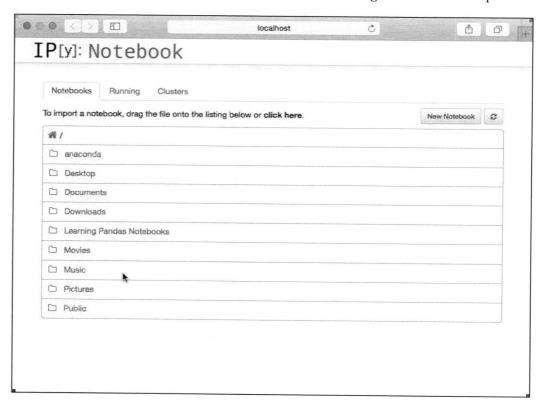

The default notebook shows the contents of the folder where the command was executed. Clicking on the **New Notebook** button will present you with a notebook where you can start entering your pandas code. The following screenshot shows the IPython Notebook where we will enter the pandas code:

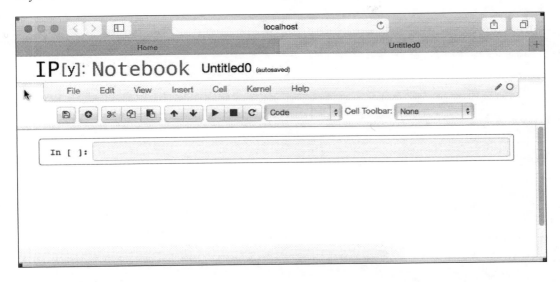

Within the input box, enter the three lines of code from the earlier example and then press *Shift + Enter* to run the code in that block. The server will execute the code and return the output to the browser:

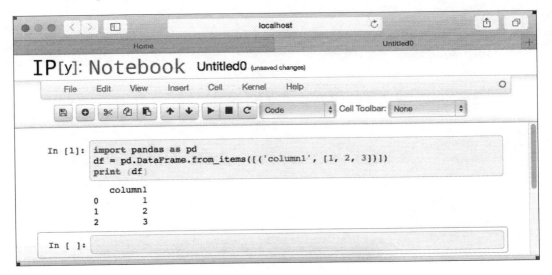

Additionally, after a brief period of time, the code will be saved automatically (you can save explicitly by clicking on the Save button). Returning to the home page, you will see the notebook created in the folder.

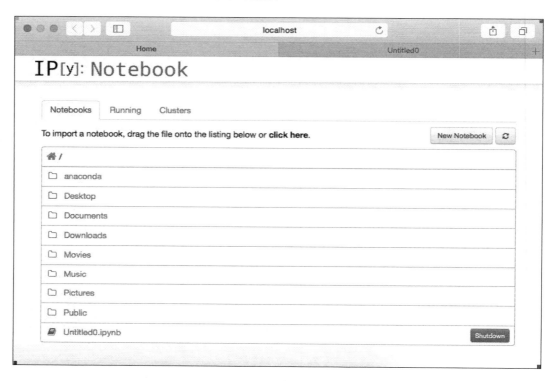

Clicking on the notebook's link will take you back to the notebook for additional editing and execution.

Installing and running IPython Notebooks

The examples for the book consist of an IPython Notebook per chapter, as well as some data files used by various code examples. To install and run the notebooks, simply unzip the notebook files in a directory and then start the IPython Notebook server from that directory. This should present you with something similar to the following screenshot:

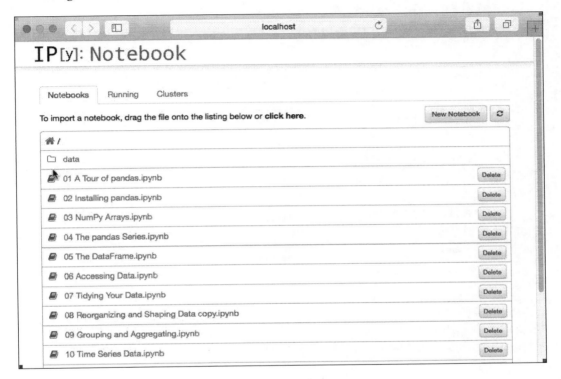

To view the samples for a chapter, click on the link for that chapter. The following screenshot shows the examples for *Chapter 1, A Tour of pandas*:

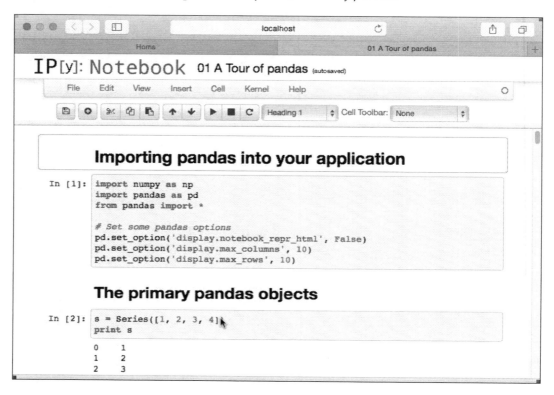

I'll leave exploring the IPython Notebook functionality in more detail to you. If you are reading this book and are interested in pandas, I believe you will find IPython Notebooks fascinating.

To get more examples on IPython Notebooks, you can check out the following resources:

- There are examples on the notebook site at http://ipython.org/notebook.html

- There are several good Packt Publishing books on the subject (http://ipython.org/books.html)

- There are many great notebooks published for review at https://github.com/ipython/ipython/wiki/A-gallery-of-interesting-IPython-Notebooks

- Additionally, Wakari, which is covered in the next section, also has its own gallery of examples at `https://wakari.io/gallery`

- Last, but not least, the nbviewer site at `http://nbviewer.ipython.org/` is a great means of sharing notebooks and has many useful notebooks to examine and learn from

Using Wakari for pandas

Another option for learning pandas and running the examples in this book is to utilize the Wakari web-based Python Data Analysis platform. This service is freemium and it only takes a few minutes to create an account. All the examples in this book can be run with a free account. Wakari is available at `https://wakari.io/`.

On registering for the service, you will be presented with the following web interface for managing IPython Notebooks:

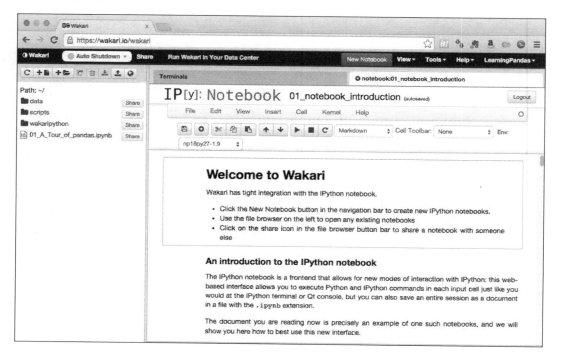

All of the functionality provided by the local IPython Notebook server installed by Anaconda is available, and much more—including viewing and managing remote Python terminals and the ability to select different Python distributions. At the time of writing, this was Anaconda 2.7 with pandas 0.15.1, the most recent versions of both.

You can upload the workbooks and data files provided with the text to your account and run/edit them immediately, without having to go through installing Python or pandas. Additionally, the examples for the text are available publically on Wakari. The main index for the notebooks is at `https://wakari.io/sharing/bundle/ LearningPandas/LearningPandas_Index`. As an example, the first chapter's examples are at `https://wakari.io/sharing/bundle/LearningPandas/01_A_ Tour_of_pandas`.

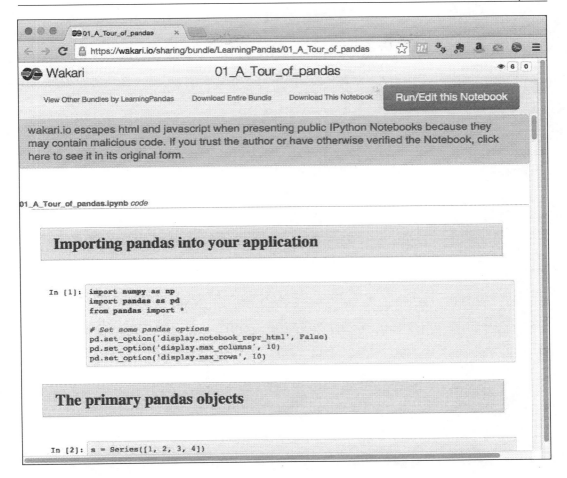

Summary

In this chapter, we discussed from where we can get pandas and how to install pandas using the Anaconda Python distribution on Windows, Mac, and Linux. We also examined how to update the pandas packages with the conda package manager and created a small pandas program that we can run in the IPython console. We then discussed how to run the IPython Notebook server to provide a rich web interface to develop pandas applications. We closed the chapter with a brief introduction to using the Wakari online service to build pandas applications on the Web.

In the next chapter, we will dive into using NumPy arrays, which are a fundamental core of pandas. Getting an understanding of NumPy arrays will therefore set you up well to understand pandas operations and data structures that are presented in *Chapter 4, The pandas Series Object* and in the later chapters.

3
NumPy for pandas

Numerical Python (NumPy) is an open source Python library for scientific computing. NumPy provides a host of features that allow a Python programmer to work with high-performance arrays and matrices. NumPy arrays are stored more efficiently than Python lists and allow mathematical operations to be vectorized, which results in significantly higher performance than with looping constructs in Python.

pandas builds upon functionality provided by NumPy. The pandas library relies heavily on the NumPy array for the implementation of the pandas `Series` and `DataFrame` objects, and shares many of its features such as being able to slice elements and perform vectorized operations. It is therefore useful to spend some time going over NumPy arrays before diving into pandas.

In this chapter, we will cover the following topics about NumPy arrays:

- Installing and importing NumPy
- Benefits and characteristics of NumPy arrays
- Creating NumPy arrays and performing basic array operations
- Selecting array elements
- Logical operation on arrays
- Slicing arrays
- Reshaping arrays
- Combining arrays
- Splitting arrays
- Useful numerical methods of NumPy arrays

Installing and importing NumPy

Since NumPy is a prerequisite for pandas, and you have already installed pandas, NumPy is ready to be used. All that is required to do to use NumPy is to import the library and so all that is required for the examples in this chapter and for most of this book is the following import command:

```
In [1]:
    # this allows us to access numpy using the
    # np. prefix
    import numpy as np
```

This makes the top-level functions of NumPy available in the `np` namespace. This is a common practice when using NumPy, and this book will follow this convention for accessing NumPy functionality.

Benefits and characteristics of NumPy arrays

NumPy arrays have several advantages over Python lists. These benefits are focused on providing high-performance manipulation of sequences of homogenous data items. Several of these benefits are as follows:

- Contiguous allocation in memory
- Vectorized operations
- Boolean selection
- Sliceability

Contiguous allocation in memory provides benefits in performance by ensuring that all elements of an array are directly accessible at a fixed offset from the beginning of the array. This also is a computer organization technique that facilities providing vectorized operations across arrays.

Vectorized operation is a technique of applying an operation across all or a subset of elements without explicit coding of loops. Vectorized operations are often orders of magnitude more efficient in execution as compared to loops implemented in a higher-level language. They are also excellent for reducing the amount of code that needs to be written, which also helps in minimizing coding errors.

To demonstrate both of these benefits, the following example calculates the time required by the `for` loop in Python to square a list consisting of 100,000 sequential integers:

```
In [2]:
    # a function that squares all the values
    # in a sequence
    def squares(values):
        result = []
        for v in values:
            result.append(v * v)
        return result


    # create 100,000 numbers using python range
    to_square = range(100000)
    # time how long it takes to repeatedly square them all
    %timeit squares(to_square)


    100 loops, best of 3: 14 ms per loop
```

Using NumPy and vectorized arrays, the example can be rewritten as follows.

```
In [3]:
    # now lets do this with a numpy array
    array_to_square = np.arange(0, 100000)
    # and time using a vectorized operation
    %timeit array_to_square ** 2


    10000 loops, best of 3: 77.4 µs per loop
```

Vectorization of the operation made our code simpler and also performed roughly 158 times faster!

This brings up something to keep in mind when working with data in NumPy and pandas: if you find yourself coding a loop to iterate across elements of a NumPy array, or a pandas `Series` or `DataFrame`, then you are, as they say, **doing it wrong**. Always keep in mind to write code that makes use of vectorization. It is almost always faster, as well as more elegantly expressed in a vectorized manner.

Boolean selection is a common pattern that we will see with NumPy and pandas where selection of elements from an array is based on specific logical criteria. This consists of calculating an array of Boolean values where `True` represents that the given item should be in the result set. This array can then be used to efficiently select the matching items.

Sliceability provides the programmer with a very efficient means to specify multiple elements in an array using a convenient notation. Slicing becomes invaluable when working with data in an ad hoc manner. The slicing process also benefits from being able to take advantage of the contiguous memory allocation of arrays to optimize access to series of items.

Creating NumPy arrays and performing basic array operations

A NumPy array can be created using multiple techniques. The following code creates a new NumPy array object from a Python list:

```
In [4]:
    # a simple array
    a1 = np.array([1, 2, 3, 4, 5])
    a1

Out[4]:
    array([1, 2, 3, 4, 5])

In [5]:
    # what is its type?
    type(a1)

Out[5]:
    numpy.ndarray

In [6]:
    # how many elements?
    np.size(a1)

Out[6]:
    5
```

In NumPy, n-dimensional arrays are denoted as ndarray, and this one contains five elements, as is reported by the np.size() function.

NumPy arrays must have all of their elements of the same type. If you specify different types in the list, NumPy will try to coerce all the items to the same type. The following code example demonstrates using integer and floating-point values to initialize the array, which are then converted to floating-point numbers by NumPy:

```
In [7]:
    # any float in the sequences makes
    # it an array of floats
    a2 = np.array([1, 2, 3, 4.0, 5.0])
    a2
```

```
Out[7]:
    array([ 1.,   2.,   3.,   4.,   5.])
```

```
In [8]:
    # array is all of one type (float64 in this case)
    a2.dtype
```

```
Out[8]:
    dtype('float64')
```

The types of the items in an array can be checked with the dtype property, which in this example shows that NumPy converted all the items to float64.

An array of a specific size can be created in multiple ways. The following code uses a single item Python list to initialize an array of 10 items:

```
In [9]:
    # shorthand to repeat a sequence 10 times
    a3 = np.array([0]*10)
    a3
```

```
Out[9]:
    array([0, 0, 0, 0, 0, 0, 0, 0, 0, 0])
```

An array can also be initialized with sequential values using the Python `range()` function. The following code initializes with ten items from `0` through `9`:

```
In [10]:
    # convert a python range to numpy array
    np.array(range(10))
```

```
Out[10]:
    array([0, 1, 2, 3, 4, 5, 6, 7, 8, 9])
```

Since the last two examples use a Python list, this is not the most efficient manner to allocate the array. To efficiently create an array of a specific size that is initialized with zeros, use the `np.zeros()` function as shown in the following code:

```
In [11]:
    # create a numpy array of 10 0.0's
    np.zeros(10)
```

```
Out[11]:
    array([ 0., 0., 0., 0., 0., 0., 0., 0., 0., 0.])
```

The default is to create floating-point numbers. This can be changed to integers using the `dtype` parameter, as shown in the following example:

```
In [12]:
    # force it to be of int instead of float64
    np.zeros(10, dtype=int)
```

```
Out[12]:
    array([0, 0, 0, 0, 0, 0, 0, 0, 0, 0])
```

NumPy provides the `np.arange()` function to create a NumPy array consisting of sequential values from a specified start value up to, but not including, the specified end value:

```
In [13]:
    # make "a range" starting at 0 and with 10 values
    np.arange(0, 10)
```

```
Out[13]:
    array([0, 1, 2, 3, 4, 5, 6, 7, 8, 9])
```

A `step` value can also be provided to `np.arange()`. The following example demonstrates the generation of even numbers between `0` and `10`, and also another allocation of an array of decreasing values by specifying a step of `-1`:

```
In [14]:
    # 0 <= x < 10 increment by two
    np.arange(0, 10, 2)
```

```
Out[14]:
    array([0, 2, 4, 6, 8])
```

```
In [15]:
    # 10 >= x > 0, counting down
    np.arange(10, 0, -1)
```

```
Out[15]:
    array([10,  9,  8,  7,  6,  5,  4,  3,  2,  1])
```

The `np.linspace()` function is similar to `np.arange()`, but generates an array of a specific number of items between the specified start and stop values:

```
In [16]:
# evenly spaced #'s between two intervals
np.linspace(0, 10, 11)
```

```
Out[16]:
    array([  0.,   1.,   2.,   3.,   4.,   5.,   6.,   7.,   8.,   9.,
        10.])
```

 Note that the datatype of the array by default is float, and that the start and end values are inclusive.

NumPy arrays will vectorize many mathematical operators. The following example creates a 10-element array and then multiplies each element by a constant:

```
In [17]:
    # multiply numpy array by 2
    a1 = np.arange(0, 10)
```

```
a1 * 2
```

Out[17]:

```
array([ 0,  2,  4,  6,  8, 10, 12, 14, 16, 18])
```

It is also possible to apply a mathematical operator across two arrays:

In [18]:

```
# add two numpy arrays
a2 = np.arange(10, 20)
a1 + a2
```

Out[18]:

```
array([10, 12, 14, 16, 18, 20, 22, 24, 26, 28])
```

NumPy arrays are n-dimensional, but for purposes of pandas, we will be most interested in one- and two-dimensional arrays. This is because the pandas `Series` and `DataFrame` objects operate similarly to one-and two-dimensional arrays, respectively.

To create a two-dimensional NumPy array, you can pass in a list of lists as shown in the following example:

In [19]:

```
# create a 2-dimensional array (2x2)
np.array([[1,2], [3,4]])
```

Out[19]:

```
array([[1, 2],
       [3, 4]])
```

A more convenient and efficient means is to use the NumPy array's `.reshape()` method to reorganize a one-dimensional array into two dimensions.

In [20]:

```
# create a 1x20 array, and reshape to a 5x4 2d-array
m = np.arange(0, 20).reshape(5, 4)
m
```

Out[20]:

```
array([[ 0,  1,  2,  3],
```

```
       [ 4,    5,    6,    7],
       [ 8,    9,   10,   11],
       [12,   13,   14,   15],
       [16,   17,   18,   19]])
```

As we have seen, the number of items in an array can be determined by the `np.size()` function. As the next example demonstrates, for a two-dimensional array, this will return the product of all of the dimensions of the array, which will be equivalent to the total number of items it contains:

In [21]:
```
# size of any dimensional array is the # of elements
np.size(m)
```

Out[21]:
```
20
```

To determine the number of rows in a two-dimensional array, we can pass 0 as another parameter:

In [22]:
```
# can ask the size along a given axis (0 is rows)
np.size(m, 0)
```

Out[22]:
```
5
```

To determine the number of columns in a two-dimensional array, we can pass the value 1:

In [23]:
```
# and 1 is the columns
np.size(m, 1)
```

Out[23]:
```
4
```

Selecting array elements

NumPy arrays can have their elements accessed via the `[]` operator. There are many variants of this operator that we will see throughout this book, but the basic access to array elements is by passing the zero-based offset of the desired element:

```
In [24]:
    # select 0-based elements 0 and 2
    a1[0], a1[2]
```

```
Out[24]:
    (0, 2)
```

Elements in a two-dimensional array can be used by making use of two values separated by a comma, with the row first and column second:

```
In [25]:
    # select an element in 2d array at row 1 column 2
    m[1, 2]
```

```
Out[25]:
    6
```

It is possible to retrieve an entire row of a two-dimensional array using just a single value representing the row and omitting the column component:

```
In [26]:
# all items in row 1
m[1,]
```

```
Out[26]:
array([4, 5, 6, 7])
```

It is possible to retrieve an entire column of a two-dimensional array using the `:` symbol for the row (just omitting the row value is a syntax error):

```
In [27]:
    # all items in column 2
    m[:,2]
```

```
Out[27]:
    array([ 2,  6, 10, 14, 18])
```

Logical operations on arrays

Logical operations can be applied to arrays to test the array values against specific criteria. The following code tests if the values of the array are less than 2:

```
In [28]:
    # which items are less than 2?
    a = np.arange(5)
    a < 2
```

```
Out[28]:
    array([ True,  True, False, False, False], dtype=bool)
```

Note that this has resulted in an array of Boolean values. The value of each item in the array is the result of the logical operation on the respective array element.

It is worth pointing out that this does not work with more complicated expressions, such as this:

```
In [29]:
    # this is commented as it will cause an exception
    # print (a<2 or a>3)
```

This can be made to work by using parentheses around the logical conditions and using | instead of or:

```
In [30]:
    # less than 2 or greater than 3?
    (a<2) | (a>3)
```

```
Out[30]:
    array([ True,  True, False, False,  True], dtype=bool)
```

NumPy provides the np.vectorize() function, which applies an expression or function to an array in a vectorized manner. The following code demonstrates the use of np.vectorize() to apply a function named exp() to each item in the array:

```
In [31]:
    # create a function that is applied to all array elements
    def exp (x):
        return x<3 or x>3
```

```
# np.vectorize applies the method to all items in an array
np.vectorize(exp)(a)
```

Out[31]:

```
array([ True,   True,   True, False,   True], dtype=bool)
```

 Note that only the function representing the expression is passed to np.vectorize(). The array is then passed as a parameter to the object that results from that operation.

A specific use of this type of an array of Boolean values is to select the elements from an array where the value in the Boolean array is True. This is referred to as **Boolean selection** and can be performed by passing the Boolean value array to the [] operator of the array from which the values are to be selected.

In [32]:

```
# boolean select items < 3
r = a<3
# applying the result of the expression to the [] operator
# selects just the array elements where there is a matching True
a[r]
```

Out[32]:

```
array([0, 1, 2])
```

A very good feature of a Boolean array is the ability to count the number of the True values using the np.sum() function. The following code computes that there are three elements in the array that are less than the value 3:

In [33]:

```
# np.sum treats True as 1 and False as 0
# so this is how many items are less than 3
np.sum(a < 3)
```

Out[33]:

```
3
```

Arrays can also be compared to other arrays:

```
In [34]:
    # This can be applied across two arrays
    a1 = np.arange(0, 5)
    a2 = np.arange(5, 0, -1)
    a1 < a2
```

```
Out[34]:
    array([ True,  True,  True, False, False], dtype=bool)
```

This also works across multi-dimensional arrays:

```
In [35]:
    # and even multi dimensional arrays
    a1 = np.arange(9).reshape(3, 3)
    a2 = np.arange(9, 0 , -1).reshape(3, 3)
    a1 < a2
```

```
Out[35]:
    array([[ True,  True,  True],
        [ True,  True, False],
        [False, False, False]], dtype=bool)
```

Slicing arrays

NumPy arrays support a feature called slicing. Slicing retrieves zero or more items from an array, and the items also don't need to be sequential, whereas the normal array element operator [] can only retrieve one value. This is very convenient as it provides an ability to efficiently select multiple items from an array without the need to implement Python loops.

Slicing overloads the normal array [] operator to accept what is referred to as a slice object. A slice object is created using a syntax of start:end:step. Each component of the slice is optional and, as we will see, this provides convenient means to select entire rows or columns by omitting the component of the slice.

To begin with the demonstrations, the following code creates a ten-element array and selects items in zero-based positions from 3 up to, but not including, position 8:

```
In [36]:
    # get all items in the array from position 3
    # up to position 8 (but not inclusive)
    a1 = np.arange(1, 10)
    a1[3:8]
```

```
Out[36]:
    array([4, 5, 6, 7, 8])
```

This example has omitted specifying the step value, which uses the default value of 1. To demonstrate using other values for step, the following code selects every other element in the array:

```
In [37]:
    # every other item
    a1[::2]
```

```
Out[37]:
    array([1, 3, 5, 7, 9])
```

By omitting the start and end, NumPy chooses 0 through the length of the array as those values and then retrieves every other item. Changing this slightly, a negative step value of -1 will conveniently reverse the array:

```
In [38]:
# in reverse order
    a1[::-1]
```

```
Out[38]:
    array([9, 8, 7, 6, 5, 4, 3, 2, 1])
```

When using a negative step value, it is important that the start value is greater than the end value. Also, note that the following example is not equivalent to the preceding example:

```
In [39]:
    # note that when in reverse, this does not include
    # the element specified in the second component of the slice
```

```
# that is, there is no 1 printed in this
a1[9:0:-1]
```

Out[39]:

```
array([9, 8, 7, 6, 5, 4, 3, 2])
```

In this scenario, the 0 value in the array was not retrieved. This is because the end value is not inclusive, so when iterating by -1 from 9, NumPy stops at 0 before returning the value at that position in the array.

To select all the items starting at a position until the end of the array, simply specify the start position and leave end unspecified. The following code selects items from position 5 through the end of the array:

In [40]:

```
# all items from position 5 onwards
a1[5:]
```

Out[40]:

```
array([6, 7, 8, 9])
```

To select the first n element in an array, simply leave the start position unspecified and set end to be the value of n. The following selects the first five items in the array:

In [41]:

```
# the items in the first 5 positions
a1[:5]
```

Out[41]:

```
array([1, 2, 3, 4, 5])
```

Two-dimensional arrays can also be sliced. We have already seen how to select a specific element from a two-dimensional array, and how to select a specific row. The column selection example that we saw actually used the slice notation. To revisit that, the following code selects items from the second column of a matrix:

In [42]:

```
# we saw this earlier
# : in rows specifier means all rows
# so this gets items in column position 1, all rows
```

```
    m[:,1]
```

```
Out[42]:
    array([ 1,   5,   9,  13,  17])
```

To the left of the comma is a slice object for the rows, and to the right is one for the columns. The following code selects columns in position 2 through 3 of the matrix:

```
In [43]:
    # in all rows, but for all columns in positions
    # 1 up to but not including 3
    m[:,1:3]
```

```
Out[43]:
    array([[ 1,   2],
           [ 5,   6],
           [ 9,  10],
           [13,  14],
           [17,  18]])
```

Rows can also be sliced, and the `step` value is valid for both rows and columns. The following code returns rows in position 3 and 4:

```
In [44]:
    # in row positions 3 up to but not including 5, all columns
    m[3:5,:]
```

```
Out[44]:
    array([[12, 13, 14, 15],
           [16, 17, 18, 19]])
```

Both columns and rows can be sliced at the same time:

```
In [45]:
    # combined to pull out a sub matrix of the matrix
    m[3:5,1:3]
```

```
Out[45]:
    array([[13, 14],
           [17, 18]])
```

It is also possible to select specific rows or columns by passing a Python list as an element of the slice. The following code explicitly selects by position the first, third, and fourth rows:

```
In [46]:
    # using a python array, we can select
    # non-contiguous rows or columns
    m[[1,3,4],:]


Out[46]:
    array([[ 4,  5,  6,  7],
           [12, 13, 14, 15],
           [16, 17, 18, 19]])
```

Reshaping arrays

NumPy makes it simple to change the shape of your arrays. Earlier in this chapter, we briefly saw the .reshape() method of the NumPy array and how it can be used to reshape a one-dimensional array into a matrix. It is also possible to convert from a matrix back to an array. The following example demonstrates this by creating a nine-element array, reshaping it into a *3 x 3* matrix, and then back to a *1 x 9* array:

```
In [47]:
    # create a 9 element array (1x9)
    a = np.arange(0, 9)
    # and reshape to a 3x3 2-d array
    m = a.reshape(3, 3)
  m


Out[47]:
    array([[0, 1, 2],
           [3, 4, 5],
           [6, 7, 8]])


In [48]:
    # and we can reshape downward in dimensions too
```

```
reshaped = m.reshape(9)
reshaped
```

Out[48]:

```
array([0, 1, 2, 3, 4, 5, 6, 7, 8])
```

 Note that .reshape() returns a new array with a different shape. The original array's shape remains unchanged.

The .reshape() method is not the only means of reorganizing data. Another means is the .ravel() method that will flatten a matrix to one dimension as shown in the following example:

In [49]:

```
# .ravel will generate array representing a flattened 2-d array
raveled = m.ravel()
raveled
```

Out[49]:

```
array([0, 1, 2, 3, 4, 5, 6, 7, 8])
```

In [50]:

```
# it does not alter the shape of the source
m
```

Out[50]:

```
array([[0, 1, 2],
       [3, 4, 5],
       [6, 7, 8]])
```

The preceding code has performed the same operation as using the previous .reshape() example, but without the need to pass the number of items in the matrix. Again, the shape of the original matrix is unchanged.

Even though .reshape() and .ravel() do not change the shape of the original array or matrix, they do actually return a one-dimensional view into the specified array or matrix. If you change an element in this view, the value in the original array or matrix is changed. The following example demonstrates this ability to change items of the original matrix through the view:

```
In [51]:
    # but it will be a view into the source
    # so items changed in the result of the ravel
    # are changed in the original object
    # reshape m to an array
    reshaped = m.reshape(np.size(m))
    # ravel into an array
    raveled = m.ravel()
    # change values in either
    reshaped[2] = 1000
    raveled[5] = 2000
    # and they show as changed in the original
    m
```

```
Out[51]:
    array([[   0,    1, 1000],
           [   3,    4, 2000],
           [   6,    7,    8]])
```

The .flatten() method functions similarly to .ravel() but instead returns a new array with copied data instead of a view. Changes to the result do not change the original matrix:

```
In [52]:
    # flattened is like ravel, but a copy of the data,
    # not a view into the source
    m2 = np.arange(0, 9).reshape(3,3)
    flattened = m2.flatten()
    # change in the flattened object
    flattened[0] = 1000
    flattened
```

```
Out[52]:
```

```
array([1000,    1,    2,    3,    4,    5,    6,    7,    8])
```

In [53]:
```
# but not in the original
m2
```

Out[53]:
```
array([[0, 1, 2],
       [3, 4, 5],
       [6, 7, 8]])
```

The .shape property returns a tuple representing the shape of the array:

In [54]:
```
# we can reshape by assigning a tuple to the .shape property
# we start with this, which has one dimension
flattened.shape
```

Out[54]:
```
(9,)
```

The property can also be assigned a tuple, which will force the array to reshape itself as specified:

In [55]:
```
# and make it 3x3
flattened.shape = (3, 3)
# it is no longer flattened
flattened
```

Out[55]:
```
array([[1000,    1,    2],
       [   3,    4,    5],
       [   6,    7,    8]])
```

In linear algebra, it is common to transpose a matrix. This can be performed with the `.transpose()` method, as shown here:

```
In [56]:
    # transpose a matrix
    flattened.transpose()
```

```
Out[56]:
    array([[1000,    3,    6],
           [   1,    4,    7],
           [   2,    5,    8]])
```

Alternatively, this can also be performed with the `.T` property:

```
In [57]:
    # can also use .T property to transpose
    flattened.T
```

```
Out[57]:
    array([[1000,    3,    6],
           [   1,    4,    7],
           [   2,    5,    8]])
```

The `.resize()` method functions similarly to the `.reshape()` method, except that while reshaping returns a new array with data copied into it, `.resize()` performs an in-place reshaping of the array.:

```
In [58]:
    # we can also use .resize, which changes shape of
    # an object in-place
    m = np.arange(0, 9).reshape(3,3)
    m.resize(1, 9)
    m # my shape has changed
```

```
Out[58]:
    array([[0, 1, 2, 3, 4, 5, 6, 7, 8]])
```

Combining arrays

Arrays can be combined in various ways. This process in NumPy is referred to as stacking. Stacking can take various forms, including horizontal, vertical, and depth-wise stacking. To demonstrate this, we will use the following two arrays (a and b):

```
In [59]:
    # creating two arrays for examples
    a = np.arange(9).reshape(3, 3)
    b = (a + 1) * 10
    a

Out[59]:
    array([[0, 1, 2],
           [3, 4, 5],
           [6, 7, 8]])

In [60]:
    b

Out[60]:
    array([[10, 20, 30],
           [40, 50, 60],
           [70, 80, 90]])
```

Horizontal stacking combines two arrays in a manner where the columns of the second array are placed to the right of those in the first array. The function actually stacks the two items provided in a two-element tuple. The result is a new array with data copied from the two that are specified:

```
In [61]:
    # horizontally stack the two arrays
    # b becomes columns of a to the right of a's columns
    np.hstack((a, b))

Out[61]:
    array([[ 0,  1,  2, 10, 20, 30],
           [ 3,  4,  5, 40, 50, 60],
           [ 6,  7,  8, 70, 80, 90]])
```

This functionally is equivalent to using the `np.concatenate()` function while specifying `axis = 1`:

```
In [62]:
    # identical to concatenate along axis = 1
    np.concatenate((a, b), axis = 1)
```

```
Out[62]:
    array([[ 0,  1,  2, 10, 20, 30],
           [ 3,  4,  5, 40, 50, 60],
           [ 6,  7,  8, 70, 80, 90]])
```

Vertical stacking returns a new array with the contents of the second array as appended rows of the first array:

```
In [63]:
# vertical stack, adding b as rows after a's rows
np.vstack((a, b))
```

```
Out[63]:
array([[ 0,  1,  2],
       [ 3,  4,  5],
       [ 6,  7,  8],
       [10, 20, 30],
       [40, 50, 60],
       [70, 80, 90]])
```

Like `np.hstack()`, this is equivalent to using the concatenate function, except specifying `axis=0`:

```
In [64]:
    # concatenate along axis=0 is the same as vstack
    np.concatenate((a, b), axis = 0)
```

```
Out[64]:
    array([[ 0,  1,  2],
           [ 3,  4,  5],
           [ 6,  7,  8],
```

```
      [10, 20, 30],
      [40, 50, 60],
      [70, 80, 90]])
```

Depth stacking takes a list of arrays and arranges them in order along an additional axis referred to as the depth:

```
In [65]:
    # dstack stacks each independent column of a and b
    np.dstack((a, b))
```

```
Out[65]:
    rray([[[ 0, 10],
           [ 1, 20],
           [ 2, 30]],

          [[ 3, 40],
           [ 4, 50],
           [ 5, 60]],

          [[ 6, 70],
           [ 7, 80],
           [ 8, 90]]])
```

Column stacking performs a horizontal stack of two one-dimensional arrays, making each array a column in the resulting array:

```
In [66]:
    # set up 1-d array
    one_d_a = np.arange(5)
    one_d_a
```

```
Out[66]:
    array([0, 1, 2, 3, 4])
```

```
In [67]:
    # another 1-d array
    one_d_b = (one_d_a + 1) * 10
```

```
    one_d_b

Out[67]:
    array([10, 20, 30, 40, 50])

In [68]:
    # stack the two columns
    np.column_stack((one_d_a, one_d_b))

Out[68]:
    array([[ 0, 10],
           [ 1, 20],
           [ 2, 30],
           [ 3, 40],
           [ 4, 50]])
```

Row stacking returns a new array where each one-dimensional array forms one of the rows of the new array:

```
In [69]:
    # stack along rows
    np.row_stack((one_d_a, one_d_b))

Out[69]:
    array([[ 0,  1,  2,  3,  4],
           [10, 20, 30, 40, 50]])
```

Splitting arrays

Arrays can also be split into multiple arrays along the horizontal, vertical, and depth axes using the np.hsplit(), np.vsplit(), and np.dsplit() functions. We will only look at the np.hsplit() function as the others work similarly.

The np.hsplit() function takes the array to split as a parameter, and either a scalar value to specify the number of arrays to be returned, or a list of column indexes to split the array upon.

If splitting into a number of arrays, each array returned will have the same count of columns. The source array must have a number of columns that is a multiple of the specified value.

To demonstrate this, we will use the following array with four columns and three rows:

```
In [70]:
# sample array
a = np.arange(12).reshape(3, 4)
a
```

```
Out[70]:
array([[ 0,  1,  2,  3],
       [ 4,  5,  6,  7],
       [ 8,  9, 10, 11]])
```

We can split this into four arrays, each representing the values in a specific column:

```
In [71]:
    # horiz split the 2-d array into 4 array columns
    np.hsplit(a, 4)
```

```
Out[71]:
    [array([[0],
            [4],
            [8]]), array([[1],
            [5],
            [9]]), array([[ 2],
            [ 6],
            [10]]), array([[ 3],
            [ 7],
            [11]])]
```

 The result is actually an array containing the four specified arrays.

Using a value of 2 returns two matrices with two columns each:

```
In [72]:
    # horiz split into two array columns
    np.hsplit(a, 2)

Out[72]:
    [array([[0, 1],
            [4, 5],
            [8, 9]]), array([[ 2,  3],
            [ 6,  7],
            [10, 11]])]
```

Also, the following code splits an array along specific columns:

```
In [73]:
    # split at columns 1 and 3
    np.hsplit(a, [1, 3])

Out[73]:
    [array([[0],
            [4],
            [8]]), array([[ 1,  2],
            [ 5,  6],
            [ 9, 10]]), array([[ 3],
            [ 7],
            [11]])]
```

The np.split() function performs an identical task when using axis=1:

```
In [74]:
    # along the rows
    np.split(a, 2, axis = 1)

Out[74]:
    [array([[0, 1],
            [4, 5],
            [8, 9]]), array([[ 2,  3],
            [ 6,  7],
            [10, 11]])]
```

Vertical splitting works similarly to horizontal splitting, except against the vertical axis, which can be seen here:

```
In [75]:
    # new array for examples
    a = np.arange(12).reshape(4, 3)
    a

Out[75]:
    array([[ 0,  1,  2],
           [ 3,  4,  5],
           [ 6,  7,  8],
           [ 9, 10, 11]])
```

We can split this by 4 and get the four arrays representing the rows:

```
In [76]:
    # split into four rows of arrays
    np.vsplit(a, 4)

Out[76]:
    [array([[0, 1, 2]]),
     array([[3, 4, 5]]),
     array([[6, 7, 8]]),
     array([[ 9, 10, 11]])]
```

Alternately, splitting by 2, retrieving two arrays of two rows each:

```
In [77]:
    # into two rows of arrays
    np.vsplit(a, 2)

Out[77]:
    [array([[0, 1, 2],
           [3, 4, 5]]), array([[ 6,  7,  8],
           [ 9, 10, 11]])]
```

Splitting can also be performed on specific rows:

```
In [78]:
    # split along axis=0
    # row 0 of original is row 0 of new array
    # rows 1 and 2 of original are row 1
    np.vsplit(a, [1, 3])


Out[78]:
    [array([[0, 1, 2]]), array([[3, 4, 5],
           [6, 7, 8]]), array([[ 9, 10, 11]])]
```

Likewise, the split command does the same when specifying axis=0:

```
In [79]:
    # split can specify axis
    np.split(a, 2, axis = 0)


Out[79]:
    [array([[0, 1, 2],
           [3, 4, 5]]), array([[ 6,  7,  8],
           [ 9, 10, 11]])]
```

Depth splitting splits three-dimensional arrays. To demonstrate this, we will use the following three-dimensional array:

```
In [80]:
    # 3-d array
    c = np.arange(27).reshape(3, 3, 3)
    c


Out[80]:
    array([[[ 0,  1,  2],
           [ 3,  4,  5],
           [ 6,  7,  8]],

          [[ 9, 10, 11],
           [12, 13, 14],
```

```
            [15, 16, 17]],

          [[18, 19, 20],
           [21, 22, 23],
           [24, 25, 26]]])
```

This array can be depth split by 3:

```
In [81]:
    # split into 3
    np.dsplit(c, 3)

Out[81]:
    [array([[[ 0],
            [ 3],
            [ 6]],

           [[ 9],
            [12],
            [15]],

           [[18],
            [21],
            [24]]]), array([[[ 1],
            [ 4],
            [ 7]],

           [[10],
            [13],
            [16]],

           [[19],
            [22],
            [25]]]), array([[[ 2],
            [ 5],
```

```
    [ 8]],

   [[11],
    [14],
    [17]],

   [[20],
    [23],
    [26]]])]
```

Useful numerical methods of NumPy arrays

NumPy arrays have many functions that can be applied to the arrays. Many of these are statistical functions that you can use for data analysis. The following example describes several of the useful functions.

 Note that most of these functions work on multi-dimensional arrays, and the axis to which the function is applied to is specified by the `axis` parameter. We will examine this for the `.min()` and `.max()` functions, but note that the `axis` parameter applies to many other NumPy functions.

The `.min()` and `.max()` methods return the minimum and maximum values in an array. The `.argmax()` and `.argmin()` functions return the position of the maximum or minimum value in the array:

```
In [82]:
    # demonstrate some of the properties of NumPy arrays
    m = np.arange(10, 19).reshape(3, 3)
    print (a)
    print ("{0} min of the entire matrix".format(m.min()))
    print ("{0} max of entire matrix".format(m.max()))
    print ("{0} position of the min value".format(m.argmin()))
    print ("{0} position of the max value".format(m.argmax()))
    print ("{0} mins down each column".format(m.min(axis = 0)))
    print ("{0} mins across each row".format(m.min(axis = 1)))
    print ("{0} maxs down each column".format(m.max(axis = 0)))
```

```
print ("{0} maxs across each row".format(m.max(axis = 1)))


[[ 0  1  2]
 [ 3  4  5]
 [ 6  7  8]
 [ 9 10 11]]
10 min of the entire matrix
18 max of entire matrix
0 position of the min value
8 position of the max value
[10 11 12] mins down each column
[10 13 16] mins across each row
[16 17 18] maxs down each column
[12 15 18] maxs across each row
```

The .mean(), .std(), and .var() methods compute the mathematical mean, standard deviation, and variance of the values in an array:

```
In [83]:
    # demonstrate included statistical methods
    a = np.arange(10)
    a


Out[83]:
    array([0, 1, 2, 3, 4, 5, 6, 7, 8, 9])


In [84]:
    a.mean(), a.std(), a.var()


Out[84]:
    (4.5, 2.8722813232690143, 8.25)
```

The sum and products of all the elements in an array can be computed with the `.sum()` and `.prod()` methods:

```
In [85]:
    # demonstrate sum and prod
    a = np.arange(1, 6)
    a


    Out[85]:
    array([1, 2, 3, 4, 5])
```

```
In [86]:
    a.sum(), a.prod()


Out[86]:
    (15, 120)
```

The cumulative sum and products can be computed with the `.cumsum()` and `.cumprod()` methods:

```
In [87]:
    a # and cumulative sum and prod
    a.cumsum(), a.cumprod()


Out[87]:
    (array([ 1,  3,  6, 10, 15]), array([ 1,   2,   6, 24, 120]))
```

The `.all()` method returns `True` if all elements of an array are true, and `.any()` returns `True` if any element of the array is true.

```
In [88]:
    # applying logical operators
    a = np.arange(10)
    (a < 5).any() # any < 5?


Out[88]:
    True


In [89]:
```

```
(a < 5).all() # all < 5? (a < 5).any() # any < 5?
```

Out[89]:

    False

The `.size` property returns the number of elements in the array across all dimensions:

In [90]:

```
# size is always the total number of elements
np.arange(10).reshape(2, 5).size
```

Out[90]:

    10

Also, `.ndim` returns the overall dimensionality of an array:

In [91]:

```
# .ndim will give you the total # of dimensions
np.arange(10).reshape(2,5).ndim
```

Out[91]:

    2

There are a number of valuable statistical functions, as well as a number of descriptive statistical functions besides those demonstrated here. This was meant to be a brief overview of NumPy arrays, and the next two chapters on pandas `Series` and `DataFrame` objects will dive deeper into these additional methods.

Summary

In this chapter, we have examined NumPy arrays to get an understanding of their capabilities to manipulate data and performe operations on data including selecting elements, vectorization, Boolean selection, reshaping, stacking, concatenation, splitting, and slicing. NumPy has many other features, but these are the ones that are important to understand as they will set a frame of reference for understanding the operation of pandas `Series` and `DataFrame` objects. All the concepts covered in this chapter will be examined in much more detail in the next two chapters, where they are applied to pandas objects, which extend these capabilities to provide a much richer and more expressive means of representing and manipulating data than is offered with NumPy arrays.

4
The pandas Series Object

pandas is a high-performance library that provides a comprehensive set of data structures for manipulating tabular data, providing high-performance indexing, automatic alignment, reshaping, grouping, joining, and statistical analyses capabilities.

The two primary data structures in pandas are the `Series` and the `DataFrame` objects. In this chapter, we will examine the `Series` object and how it builds on the features of a NumPy `ndarray` to provide operations such as indexing, axis labeling, alignment, handling of missing data, and merging across multiple series of data.

In this chapter, we will cover the following topics:

- Creating and initializing a `Series` and its index
- Determining the shape of a `Series` object
- Heads, tails, uniqueness, and counts of values
- Looking up values in a `Series` object
- Boolean selection
- Alignment via index labels
- Arithmetic operations on a `Series` object
- Reindexing a `Series` object
- Applying arithmetic operations on `Series` objects
- The special case of Not-A-Number (`NaN`)
- Slicing `Series` objects

The Series object

The `Series` is the primary building block of pandas. A `Series` represents a one-dimensional labeled indexed array based on the NumPy `ndarray`. Like an array, a `Series` can hold zero or more values of any single data type.

A pandas `Series` deviates from NumPy arrays by adding an associated set of labels that are used to index and efficiently access the elements of the array by the label values instead of just by the integer position. This labeled index is a key feature of pandas `Series` (and, as we will see, also a `DataFrame`) and adds significant power for accessing the elements of the `Series` over a NumPy array.

A `Series` always has an index even if one is not specified. In this default case, pandas will create an index that consists of sequential integers starting from zero. This default behavior will make a `Series` initially appear to be very similar to a NumPy array. This is by design, as a `Series` was derived from a NumPy array. This allowed a `Series` to be used by existing NumPy array code that used integer-based position lookup. In recent versions of pandas, this derivation from `ndarray` has been removed, but the `Series` still remains mostly API compatible.

Even though a `Series` with a default integer index will appear identical to a NumPy array, access to elements is not by integer position but using values in the index (referred to as labels). The pandas library will use the provided labels to perform a lookup of values for those labels. Unlike an array, index labels do not need to be integers, they can have repeated labels, can have hierarchical sets of labels, and are integrally utilized in a pandas concept, known as automatic alignment of values by index label.

This automatic alignment is arguably the most significant change that a `Series` makes over `ndarray`. Operations applied across multiple pandas objects (a simple example can be addition) are not blindly applied to the values in order by position in the `Series`. The pandas library will first align the two pandas objects by the index labels and then apply the operation values with aligned labels. This is in a way, a simple type of join and allows you to associate data with common index labels without any effort.

A pandas index is a first-class component of pandas. pandas provides various specializations of indexes for different data types with each being highly optimized for that specific type of data, be it integers, floats, strings, `datetime` objects, or any type of hashable pandas object. Additionally, a `Series` can be reindexed into other types of indexes, effectively providing different views into the `Series` object using different indexes.

This ability to dynamically construct alternative views on data using ad hoc indexes establishes an environment for interactive data manipulation, where data can stay in a single structure but can be easily morphed into different views. This facilitates creating a very interactive environment to play with information and intuitively discovering meaning without having to be overburdened by its structure, such as with relational tools such as SQL.

Importing pandas

Importing pandas into your application is simple. The following code is a fairly standard convention that is used:

```
In [1]:
    # bring in NumPy and pandas
    import numpy as np
    import pandas as pd
```

Importing of both NumPy and pandas is fairly common, with their objects mapped into the np and pd namespaces, respectively. It is also common to import several classes from pandas into the global namespace, but for the purpose of this text, we will explicitly reference all objects through the pd namespace prefix.

pandas also provides several options that can be set to control the formatting of output. The notebooks in this book will use the following code or a slight variant to control the representation of the rendering, as well as setting a maximum number of rows and columns to be displayed in the output any code example.

```
In [2]:
    # Set some pandas options for controlling output display
    pd.set_option('display.notebook_repr_html', False)
    pd.set_option('display.max_columns', 10)
    pd.set_option('display.max_rows', 10)
```

Creating Series

A Series can be created and initialized by passing either a scalar value, a NumPy ndarray, a Python list, or a Python Dict as the data parameter of the Series constructor. This is the default parameter and does not need to be specified if it is the first item.

The index parameter of the constructor assigns a user defined index to the Series that functions similar to a database index. This index provides a means to look up elements in the Series by index label and not by the elements' position in the array.

If you do not specify an index at the creation of a Series, the Series object will construct an index automatically using integer values starting from zero and increasing by one for each item in the Series.

The simplest means of creating a Series is from a scalar value. A Series with a single value has important uses in various mathematical operations such as applying a unified value across all the elements of another Series or DataFrame. The following code creates a one-item Series from the scalar value 1:

```
In [3]:
    # create one item Series
    s1 = pd.Series(2)
    s1


Out[3]:
    0    2
    dtype: int64
```

Note the output when the series s1 is printed. Two integers are displayed. The 0 value is the index label of the single item in the Series whose value is 2. The data type of the Series object is also shown as being int64. The index label is what we can use to retrieve the associated value from the Series:

```
In [4]:
    # get value with label 0
    s1[0]


Out[4]:
    2
```

This looks like a normal array access of the item at position zero in the array, but pandas really references the index of the Series for a label of value 0 and then returns the matching values.

The following example creates a `Series` from a Python list:

```
In [5]:
    # create a series of multiple items from a list
    s2 = pd.Series([1, 2, 3, 4, 5])
    s2
```

```
Out[5]:
    0    1
    1    2
    2    3
    3    4
    4    5
    dtype: int64
```

Since an index was not specified at the time of creation, pandas created an index for us with sequential zero-based integer values.

The array of values in the `Series` can be retrieved using the `.values` property, as shown here:

```
In [6]:
    # get the values in the Series
    s2.values
```

```
Out[6]:
    array([1, 2, 3, 4, 5])
```

Also, the index of the series can be retrieved with the `.index` property:

```
In [7]:
    # get the index of the Series
    s2.index
```

```
Out[7]:
    Int64Index([0, 1, 2, 3, 4], dtype='int64')
```

This informs us that the type of index created by pandas is `Int64Index`, it also informs about the labels in the index and their data type.

pandas will create different index types based on the type of data identified in the index parameter. These different index types are optimized to perform indexing operations for that specific data type. To specify the index at the time of creation of the Series, use the index parameter of the constructor. The following example creates a Series and assigns strings to each label of the index:

```
In [8]:
    # explicitly create an index
    # index is alpha, not integer
    s3 = pd.Series([1, 2, 3], index=['a', 'b', 'c'])
    s3

Out[8]:
    a    1
    b    2
    c    3
    dtype: int64

In [9]:
    s3.index

Out[9]:
    Index([u'a', u'b', u'c'], dtype='object')
```

The type of items in the index that are created are now of type object. The following example retrieves the value of the item in the Series with index label 'c':

```
In [10]:
    # lookup by label value, not integer position
    s3['c']

Out[10]:
    3
```

A `Series` created from a single scalar value is useful, as it allows you to apply an operation and a single value across all elements of a `Series`. When creating a `Series` object with a scalar and specifying an index with multiple labels, pandas will copy the scalar value to associate with each index label. The following code demonstrates this by creating a `Series` with a scalar value and an index based on an already existing index:

```
In [11]:
    # create Series from an existing index
    # scalar value with be copied at each index label
    s4 = pd.Series(2, index=s2.index)
    s4
```

```
Out[11]:
    0    2
    1    2
    2    2
    3    2
    4    2
    dtype: int64
```

It is a common practice to initialize the `Series` objects using NumPy `ndarrays`, and with various NumPy functions that create arrays. The following code creates a `Series` from five normally distributed values:

```
In [12]:
    # generate a Series from 5 normal random numbers
    np.random.seed(123456)
    pd.Series(np.random.randn(5))
```

```
    Out[12]:
    0     0.469112
    1    -0.282863
    2    -1.509059
    3    -1.135632
    4     1.212112
    dtype: float64
```

NumPy also provides several convenient functions to create arrays (and hence
`Series` objects). The `np.linspace()` method creates an array of values between
two specified values:

```
In [13]:
    # 0 through 9
    pd.Series(np.linspace(0, 9, 10))
```

```
Out[13]:
    0    0
    1    1
    2    2
    3    3
    4    4
    5    5
    6    6
    7    7
    8    8
    9    9
    dtype: float64
```

Likewise, the `np.arange()` method creates an array of values between two
specified values:

```
In [14]:
    # 0 through 8
    pd.Series(np.arange(0, 9))
```

```
Out[14]:
    0    0
    1    1
    2    2
    3    3
    4    4
    5    5
    6    6
    7    7
    8    8
    dtype: int64
```

Finally, a `Series` can be directly initialized from a Python dictionary. The keys of the dictionary are used as the index labels for the `Series`:

```
In [15]:
    # create Series from dict
    s6 = pd.Series({'a': 1, 'b': 2, 'c': 3, 'd': 4})
    s6

Out[15]:
    a    1
    b    2
    c    3
    d    4
    dtype: int64
```

Size, shape, uniqueness, and counts of values

The number of items in a `Series` object can be determined by several techniques. To demonstrate this, we will use the following `Series`:

```
In [16]:
    # example series, which also contains a NaN
    s = pd.Series([0, 1, 1, 2, 3, 4, 5, 6, 7, np.nan])
    s

Out[16]:
    0      0
    1      1
    2      1
    3      2
    4      3
    5      4
    6      5
    7      6
    8      7
    9    NaN
    dtype: float64
```

The length can be determined using the `len()` function:

```
In [17]:
    # length of the Series
    len(s)
```

```
Out[17]:
    10
```

Alternately, the length can be determined using the `.size` property:

```
In [18]:
    # .size is also the # of items in the Series
    s.size
```

```
Out[18]:
    10
```

The `.shape` property returns a tuple where the first item is the number of items:

```
In [19]:
    # .shape is a tuple with one value
    s.shape
```

```
Out[19]:
    (10,)
```

The number of the values that are not part of the NaN can be found by using the `.count()` method:

```
In [20]:
    # count() returns the number of non-NaN values
    s.count()
```

```
Out[20]:
    9
```

To determine all of the unique values in a `Series`, pandas provides the `.unique()` method:

```
In [21]:
    # all unique values
```

```
    s.unique()
```

Out[21]:

```
    array([ 0.,    1.,    2.,    3.,    4.,    5.,    6.,    7.,    nan])
```

Also, the count of each of the unique items in a `Series` can be obtained using
`.value_counts()`:

In [22]:

```
    # count of non-NaN values, returned max to min order
    s.value_counts()
```

Out[22]:

```
    1    2
    7    1
    6    1
    5    1
    4    1
    3    1
    2    1
    0    1
    dtype: int64
```

Peeking at data with heads, tails, and take

pandas provides the `.head()` and `.tail()` methods to examine just the first few,
or last, records in a `Series`. By default, these return the first or last five rows,
respectively, but you can use the n parameter or just pass an integer to specify
the number of rows:

In [23]:

```
    # first five
    s.head()
```

Out[23]:

```
    0    0
    1    1
```

```
    2    1
    3    2
    4    3
    dtype: float64
```

In [24]:
```
    # first three
    s.head(n = 3) # s.head(3) is equivalent
```

Out[24]:
```
    0    0
    1    1
    2    1
    dtype: float64
```

In [25]:
```
    # last five
    s.tail()
```

Out[25]:
```
    5      4
    6      5
    7      6
    8      7
    9    NaN
    dtype: float64
```

In [26]:
```
    # last 3
    s.tail(n = 3) # equivalent to s.tail(3)
```

Out[26]:
```
    7      6
    8      7
    9    NaN
    dtype: float64
```

The `.take()` method will return the rows in a series that correspond to the zero-based positions specified in a list:

```
In [27]:
    # only take specific items
    s.take([0, 3, 9])

Out[27]:
    0      0
    3      2
    9    NaN
    dtype: float64
```

Looking up values in Series

Values in a `Series` object can be retrieved using the `[]` operator and passing either a single index label or a list of index labels. The following code retrieves the value associated with the index label `'a'` of the `s3` series defined earlier:

```
In [28]:
    # single item lookup
    s3['a']

Out[28]:
    1
```

Accessing this `Series` using an integer value will perform a zero-based position lookup of the value:

```
In [29]:
    # lookup by position since the index is not an integer
    s3[1]

Out[29]:
    2
```

This is because pandas determines that the specified value is an integer and that the index is not an integer-based index. Given this, pandas decides to perform a lookup by position and not by index label.

To retrieve multiple items, you can pass a list of index labels via the `[]` operator. Instead of a single value, the result will be a new `Series` with both index labels and values, and data copied from the original `Series`.

```
In [30]:
    # multiple items
    s3[['a', 'c']]
```

```
Out[30]:
    a    1
    c    3
    dtype: int64
```

To elaborate on the use of integers for lookup based on either label or position, we can examine operations using the following `Series` where the index labels are integers but not starting from 0.

```
In [31]:
    # series with an integer index, but not starting with 0
    s5 = pd.Series([1, 2, 3], index=[10, 11, 12])
    s5
```

```
Out[31]:
    10    1
    11    2
    12    3
    dtype: int64
```

Also, the following code looks up the value at the index label of 11. Label-based lookup is performed because the type of the index is integer, as well as the value passed to the `[]` operator is integer:

```
In [32]:
    # by value as value passed and index are both integer
    s5[11]
```

```
Out[32]:
    2
```

If this was performed using a zero-based position lookup, an exception would be thrown as the Series only contains three items.

To alleviate the potential confusion in determining label-based lookup versus position-based lookup, index label based lookup can be enforced using the `.loc[]` accessor:

```
In [33]:
    # force lookup by index label
    s5.loc[12]


Out[33]:
    3
```

Lookup by position can be enforced using the `.iloc[]` accessor:

```
In [34]:
    # forced lookup by location / position
    s5.iloc[1]


Out[34]:
    2
```

These two options also function using lists, as shown in the following example:

```
In [35]:
    # multiple items by label (loc)
    s5.loc[[12, 10]]


Out[35]:
    12    3
    10    1
    dtype: int64


In [36]:
    # multiple items by location / position (iloc)
    s5.iloc[[0, 2]]


Out[36]:
```

```
10      1
12      3
dtype: int64
```

If a location/position passed to .iloc[] in a list is out of bounds, an exception will be thrown. This is different than with .loc[], which if passed a label that does not exist, will return NaN as the value for that label:

In [37]:

```
# -1 and 15 will be NaN
s5.loc[[12, -1, 15]]
```

Out[37]:

```
    12      3
    -1      NaN
    15      NaN
dtype: float64
```

When looking to write the highest performance code for accessing items in a Series, it is recommended that you use the .loc[] method using lookup by integer position.

A Series also has a property .ix that can be used to look up items either by label or by zero-based array position. To demonstrate this, let's revisit the s3 series:

In [38]:

```
# reminder of the contents of s3
s3
```

Out[38]:

```
    a      1
    b      2
    c      3
dtype: int64
```

The following example looks up by index label:

```
In [39]:
    # label based lookup
    s3.ix[['a', 'c']]

Out[39]:
    a    1
    c    3
    dtype: int64
```

The following example looks up by position:

```
In [40]:
    # position based lookup
    s3.ix[[1, 2]]

Out[40]:
    b    2
    c    3
    dtype: int64
```

This can become complicated if the indexes are integers and you pass a list of integers to .ix. Since they are of the same type, the lookup will be by index label instead of position:

```
In [41]:
    # this looks up by label and not position
    # note that 1,2 have NaN as those labels do not exist
    # in the index
    s5.ix[[1, 2, 10, 11]]

Out[41]:
    1     NaN
    2     NaN
    10    1
    11    2
    dtype: float64
```

This has reverted to label value lookup, and since there were no elements for labels 1 and 2, NaN was returned.

 Use of .ix is generally frowned upon by many practitioners due to this issue. It is recommended to use the .loc or .iloc[] techniques. Additionally, they are also better performing than .ix.

Alignment via index labels

A fundamental difference between a NumPy ndarray and a pandas Series is the ability of a Series to automatically align data from another Series based on label values before performing an operation.

We will examine alignment using the following two Series objects:

```
In [42]:
    s6 = pd.Series([1, 2, 3, 4], index=['a', 'b', 'c', 'd'])
    s6
```

```
Out[42]:
    a    1
    b    2
    c    3
    d    4
    dtype: int64
```

```
In [43]:
    s7 = pd.Series([4, 3, 2, 1], index=['d', 'c', 'b', 'a'])
    s7
```

```
Out[43]:
    d    4
    c    3
    b    2
    a    1
    dtype: int64
```

The following code adds the values in the two series:

```
In [44]:
    # add them
    s6 + s7
```

```
Out[44]:
    a    2
    b    4
    c    6
    d    8
    dtype: int64
```

The process of adding two `Series` objects differs from the process of addition of arrays as it first aligns data based on index label values instead of simply applying the operation to elements in the same position. This becomes significantly powerful when using pandas `Series` to combine data based on labels instead of having to first order the data manually.

 Also worth noting is the order of the items in the index resulting from the addition. The two `Series` in the addition had the same labels but were ordered differently. The index in the result is arranged in ascending order.

This is a very different result than what it would have been if it were two pure NumPy arrays being added. A NumPy `ndarray` would add the items in identical positions of each array resulting in different values:

```
In [45]:
    # see how different from adding numpy arrays
    a1 = np.array([1, 2, 3, 4])
    a2 = np.array([4, 3, 2, 1])
    a1 + a2
```

```
Out[45]:
    array([5, 5, 5, 5])
```

Arithmetic operations

Arithmetic operations (+, -, /, *, and so on) can be applied either to a `Series` or between two `Series` objects. When applied to a single Series, the operation is applied to all of the values in that `Series`. The following code demonstrates arithmetic operations applied to a `Series` object by multiplying the values in s3 by 2. The result is a new `Series` with the new values (s3 is unchanged).

```
In [46]:
    # multiply all values in s3 by 2
    s3 * 2
```

```
Out[46]:
    a    2
    b    4
    c    6
    dtype: int64
```

The preceding code is also roughly equivalent to the following code, which creates a new series from a scalar value using the index from s3. It has the same result, but it is not as efficient, as alignment is performed between the Series objects instead of a simple vectorization of the multiplication:

```
In [47]:
    # scalar series using s3's index
    t = pd.Series(2, s3.index)
    s3 * t
```

```
Out[47]:
    a    2
    b    4
    c    6
    dtype: int64
```

To reinforce the point that alignment is being performed when applying arithmetic operations across two `Series` objects, look at the following two Series as examples:

```
In [48]:
    # we will add this to s9
    s8 = pd.Series({'a': 1, 'b': 2, 'c': 3, 'd': 5})
    s8

Out[48]:
    a    1
    b    2
    c    3
    d    5
    dtype: int64

In [49]:
    # going to add this to s8
    s9 = pd.Series({'b': 6, 'c': 7, 'd': 9, 'e': 10})
    s9

Out[49]:
    b     6
    c     7
    d     9
    e    10
    dtype: int64
```

These two Series objects only have intersecting index labels 'b', 'c', and 'd'. We will add the two series results in the following example:

```
In [50]:
    # NaN's result for a and e
    # demonstrates alignment
    s8 + s9

Out[50]:
    a    NaN
```

```
b      8
c     10
d     14
e     NaN
dtype: float64
```

Since s8 has an 'a' label and s9 does not, the result is NaN. Likewise with s9 having an 'e' label and s8 not having the label. The NaN value is, by default the result of any pandas arithmetic operation where an index label does not align with the other Series.

The matching of labels and returning NaN where there are no matches is essential to how pandas operates as compared to arrays in NumPy. The tasks performed with pandas using Series (and DataFrame) objects are often such that multiple sets of data need to be aligned, and if there are no matching labels during alignment, then the operation should not fail. Hence, pandas returns NaN in those situations.

This is actually common as datasets used in various statistical, financial, and data science domains often are incomplete, and more graceful techniques are required than to throw exceptions. pandas makes the assumption to return NaN in these cases. To facilitate handling of the NaN values in data and as the result of alignment, pandas changes the way that operations handle NaN by default. We will examine this in the next section of this chapter.

The last example of alignment during arithmetical operations demonstrates the situation where the two Series objects have duplicate index labels. The following two Series objects each have two 'a' labels:

```
In [51]:
    # going to add this to s11
    s10 = pd.Series([1.0, 2.0, 3.0], index=['a', 'a', 'b'])
    s10
```

```
Out[51]:
    a      1
    a      2
    b      3
    dtype: float64
```

```
In [52]:
    # going to add this to s10
```

```
s11 = pd.Series([4.0, 5.0, 6.0], index=['a', 'a', 'c'])
s11
```

Out[52]:

```
a    4
a    5
c    6
dtype: float64
```

When the two `Series` objects are added (or any other operation performed), the resulting `Series` has four `'a'` index labels.

In [53]:

```
# will result in four 'a' index labels
s10 + s11
```

Out[53]:

```
a    5
a    6
a    6
a    7
b    NaN
c    NaN
dtype: float64
```

The reason for this is that during alignment, pandas actually performs a Cartesian product of the sets of all unique index labels in both `Series` objects, and then applies the specified operation on all items in the products. To explain why there are four `'a'` index values, s10 contains two `'a'` labels, and s11 also contains two `'a'` labels. Every combination of `'a'` labels in each will be calculated, resulting in four `'a'` labels. There is one `'b'` label from s10 and one `'c'` label from s11. Since there is no matching label for either in the other Series object, they only result in a single row in the resulting Series object. Each combination of values for `'a'` in both Series are computed, resulting in the four values: *1+4, 1+5, 2+4* and *2+5*.

So, remember that an index can have duplicate labels, and during alignment this will result in a number of index labels equivalent to the products of the number of the labels in each `Series`.

The special case of Not-A-Number (NaN)

pandas mathematical operators and functions handle NaN in a special manner (compared to NumPy) that does not break the computations. pandas is lenient with missing data assuming that it is a common situation.

To demonstrate the difference, we can examine the following code, which calculates the mean of a NumPy array:

```
In [54]:
    # mean of numpy array values
    nda = np.array([1, 2, 3, 4, 5])
    nda.mean()
```

```
Out[54]:
    3.0
```

The result is as expected. The following code replaces one value with a NaN value:

```
In [55]:
    # mean of numpy array values with a NaN
    nda = np.array([1, 2, 3, 4, np.NaN])
    nda.mean()
```

```
Out[55]:
    nan
```

When encountering a NaN value, NumPy simply returns NaN. pandas changes this, so that NaN values are ignored:

```
In [56]:
    # ignores NaN values
    s = pd.Series(nda)
    s.mean()
```

```
Out[56]:
    2.5
```

In this case, pandas override the mean function of the `Series` object so that NaN values are simply ignored. They are not counted as a 0 value; as shown here with calculating the mean, it does not get factored into the count of items used in the result. This behavior is similar to how other statistical languages, such as R, function. It is expected that data will be missing, and that you will "tidy" the data over progressive iterations, but until then you will still be able to produce analysis with data that is not tidy. Often, the conclusion you want to draw can be seen even with untidy data, and pandas will not work against you by determining this earlier in the analysis.

However, to provide some amount of backwards compatibility, the pandas library's functions such as `.mean()` support a parameter `skipna` that can force the operation to be the same as with NumPy:

```
In [57]:
    # handle NaN values like NumPy
    s.mean(skipna=False)
```

```
Out[57]:
    nan
```

Boolean selection

Items in a `Series` can be selected, based on the value instead of index labels, via the utilization of a Boolean selection. A Boolean selection applies a logical expression to the values of the Series and returns a new Series of Boolean values representing the result for each value. The following code demonstrates identifying items in a Series where the values are greater than 5:

```
In [58]:
    # which rows have values that are > 5?
    s = pd.Series(np.arange(0, 10))
    s > 5
```

```
Out[58]:
    0    False
    1    False
    2    False
    3    False
    4    False
    5    False
```

```
6        True
7        True
8        True
9        True
dtype: bool
```

To obtain the rows in the `Series` where the logical expression is `True`, simply pass the result of the Boolean expression to the `[]` operator of the `Series`. The result will be a new `Series` with a copy of index and value for the selected rows:

```
In [59]:
    # select rows where values are > 5
    logicalResults = s > 5
    s[logicalResults]

Out[59]:
    6        6
    7        7
    8        8
    9        9
    dtype: int64
```

pandas performs this Boolean selection by overloading the `Series` object's `[]` operator so that when passed a `Series` object consisting of boolean values it knows to return only the values in the outer Series (in this cases s) where the labels in the `Series` object are passed to a `[]` operator have True values.

This is actually very similar to how selection works in R, and can feel a bit unnatural at first for someone using a procedural or statistical programming language. However, this turns out to be very valuable and efficient in expressing many types of data analysis algorithms, and very convenient for extracting subsets of data based on its contents.

There is a shortcut syntax to perform the operation. You can use the name of the `Series` inside of the `[]` operator, as follows.

```
In [60]:
    # a little shorter version
    s[s > 5]

Out[60]:
```

```
6      6
7      7
8      8
9      9
dtype: int64
```

Unfortunately, multiple logical operators cannot be used in a normal Python syntax. As an example, the following causes an exception to be thrown:

```
In [61]:
    # commented as it throws an exception
    # s[s > 5 and s < 8]
```

There are technical reasons for why the preceding code does not work. The solution is to express the equation differently, putting parentheses around each of the logical conditions and using different operators for and/or ('|' and '&').

```
In [62]:
    # correct syntax
    s[(s > 5) & (s < 8)]
```

```
Out[62]:
    6      6
    7      7
    dtype: int64
```

It is possible to determine whether all the values in a `Series` match a given expression using the `.all()` method. The following asks if all elements in the series are greater than or equal to 0:

```
In [63]:
# are all items >= 0?
(s >= 0).all()
```

```
Out[63]:
    True
```

The .any() method returns True if any values satisfy the expressions. The following asks if any elements are less than 2:

```
In [64]:
    # any items < 2?
    s[s < 2].any()


Out[64]:
    True
```

> Note that I used a slightly different syntax than with the .all() example. Both are correct and you can use whichever suits your style better.

There is something important going on here that is worth mentioning. The result of these logical expressions is a Boolean selection, a Series of True and False values. The .sum() method of a Series, when given a series of Boolean values, will treat True as 1 and False as 0. The following demonstrates using this to determine the number of items in a Series that satisfy a given expression:

```
In [65]:
# how many values < 2?
(s < 2).sum()


Out[65]:
    2
```

Reindexing a Series

Reindexing in pandas is a process that makes the data in a Series or DataFrame match a given set of labels. This is core to the functionality of pandas as it enables label alignment across multiple objects, which may originally have different indexing schemes.

This process of performing a reindex includes the following steps:

1. Reordering existing data to match a set of labels.
2. Inserting NaN markers where no data exists for a label.
3. Possibly, filling missing data for a label using some type of logic (defaulting to adding NaN values).

Here is a simple example of reindexing a `Series`. The following `Series` has an index with numerical values, and the index is modified to be alphabetic by simply assigning a list of characters to the `.index` property. This makes the values accessible via the character labels in the new index:

```
In [66]:
    # sample series of five items
    s = pd.Series(np.random.randn(5))
    s
```

```
Out[66]:
    0    -0.173215
    1     0.119209
    2    -1.044236
    3    -0.861849
    4    -2.104569
    dtype: float64
```

```
In [67]:
    # change the index
    s.index = ['a', 'b', 'c', 'd', 'e']
    s
```

```
Out[67]:
    a    -0.173215
    b     0.119209
    c    -1.044236
    d    -0.861849
    e    -2.104569
    dtype: float64
```

 The number of elements in the list being assigned to the `.index` property must match the number of rows, or else an exception will be thrown.

Now, let's examine a slightly more practical example. The following code concatenates two `Series` objects resulting in duplicate index labels, which may not be desired in the resulting `Series`:

```
In [68]:
    # concat copies index values verbatim,
    # potentially making duplicates
    np.random.seed(123456)
    s1 = pd.Series(np.random.randn(3))
    s2 = pd.Series(np.random.randn(3))
    combined = pd.concat([s1, s2])
    combined

Out[68]:
    0     0.469112
    1    -0.282863
    2    -1.509059
    0    -1.135632
    1     1.212112
    2    -0.173215
    dtype: float64
```

To fix this, the following creates a new index for the concatenated result which has sequential and distinct values.

```
In [69]:
    # reset the index
    combined.index = np.arange(0, len(combined))
    combined

Out[69]:
    0     0.469112
    1    -0.282863
    2    -1.509059
    3    -1.135632
    4     1.212112
    5    -0.173215
    dtype: float64
```

Reindexing using the .index property in-place modifies the Series.

Greater flexibility in creating a new index is provided using the .reindex() method. An example of the flexibility of .reindex() over assigning the .index property directly is that the list provided to .reindex() can be of a different length than the number of rows in the Series:

```
In [70]:
    np.random.seed(123456)
    s1 = pd.Series(np.random.randn(4), ['a', 'b', 'c', 'd'])
    # reindex with different number of labels
    # results in dropped rows and/or NaN's
    s2 = s1.reindex(['a', 'c', 'g'])
    s2

Out[70]:
    a      0.469112
    c     -1.509059
    g           NaN
    dtype: float64
```

There are several things here that are important to point out about .reindex(). First is that the result of a .reindex() method is a new Series. This new Series has an index with labels that are provided as the parameter to .reindex(). For each item in the given parameter list, if the original Series contains that label, then the value is assigned to that label. If the label does not exist in the original Series, pandas assigns a NaN value. Rows in the Series without a label specified in the parameter of .reindex() is not included in the result.

To demonstrate that the result of .reindex() is a new Series object, changing a value in s2 does not change the values in s1:

```
In [71]:
    # s2 is a different Series than s1
    s2['a'] = 0
    s2

Out[71]:
    a      0.000000
```

```
    c    -1.509059
    g           NaN
    dtype: float64
```

In [72]:

```
    # this did not modify s1
    s1
```

Out[72]:

```
    a     0.469112
    b    -0.282863
    c    -1.509059
    d    -1.135632
    dtype: float64
```

Reindexing is also useful when you want to align two Series to perform an operation on matching elements from each series; however, for some reason, the two Series had index labels that will not initially align.

The following example demonstrates this, where the first Series has indexes as sequential integers, but the second has a string representation of what would be the same values:

In [73]:

```
    # different types for the same values of labels
    # causes big trouble
    s1 = pd.Series([0, 1, 2], index=[0, 1, 2])
    s2 = pd.Series([3, 4, 5], index=['0', '1', '2'])
    s1 + s2
```

Out[73]:

```
    0    NaN
    1    NaN
    2    NaN
    0    NaN
    1    NaN
    2    NaN
    dtype: float64
```

This is almost a catastrophic failure in accomplishing the desired result, and exemplifies a scenario where data may have been retrieved from two different systems that used different representations for the index labels. The reasons why this happens in pandas are as follows:

1. pandas first tries to align by the indexes and finds no matches, so it copies the index labels from the first series and tries to append the indexes from the second series.

2. However, since they are a different type, it defaults back to a zero-based integer sequence that results in duplicate values.

3. Finally, all values are NaN because the operation tries to add the item in the first series with the integer label 0, which has a value of 0, but can't find the item in the other series and therefore, the result is NaN (and this fails six times in this case).

Once this situation is identified, it becomes a fairly trivial situation to fix by reindexing the second series:

```
In [74]:
    # reindex by casting the label types
    # and we will get the desired result
    s2.index = s2.index.values.astype(int)
    s1 + s2

Out[74]:
    0    3
    1    5
    2    7
    dtype: int64
```

The default action of inserting NaN as a missing value during reindexing can be changed by using the `fill_value` parameter of the method. The following example demonstrates using 0 instead of NaN:

```
In [75]:
    # fill with 0 instead of NaN
    s2 = s.copy()
    s2.reindex(['a', 'f'], fill_value=0)

Out[75]:
```

```
a    -0.173215
f     0.000000
dtype: float64
```

When performing a reindex on ordered data such as a time series, it is possible to perform interpolation or filling of values. There will be a more elaborate discussion on interpolation and filling in *Chapter 10, Time-series Data*, but the following examples introduce the concept using this Series:

```
In [76]:
    # create example to demonstrate fills
    s3 = pd.Series(['red', 'green', 'blue'], index=[0, 3, 5])
    s3

Out[76]:
    0       red
    3     green
    5      blue
    dtype: object
```

The following example demonstrates forward filling, often referred to as "last known value." The Series is reindexed to create a contiguous integer index, and using the method='ffill' parameter, any new index labels are assigned the previously known values that are not part of NaN value from earlier in the Series object:

```
In [77]:
    # forward fill example
    s3.reindex(np.arange(0,7), method='ffill')

Out[77]:
    0       red
    1       red
    2       red
    3     green
    4     green
    5      blue
    6      blue
    dtype: object
```

The following example fills backward using `method='bfill'`:

```
In [78]:
    # backwards fill example
    s3.reindex(np.arange(0,7), method='bfill')
```

```
Out[78]:
    0       red
    1     green
    2     green
    3     green
    4      blue
    5      blue
    6       NaN
    dtype: object
```

Modifying a Series in-place

There are several ways that an existing `Series` can be modified in-place, having either its values changed or having rows added or deleted. In-place modification of a `Series` is a slightly controversial topic. When possible, it is preferred to perform operations that return a new Series with the modifications represented in the new Series. However, it is possible to change values and add/remove rows in-place, and they will be explained here briefly.

A new item can be added to a `Series` by assigning a value to an index label that does not already exist. The following code creates a `Series` object and adds a new item to the series:

```
In [79]:
    # generate a Series to play with
    np.random.seed(123456)
    s = pd.Series(np.random.randn(3), index=['a', 'b', 'c'])
    s
```

```
Out[79]:
    a     0.469112
    b    -0.282863
    c    -1.509059
```

```
dtype: float64
```

In [80]:
```
# change a value in the Series
# this is done in-place
# a new Series is not returned that has a modified value
s['d'] = 100
s
```

Out[80]:
```
a         0.469112
b        -0.282863
c        -1.509059
d       100.000000
dtype: float64
```

The value at a specific index label can be changed by assignment:

In [81]:
```
# modify the value at 'd' in-place
s['d'] = -100
s
```

Out[81]:
```
a         0.469112
b        -0.282863
c        -1.509059
d      -100.000000
dtype: float64
```

Items can be removed from a `Series` using the `del()` function and passing the index label(s) to be removed. The following code removes the item at index label `'a'`:

In [82]:
```
# remove a row / item
del(s['a'])
s
```

Out[82]:

```
b       -0.282863
c       -1.509059
d     -100.000000
dtype: float64
```

 To add and remove items out-of-place, you use pd.concat() to add and remove a Boolean selection.

Slicing a Series

In *Chapter 3, NumPy for pandas*, we covered techniques for NumPy array slicing. pandas Series objects also support slicing and override the slicing operators to perform their magic on Series data. Just like NumPy arrays, you can pass a slice object to the [] operator of the Series to get the specified values. Slices also work with the .loc[], .iloc[], and .ix properties and accessors.

To demonstrate slicing, we will use the following Series:

```
In [83]:
    # a Series to use for slicing
    # using index labels not starting at 0 to demonstrate
    # position based slicing
    s = pd.Series(np.arange(100, 110), index=np.arange(10, 20))
    s

Out[83]:
    10      100
    11      101
    12      102
    13      103
    14      104
    15      105
    16      106
    17      107
    18      108
    19      109
    dtype: int64
```

The slice syntax is identical to that in NumPy arrays. The following example selects rows from the `Series` by position starting from and including 0, up to but not inclusive of 6, and stepping by 2 (alternate):

```
In [84]:
    # items at position 0, 2, 4
    s[0:6:2]
```

```
Out[84]:
    10      100
    12      102
    14      104
    dtype: int64
```

This is functionally equivalent to the following code:

```
In [85]:
    # equivalent to
    s.iloc[[0, 2, 4]]
```

```
Out[85]:
    10      100
    12      102
    14      104
    dtype: int64
```

A good feature of slicing is that particular elements of the slice are optional. The following example omits the start value and selects all items within positions 0 through 4. This is also a convenient shorthand for the `.head()` function of the `Series`:

```
In [86]:
    # first five by slicing, same as .head(5)
    s[:5]

    Out[86]:
    10      100
    11      101
    12      102
```

```
13     103
14     104
dtype: int64
```

Flipping this around, you can select all the elements from a particular position to the end of the `Series`:

```
In [87]:
    # fourth position to the end
    s[4:]
```

```
Out[87]:
    14     104
    15     105
    16     106
    17     107
    18     108
    19     109
    dtype: int64
```

A step can be used in both scenarios, as can be seen here:

```
In [88]:
    # every other item in the first five positions
    s[:5:2]
```

```
Out[88]:
    10     100
    12     102
    14     104
    dtype: int64
```

```
In [89]:
    # every other item starting at the fourth position
    s[4::2]
```

```
Out[89]:
```

```
14      104
16      106
18      108
dtype: int64
```

An interesting usage of slicing is to specify a negative step. The following code returns the reverse of the `Series`:

```
In [90]:
    # reverse the Series
    s[::-1]

Out[90]:
    19      109
    18      108
    17      107
    16      106
    15      105
    14      104
    13      103
    12      102
    11      101
    10      100
    dtype: int64
```

Alternately, we can execute the following code if we want every other element, starting with position 4, in reverse:

```
In [91]:
    # every other starting at position 4, in reverse
    s[4::-2]

Out[91]:
    14      104
    12      102
    10      100
    dtype: int64
```

Negative values for the start and end of a slice have special meaning. If the series has *n* elements, then negative values for the start and end of the slice represent elements *n + start* through and not including *n + end*. This sounds a little confusing, but can be understood simply with the following example:

```
In [92]:
    # :-2, which means positions 0 through (10-2) [8]
    s[:-2]


Out[92]:
    10      100
    11      101
    12      102
    13      103
    14      104
    15      105
    16      106
    17      107
    dtype: int64
```

What we have discovered is a shorthand for selecting all of the items except for the last *n*, in this case *n* being 2 (-2 as passed to the slice). We can also pick the last *n* items in a series by using *–n* as the start and omitting the end component of the slice. This is also equivalent to using .tail(), but uses a little less typing (and this is a good thing):

```
In [93]:
    # last three items of the series
    s[-3:]


Out[93]:
    17      107
    18      108
    19      109
    dtype: int64
```

These can be combined, like in the following example, which returns all but the last row in the last four rows of the `Series`:

```
In [94]:
    # equivalent to s.tail(4).head(3)
    s[-4:-1]

Out[94]:
    16      106
    17      107
    18      108
    dtype: int64
```

An important thing to keep in mind when using slicing, is that the result of the slice is actually a view into the original `Series`. Modification of values through the result of the slice will modify the original `Series`. Consider the following example, which selects the first two elements in the `Series` and stores it into a new variable:

```
In [95]:
    copy = s.copy() # preserve s
    slice = copy[:2] # slice with first two rows
    slice

Out[95]:
    10      100
    11      101
    dtype: int64
```

Now, the assignment of a value to an element of a slice will change the value in the original `Series`:

```
In [96]:
    # change item with label 10 to 1000
    slice[11] = 1000
    # and see it in the source
    copy

Out[96]:
    10      100
    11      1000
```

```
12      102
13      103
14      104
15      105
16      106
17      107
18      108
19      109
dtype: int64
```

 Keep this in mind as it is powerful, because if you were expecting slicing to use a copy of the data you will likely be tracking down some bugs in the future.

Slicing can be performed on `Series` objects with a noninteger index. The following `Series` will be used to demonstrate this:

```
In [97]:
    # used to demonstrate the next two slices
    s = pd.Series(np.arange(0, 5),
                  index=['a', 'b', 'c', 'd', 'e'])
    s
```

```
Out[97]:
    a    0
    b    1
    c    2
    d    3
    e    4
    dtype: int64
```

Slicing with integer values will extract items based on position:

```
In [98]:
    # slices by position as the index is characters
    s[1:3]
```

```
Out[98]:
```

```
b    1
c    2
dtype: int64
```

With the noninteger index, it is also possible to slice with values in the same type of the index:

```
In [99]:
    # this slices by the strings in the index
    s['b':'d']

Out[99]:
    b    1
    c    2
    d    3
    dtype: int64
```

Summary

In this chapter, you learned about the pandas `Series` object and how it provides capabilities beyond that of the NumPy array. We examined how to create and initialize a `Series` and its associated index. Using a Series, we then looked at how to manipulate the data in one or more `Series` objects, including alignment by labels, various means of rearranging and changing data, and applying arithmetical operations. We closed with examining how to reindex and perform slicing.

In the next chapter, you will learn how the `DataFrame` is used to represent multiple `Series` of data that are automatically aligned to a `DataFrame` level index, providing a uniform and automatic ability to represent multiple values for each index label.

5
The pandas DataFrame Object

The pandas DataFrame object extends the capabilities of the Series object into two-dimensions. A Series object adds an index to a NumPy array but can only associate a single data item per index label, a DataFrame integrates multiple Series objects by aligning them along common index labels. This automatic alignment by index label provides a seamless view across all the Series at each index label that has the appearance of a row in a table.

A DataFrame object can be thought of as a dictionary-like container of one or more Series objects, or as a spreadsheet, probably the best description for those new to pandas is to compare a DataFrame object to a relational database table. However, even that comparison is limited, as a DataFrame object has very distinct qualities (such as automatic data alignment of series) that make it much more capable for exploratory data analysis than either a spreadsheet or relational database table.

Because of the increased dimensionality of the DataFrame object, it becomes necessary to provide a means to select both rows and columns. Carrying over from a Series, the DataFrame uses the [] operator for selection, but it is now applied to the selection of columns of data. This means that another construct must be used to select specific rows of a DataFrame object. For those operations, a DataFrame object provides several methods and attributes that can be used in various fashions to select data by rows.

A DataFrame also introduces the concept of multiple axes, specifically the horizontal and vertical axis. Functions from pandas can then be applied to either axis, in essence stating that the operation be applied horizontally to all the values in the rows, or up and down each column.

In this chapter, we will examine the pandas DataFrame and how we can manipulate both the DataFrame and the data it represents to build a basis for performing interactive data analysis.

Specifically, in this chapter we will cover:

- Creating a `DataFrame` from scratch
- Loading sample data to demonstrate the capabilities of a `DataFrame` object
- Selecting columns of a `DataFrame` object
- Selecting rows and values of a `DataFrame` using the index
- Selecting rows of a `DataFrame` using Boolean selection
- Adding, replacing, and deleting columns from a `DataFrame`
- Adding, replacing, and deleting rows from a `DataFrame`
- Modifying scalar values in a `DataFrame`
- Arithmetic operations on the `DataFrame` objects
- Resetting and reindexing a `DataFrame`
- Hierarchically indexing a `DataFrame`
- Statistical methods of a `DataFrame`
- Summarized data and statistical methods of a `DataFrame`

Creating DataFrame from scratch

To use a `DataFrame` we first need to import pandas and set some options for output.

```
In [1]:
    # reference NumPy and pandas
    import numpy as np
    import pandas as pd

    # Set some pandas options
    pd.set_option('display.notebook_repr_html', False)
    pd.set_option('display.max_columns', 10)
    pd.set_option('display.max_rows', 10)
```

There are several ways to create a `DataFrame`. Probably the most straightforward way, is by creating it from a NumPy `array`. The following code creates a `DataFrame` from a two dimensional NumPy array.

```
In [2]:
    # create a DataFrame from a 2-d ndarray
```

```
pd.DataFrame(np.array([[10, 11], [20, 21]]))
```

Out[2]:

```
     0   1
0   10  11
1   20  21
```

Each row of the array forms a row in the `DataFrame` object. Since we did not specify an index, pandas creates a default `int64` index in the same manner as a `Series` object. Since we did not specify column names, pandas also assigns the names for each column with a zero-based integer series.

A `DataFrame` can also be initialized by passing a list of `Series` objects.

In [3]:

```
# create a DataFrame for a list of Series objects
df1 = pd.DataFrame([pd.Series(np.arange(10, 15)),
                    pd.Series(np.arange(15, 20))])
df1
```

Out[3]:

```
     0   1   2   3   4
0   10  11  12  13  14
1   15  16  17  18  19
```

The dimensions of a `DataFrame` object can be determined using its `.shape` property. A `DataFrame` is always two-dimensional. The first value informs us about the number of rows and the second value is the number of columns:

In [4]:

```
# what's the shape of this DataFrame
df1.shape  # it is two rows by 5 columns
```

Out[4]:

```
(2, 5)
```

Column names can be specified at the time of creating the `DataFrame` by using the `columns` parameter of the `DataFrame` constructor.

In [5]:

```
# specify column names
df = pd.DataFrame(np.array([[10, 11], [20, 21]]),
```

```
        columns=['a', 'b'])
df
```

```
Out[5]:
     a    b
0   10   11
1   20   21
```

The names of the columns of a `DataFrame` can be accessed with its `.columns` property:

```
In [6]:
    # what are the names of the columns?
    df.columns
```

```
Out[6]:
    Index([u'a', u'b'], dtype='object')
```

This value of the `.columns` property is actually a pandas index. The individual column names can be accessed by position.

```
In [7]:
    # retrieve just the names of the columns by position
    "{0}, {1}".format(df.columns[0], df.columns[1])
```

```
Out[7]:
    'a, b'
```

The names of the columns can be changed by assigning a list of the new names to the the `.columns` property:

```
In [8]:
    # rename the columns
    df.columns = ['c1', 'c2']
    df
```

```
Out[8]:
     c1   c2
0   10   11
1   20   21
```

Index labels can likewise be assigned using the `index` parameter of the constructor or by assigning a list directly to the `.index` property.

```
In [9]:
    # create a DataFrame with named columns and rows
    df = pd.DataFrame(np.array([[0, 1], [2, 3]]),
                      columns=['c1', 'c2'],
                      index=['r1', 'r2'])
    df
```

```
Out[9]:
        c1   c2
    r1   0   1
    r2   2   3
```

Similar to the `Series` object, the index of a `DataFrame` object can be accessed with its `.index` property:

```
In [10]:
    # retrieve the index of the DataFrame
    df.index
```

```
Out[10]:
    Index([u'r1', u'r2'], dtype='object')
```

A `DataFrame` object can also be created by passing a dictionary containing one or more `Series` objects, where the dictionary keys contain the column names and each series is one column of data:

```
In [11]:
    # create a DataFrame with two Series objects
    # and a dictionary
    s1 = pd.Series(np.arange(1, 6, 1))
    s2 = pd.Series(np.arange(6, 11, 1))
    pd.DataFrame({'c1': s1, 'c2': s2})
```

```
Out[11]:
        c1   c2
    0    1   6
    1    2   7
```

```
2    3    8
3    4    9
4    5   10
```

A `DataFrame` also performs automatic alignment of the data for each `Series` passed in by a dictionary. For example, the following code adds a third column in the `DataFrame` initialization. This third `Series` contains two values and will specify its index. When the `DataFrame` is created, each series in the dictionary is aligned with each other by the index label, as it is added to the `DataFrame` object. The code is as follows:

```
In [12]:
    # demonstrate alignment during creation
    s3 = pd.Series(np.arange(12, 14), index=[1, 2])
    df = pd.DataFrame({'c1': s1, 'c2': s2, 'c3': s3})
    df
```

```
Out[12]:
        c1   c2   c3
    0    1    6  NaN
    1    2    7   12
    2    3    8   13
    3    4    9  NaN
    4    5   10  NaN
```

The first two `Series` did not have an index specified, so they both were indexed with 0..4. The third `Series` has index values, and therefore the values for those indexes are placed in `DataFrame` in the row with the matching index from the previous columns. Then, pandas automatically filled in `NaN` for the values that were not supplied.

Example data

Where possible, the examples in this chapter will utilize several datasets provided with the code in the download for the text. These datasets make the examples a little less academic in nature. These datasets will be read from files using the `pd.read_csv()` function that will load the sample data from the file into a `DataFrame` object.

 pd.read_csv() will be more extensively examined in *Chapter 6, Accessing Data*. For now, its function is simply to load some example `DataFrame` objects.

The remainder of the samples will still utilize the `DataFrame` objects created on demand if they demonstrate the concept being examined in a better way. Let's see the brief descriptions of these datasets.

S&P 500

The first dataset we will use is a snapshot of the S&P 500 from Yahoo! Finance. The following code shows the first three lines of the file:

```
In [13]:
    # show the first three lines of the file
    !head -n 3 data/sp500.csv # on Mac or Linux
    # !type data\sp500.csv # on Windows, but will show the entire file
```

```
Out[13]:
    Symbol,Name,Sector,Price,Dividend Yield,Price/Earnings,Earnings/
    Share,Book Value,52 week low,52 week high,Market Cap,EBITDA,Price/
    Sales,Price/Book,SEC Filings
    MMM,3M Co.,Industrials,141.14,2.12,20.33,6.90,26.668,107.15,
    143.37,92.345,8.121,2.95,5.26,http://www.sec.gov/cgi-bin/browse-
    edgar?action=getcompany&CIK=MMM
    ABT,Abbott Laboratories,Health Care,39.60,1.82,25.93,1.529,15.573,
    32.70,40.49,59.477,4.359,2.74,2.55,http://www.sec.gov/cgi-bin/browse-
    edgar?action=getcompany&CIK=ABT
```

The first line is the name of the field, and the remaining 500 lines represents the values for the 500 different stocks.

For now, we will load this data into a `DataFrame` that we can used to demonstrate various operations. This code only uses four specific columns of data in the file by specifying those columns via the `usecols` parameter to `pd.read_csv()`. This makes the output for examples a bit less unwieldy.

The following reads in the data.

```
In [14]:
    # read in the data and print the first five rows
    # use the Symbol column as the index, and
    # only read in columns in positions 0, 2, 3, 7
    sp500 = pd.read_csv("data/sp500.csv",
                        index_col='Symbol',
                        usecols=[0, 2, 3, 7])
```

We can examine the first five rows of the DataFrame using the .head() method. The examples will use this method frequently to limit the number of rows in the output of the examples.

```
In [15]:
    # peek at the first 5 rows of the data using .head()
    sp500.head()
```

```
Out[15]:
```

Symbol	Sector	Price	Book Value
MMM	Industrials	141.14	26.668
ABT	Health Care	39.60	15.573
ABBV	Health Care	53.95	2.954
ACN	Information Technology	79.79	8.326
ACE	Financials	102.91	86.897

Alternatively, we can examine the last five rows with the .tail() method:

```
In [16]:
    # peek at the first 5 rows of the data using .head()
    sp500.tail()
```

```
Out[16]:
```

Symbol	Sector	Price	Book Value
YHOO	Information Technology	35.02	12.768
YUM	Consumer Discretionary	74.77	5.147
ZMH	Health Care	101.84	37.181
ZION	Financials	28.43	30.191
ZTS	Health Care	30.53	2.150

We can see that there are indeed 500 rows of data.

```
In [17]:
    # how many rows of data?
    len(sp500)
```

```
Out[17]:
    500
```

The index of the `DataFrame` consists of the symbols for the 500 stocks representing the S&P 500.

```
In [18]:
    # examine the index
    sp500.index
```

```
Out[18]:
    Index([u'MMM', u'ABT', u'ABBV', u'ACN', u'ACE', u'ACT', u'ADBE',
    u'AES', u'AET', u'AFL', u'A', u'GAS', u'APD', u'ARG', u'AKAM', u'AA',
    u'ALXN', u'ATI', u'ALLE', u'AGN', u'ADS', u'ALL', u'ALTR', u'MO',
    u'AMZN', u'AEE', u'AEP', u'AXP', u'AIG', u'AMT', u'AMP', u'ABC',
    u'AME', u'AMGN', u'APH', u'APC', u'ADI', u'AON', u'APA', u'AIV',
    u'AAPL', u'AMAT', u'ADM', u'AIZ', u'T', u'ADSK', u'ADP', u'AN',
    u'AZO', u'AVB', u'AVY', u'AVP', u'BHI', u'BLL', u'BAC', u'BCR',
    u'BAX', u'BBT', u'BEAM', u'BDX', u'BBBY', u'BMS', u'BRK-B', u'BBY',
    u'BIIB', u'BLK', u'HRB', u'BA', u'BWA', u'BXP', u'BSX', u'BMY',
    u'BRCM', u'BF-B', u'CA', u'CVC', u'COG', u'CAM', u'CPB', u'COF',
    u'CAH', u'CFN', u'KMX', u'CCL', u'CAT', u'CBG', u'CBS', u'CELG',
    u'CNP', u'CTL', u'CERN', u'CF', u'CHRW', u'CHK', u'CVX', u'CMG',
    u'CB', u'CI', u'CINF', u'CTAS', ...], dtype='object')
```

Also, there are three columns in the `DataFrame`:

```
In [19]:
    # get the columns
    sp500.columns
```

```
Out[19]:
    Index([u'Sector', u'Price', u'Book Value'], dtype='object')
```

Monthly stock historical prices

The second dataset we will use, is the adjusted closing price for MSFT and AAPL for December 2014.

```
In [20]:
    # first three lines of the file
    !head -n 3 data/omh.csv # Mac or Linux
    # !type data\omh.csv # on Windows, but prints the entire file
```

```
Out[20]:
    Date,MSFT,AAPL
    2014-12-01,48.62,115.07
    2014-12-02,48.46,114.63
```

The data is read into a `DataFrame` as follows, and the first three lines examined using a slice:

```
In [21]:
    # read in the data
    one_mon_hist = pd.read_csv("data/omh.csv")
    # examine the first three rows
    one_mon_hist[:3]
```

```
Out[21]:
            Date    MSFT    AAPL
    0   2014-12-01  48.62  115.07
    1   2014-12-02  48.46  114.63
    2   2014-12-03  48.08  115.93
```

 This type of data is referred to as a time series. We will examine time series data in depth in *Chapter 10, Time-series Data*, but for the purposes of this chapter, we will use this data simply for demonstration of manipulating a `DataFrame`.

Selecting columns of a DataFrame

Selecting the data in specific columns of a `DataFrame` is performed by using the `[]` operator. This can be passed either as a single object, or a list of objects. These objects are then used to lookup columns either by zero-based location, or by matching the objects to the values in the columns index.

Passing a single integer, or a list of integers, to `[]` will have the `DataFrame` object attempt to perform a location based lookup of the columns. The following code retrieves the data in the second and third columns:

```
In [22]:
    # get first and second columns (1 and 2) by location
    sp500[[1, 2]].head()
```

```
Out[22]:
            Price  Book Value
```

Symbol		
MMM	141.14	26.668
ABT	39.60	15.573
ABBV	53.95	2.954
ACN	79.79	8.326
ACE	102.91	86.897

Selecting columns by passing a list of values will result in another `DataFrame`, with data copied from the original `DataFrame`. This is true, even if the list only has a single integer / value, as the following code demonstrates:

```
In [23]:
    # just the price column
    sp500[[1]].head()
```

```
Out[23]:
            Price
    Symbol
    MMM     141.14
    ABT      39.60
    ABBV     53.95
    ACN      79.79
    ACE     102.91
```

```
In [24]:
    # it's a DataFrame, not a Series
    type(sp500[[1]].head())
```

```
Out[24]:
    pandas.core.frame.DataFrame
```

Note that even though we asked for just a single column by position, the value was still in a list passed to the [] operator and hence the double set of brackets [[]]. This is important, as not passing a list always results in a value based lookup of the column.

The following code, therefore, throws an exception as the columns index does not have a value of 1:

```
In [25]:
    # this is an exception, hence it is commented
    # this tries to find a column named '1'
    # not the row at position 1
    # df = sp500[1]
```

But, this would work if the dtype of the columns index is an integer and it has a value 1:

```
In [26]:
    # create a new DataFrame with integers as the column names
    # make sure to use .copy() or change will be in-place
    df = sp500.copy()
    df.columns=[0, 1, 2]
    df.head()
```

```
Out[26]:
                                    0       1       2
    Symbol
    MMM                  Industrials   141.14  26.668
    ABT                  Health Care    39.60  15.573
    ABBV                 Health Care    53.95   2.954
    ACN        Information Technology   79.79   8.326
    ACE                   Financials   102.91  86.897
```

```
In [27]:
    # this is not an exception
    df[1]
```

```
Out[27]:
    Symbol
    MMM         141.14
    ABT          39.60
    ABBV         53.95
    ...
    ZMH         101.84
```

```
ZION        28.43
ZTS         30.53
Name: 1, Length: 500, dtype: float64
```

In [28]:

```
# because the column names are actually integers
# and therefore [1] is found as a column
df.columns
```

Out[28]:

```
Int64Index([0, 1, 2], dtype='int64')
```

In the preceding code, notice the selection of a single column using a single integer; when the DataFrame has an integer column index, it returns a Series and not a DataFrame.

In [29]:

```
# this is a Series not a DataFrame
type(df[1])
```

Out[29]:

```
pandas.core.series.Series
```

If you need a DataFrame, you can pass this Series to the constructor of a new DataFrame object, or pass the single value in a list.

If the values passed to [] consist of nonintegers, then the DataFrame will attempt to match the values to the values in the columns index. The following code retrieves the Price column by name:

In [30]:

```
# get price column by name
# result is a Series
sp500['Price']
```

Out[30]:

```
Symbol
MMM       141.14
ABT        39.60
```

```
ABBV          53.95

...

ZMH          101.84

ZION          28.43

ZTS           30.53

Name: Price, Length: 500, dtype: float64
```

Like with a column selection with a single location, this returned a `Series` and not a `DataFrame` object.

Multiple columns can be selected by name by passing a list of the values, and results in a `DataFrame` (even if a single item is passed in the list). The code is as follows:

```
In [31]:
    # get Price and Sector columns
    # since a list is passed, the result is a DataFrame
    sp500[['Price', 'Sector']]


Out[31]:
            Price                  Sector
    Symbol
    MMM       141.14              Industrials
    ABT        39.60              Health Care
    ABBV       53.95              Health Care
    ACN        79.79     Information Technology
    ACE       102.91               Financials

    ...         ...                    ...
    YHOO       35.02     Information Technology
    YUM        74.77     Consumer Discretionary
    ZMH       101.84              Health Care
    ZION       28.43               Financials
    ZTS        30.53              Health Care


    [500 rows x 2 columns]
```

Columns can also be retrieved using what is referred to as attribute access. Each column in a `DataFrame` dynamically adds a property to the `DataFrame` for each column where the name of the property is the name of the column. Since this selects a single column, the resulting value is a `Series`:

```
In [32]:
    # attribute access of the column by name
    sp500.Price
```

```
Out[32]:
    Symbol
    MMM        141.14
    ABT         39.60
    ABBV        53.95
    ...
    ZMH        101.84
    ZION        28.43
    ZTS         30.53
    Name: Price, Length: 500, dtype: float64
```

Note that this will not work for the `Book Value` column, as the name has a space.

If you do want to find the zero-based location of one or more columns using the name of the column (technically, the value of the index entry of a column), use the `.get_loc()` method of the `columns` index:

```
In [33]:
    # get the position of the column with the value of Price
    loc = sp500.columns.get_loc('Price')
    loc
```

```
Out[33]:
    1
```

Selecting rows and values of a DataFrame using the index

Elements of an array or `Series` are selected using the `[]` operator. `DataFrame` overloads `[]` to select columns instead of rows, except for a specific case of slicing. Therefore, most operations of selection of one or more rows in a `DataFrame`, require alternate methods to using `[]`.

Understanding this is important in pandas, as it is a common mistake is try and select rows using `[]` due to familiarity with other languages or data structures. When doing so, errors are often received, and can often be difficult to diagnose without realizing `[]` is working along a completely different axis than with a `Series` object.

Row selection using the index on a `DataFrame` then breaks down to the following general categories of operations:

- Slicing using the `[]` operator
- Label or location based lookup using `.loc`, `.iloc`, and `.ix`
- Scalar lookup by label or location using `.at` and `.iat`

We will briefly examine each of these techniques and attributes. Remember, all of these are working against the content of the index of the `DataFrame`. There is no involvement with data in the columns in the selection of the rows. We will cover that in the next section on Boolean selection.

Slicing using the [] operator

Slicing a `DataFrame` across its index is syntactically identical to performing the same on a `Series`. Because of this, we will not go into the details of the various permutations of slices in this section, and only give representative examples applied to a `DataFrame`.

Slicing works along both positions and labels. The following code demonstrates several examples of slicing by position:

```
In [34]:
    # first five rows
    sp500[:5]


Out[34]:
                        Sector    Price   Book Value
    Symbol
```

MMM	Industrials	141.14	26.668
ABT	Health Care	39.60	15.573
ABBV	Health Care	53.95	2.954
ACN	Information Technology	79.79	8.326
ACE	Financials	102.91	86.897

The following code returns rows starting with the ABT label through the ACN label:

```
In [35]:
    # ABT through ACN labels
    sp500['ABT':'ACN']
```

```
Out[35]:
                         Sector  Price  Book Value

    Symbol
    ABT             Health Care  39.60      15.573
    ABBV            Health Care  53.95       2.954
    ACN  Information Technology  79.79       8.326
```

In general, although slicing of a DataFrame has its uses, high performance systems tend to shy away from it and use other methods. Additionally, the slice notation for rows on a DataFrame using integers can be confusing, as it looks like accessing columns by position, and hence can lead to subtle bugs.

Selecting rows by index label and location: .loc[] and .iloc[]

Rows can be retrieved via an index label value using .loc[]. This is shown in the following code:

```
In [36]:
    # get row with label MMM
    # returned as a Series
    sp500.loc['MMM']
```

```
Out[36]:
    Sector          Industrials
    Price                141.14
    Book Value           26.668
```

```
Name: MMM, dtype: object
```

```
In [37]:
    # rows with label MMM and MSFT
    # this is a DataFrame result
    sp500.loc[['MMM', 'MSFT']]
```

```
Out[37]:
                            Sector    Price   Book Value
    Symbol
    MMM                  Industrials   141.14      26.668
    MSFT    Information Technology     40.12      10.584
```

Rows can also be retrieved by location using `.iloc[]`:

```
In [38]:
    # get rows in locations 0 and 2
    sp500.iloc[[0, 2]]
```

```
Out[38]:
                  Sector    Price   Book Value
    Symbol
    MMM      Industrials   141.14      26.668
    ABBV     Health Care    53.95       2.954
```

It is possible to look up the location in the index of a specific label value, which can then be used to retrieve the row(s):

```
In [39]:
    # get the location of MMM and A in the index
    i1 = sp500.index.get_loc('MMM')
    i2 = sp500.index.get_loc('A')
    "{0} {1}".format(i1, i2)
```

```
Out[39]:
    '0 10'
```

```
In [40]:
    # and get the rows
```

```
sp500.iloc[[i1, i2]]
```

Out[40]:

	Sector	Price	Book Value
Symbol			
MMM	Industrials	141.14	26.668
A	Health Care	56.18	16.928

Selecting rows by index label and/or location: .ix[]

Like a `Series`, a `DataFrame` also contains an `.ix` property that can be used to lookup rows, either by index label or location, essentially combining `.loc` and `.iloc` in one. The following looks up rows by index label by passing a list of nonintegers:

In [41]:

```
# by label
sp500.ix[['MSFT', 'ZTS']]
```

Out[41]:

	Sector	Price	Book Value
Symbol			
MSFT	Information Technology	40.12	10.584
ZTS	Health Care	30.53	2.150

Location-based lookup can be performed by passing a list of integers:

In [42]:

```
# by location
sp500.ix[[10, 200, 450]]
```

Out[42]:

	Sector	Price	Book Value
Symbol			
A	Health Care	56.18	16.928
GIS	Consumer Staples	53.81	10.236
TRV	Financials	92.86	73.056

In general, use of .ix is not preferred due to potential confusion, and use of .loc and .iloc is recommended and gives higher performance.

Scalar lookup by label or location using .at[] and .iat[]

Scalar values can be looked up by label using .at, by passing both the row label and then the column name/value:

```
In [43]:
    # by label in both the index and column
    sp500.at['MMM', 'Price']

Out[43]:
    141.14
```

Scalar values can also be looked up by location using .iat by passing both the row location and then the column location. This is the preferred method of accessing single values and gives the highest performance.

```
In [44]:
    # by location.  Row 0, column 1
    sp500.iat[0, 1]

Out[44]:
    141.14
```

Selecting rows of a DataFrame by Boolean selection

Rows can also be selected by using Boolean selection, using an array calculated from the result of applying a logical condition on the values in any of the columns. This allows us to build more complicated selections than those based simply upon index labels or positions.

Consider the following that is an array of all companies that have a price below `100.0`.

```
In [45]:
    # what rows have a price < 100?
    sp500.Price < 100

Out[45]:
    Symbol
    MMM        False
    ABT         True
    ABBV        True
    ...
    ZMH        False
    ZION        True
    ZTS         True
    Name: Price, Length: 500, dtype: bool
```

This results in a `Series` that can be used to select the rows where the value is `True`, exactly the same way it was done with a `Series` or a NumPy array:

```
In [46]:
    # now get the rows with Price < 100
    sp500[sp500.Price < 100]

Out[46]:
                            Sector  Price  Book Value
    Symbol
    ABT                Health Care  39.60      15.573
    ABBV               Health Care  53.95       2.954
    ACN     Information Technology  79.79       8.326
    ADBE    Information Technology  64.30      13.262
    AES                  Utilities  13.61       5.781
    ...                        ...    ...         ...
    XYL                Industrials  38.42      12.127
    YHOO    Information Technology  35.02      12.768
    YUM     Consumer Discretionary  74.77       5.147
    ZION                Financials  28.43      30.191
    ZTS                Health Care  30.53       2.150

    [407 rows x 3 columns]
```

Multiple conditions can be put together using parentheses; at the same time, it is possible to select only a subset of the columns. The following retrieves the symbols and price for all stocks with a price less than 10 and greater than 0:

```
In [47]:
    # get only the Price where Price is < 10 and > 0
    r = sp500[(sp500.Price < 10) &
             (sp500.Price > 0)] [['Price']]
    r

Out[47]:
          Price
    Symbol
    FTR       5.81
    HCBK      9.80
    HBAN      9.10
    SLM       8.82
    WIN       9.38
```

Modifying the structure and content of DataFrame

The structure and content of a `DataFrame` can be mutated in several ways. Rows and columns can be added and removed, and data within either can be modified to take on new values. Additionally, columns, as well as index labels, can also be renamed. Each of these will be described in the following sections.

Renaming columns

A column can be renamed using the `.rename()` method of the `DataFrame`. The `Book Value` column is inconvenient since it has a space, so we will rename it to `BookValue`:

```
In [48]:
    # rename the Book Value column to not have a space
    # this returns a copy with the column renamed
    df = sp500.rename(columns=
                     {'Book Value': 'BookValue'})
    # print first 2 rows
```

```
df[:2]
```

Out[48]:

```
            Sector     Price   BookValue
Symbol
MMM      Industrials   141.14    26.668
ABT      Health Care    39.60    15.573
```

This has returned a new `DataFrame` object with the renamed column and data copied from the original `DataFrame`. We can verify that the original `DataFrame` did not have its column names modified:

In [49]:

```
# verify the columns in the original did not change
sp500.columns
```

Out[49]:

```
Index([u'Sector', u'Price', u'Book Value'], dtype='object')
```

To modify the `DataFrame` without making a copy, we can use the `inplace=True` parameter to `.rename()`:

In [50]:

```
# this changes the column in-place
sp500.rename(columns=
             {'Book Value': 'BookValue'},
             inplace=True)
# we can see the column is changed
sp500.columns
```

Out[50]:

```
Index([u'Sector', u'Price', u'BookValue'], dtype='object')
```

A convenient side effect of this, is that the `DataFrame` now has a `.BookValue` attribute as before renaming the column, the space prevented attribute-based access of the column:

In [51]:

```
# and now we can use .BookValue
```

```
sp500.BookValue[:5]
```

Out[51]:
```
Symbol
MMM        26.668
ABT        15.573
ABBV        2.954
ACN         8.326
ACE        86.897
Name: BookValue, dtype: float64
```

Adding and inserting columns

Columns can be added to a DataFrame using several methods. The simplest way is by merging a new Series into the DataFrame object, along the index using the [] operator assigning the Series to a new column, with a name not already in the .columns index. Note that this will modify the DataFrame in-place and not result in a copy.

Alignment of data is important to understanding this process, as pandas does not simply concatenate the Series to the DataFrame. pandas will first align the data in the DataFrame with the Series using the index from both objects, and fill in the data from the Series into the new DataFrame at the appropriate index labels.

To demonstrate this, we will add a purely demonstrative column called TwicePrice which adds a new column with a calculated value of 2.0 * the Price column. Since this modifies the DataFrame object in-place, we will also make a copy and then add the column to the copy, so as to leave the original unmodified:

In [52]:
```
# make a copy
copy = sp500.copy()
# add a new column to the copy
copy['TwicePrice'] = sp500.Price * 2
copy[:2]
```

Out[52]:

	Sector	Price	BookValue	TwicePrice
Symbol				
MMM	Industrials	141.14	26.668	282.28
ABT	Health Care	39.60	15.573	79.20

This process is actually selecting the `Price` column out of the `sp500` object, then creating another `Series` with each value of the `Price` multiplied by two. The `DataFrame` then aligns this new `Series` by label, copies the data at the appropriate labels, and adds the column at the end of the columns index.

If you want to add the column at a different location in the `DataFrame` object, instead of at the rightmost position, use the `.insert()` method of the `DataFrame`. The following code inserts the `TwicePrice` column between `Price` and `BookValue`:

```
In [53]:
    copy = sp500.copy()
    # insert sp500.Price * 2 as the
    # second column in the DataFrame
    copy.insert(1, 'TwicePrice', sp500.Price * 2)
    copy[:2]
```

```
Out[53]:
                Sector    TwicePrice    Price    BookValue
    Symbol
    MMM      Industrials     282.28    141.14     26.668
    ABT      Health Care      79.20     39.60     15.573
```

It is important to remember that this is not simply inserting a column into the `DataFrame`. The alignment process used here is performing a left join of the `DataFrame` and the `Series` by their index labels, and then creating the column and populating the data in the appropriate cells in the `DataFrame` from matching entries in the `Series`. If an index label in the `DataFrame` is not matched in the `Series`, the value used will be `NaN`. Items in the `Series` that do not have a matching label will be ignored.

The following example demonstrates this operation:

```
In [54]:
    # extract the first four rows and just the Price column
    rcopy = sp500[0:3][['Price']].copy()
    rcopy
```

```
Out[54]:
              Price
    Symbol
    MMM      141.14
    ABT       39.60
```

```
ABBV        53.95
```

In [55]:
```
# create a new Series to merge as a column
# one label exists in rcopy (MSFT), and MMM does not
s = pd.Series(
            {'MMM': 'Is in the DataFrame',
             'MSFT': 'Not in the DataFrame'} )
s
```

Out[55]:
```
MMM        Is in the DataFrame
MSFT       Not in the DataFrame
dtype: object
```

In [56]:
```
# add rcopy into a column named 'Comment'
rcopy['Comment'] = s
rcopy
```

Out[56]:
```
          Price                Comment
Symbol
MMM       141.14   Is in the DataFrame
ABT        39.60                   NaN
ABBV       53.95                   NaN
```

The labels for ABT and ABBV were not found in rcopy and therefore, the values in the result are NaN. MMM is the only value in both, so the value from rcopy is put in the result.

Replacing the contents of a column

In general, assignment of a Series to a column using the [] operator will either create a new column if the column does not already exist, or replace the contents of a column if it already exists. To demonstrate replacement, the following code replaces the Price column with the result of the multiplication, instead of creating a new column:

```
In [57]:
    copy = sp500.copy()
    # replace the Price column data with the new values
    # instead of adding a new column
    copy.Price = sp500.Price * 2
    copy[:5]
```

```
Out[57]:
                              Sector    Price   BookValue

    Symbol
    MMM                  Industrials   282.28      26.668
    ABT                  Health Care    79.20      15.573
    ABBV                 Health Care   107.90       2.954
    ACN       Information Technology   159.58       8.326
    ACE                   Financials   205.82      86.897
```

To emphasize that this is also doing an alignment, we can change the sample slightly. The following code only utilizes the prices from three of the first four rows. This will force the result to not align values for 497 of the symbols, resulting in NaN values:

```
In [58]:
    # copy all 500 rows
    copy = sp500.copy()
    # this just copies the first 2 rows of prices
    prices = sp500.iloc[[3, 1, 0]].Price.copy()
    # examine the extracted prices
    prices
```

```
Out[58]:
    Symbol
    ACN          79.79
```

```
ABT          39.60
MMM          141.14
Name: Price, dtype: float64
```

```
In [59]:
    # now replace the Prices column with prices
    copy.Price = prices
    # it's not really simple insertion, it is alignment
    # values are put in the correct place according to labels
    copy
```

```
Out[59]:
                          Sector    Price   BookValue
    Symbol
    MMM              Industrials   141.14      26.668
    ABT              Health Care    39.60      15.573
    ABBV             Health Care      NaN       2.954
    ACN   Information Technology    79.79       8.326
    ACE               Financials      NaN      86.897
    ...                      ...      ...         ...
    YHOO  Information Technology      NaN      12.768
    YUM   Consumer Discretionary      NaN       5.147
    ZMH              Health Care      NaN      37.181
    ZION              Financials      NaN      30.191
    ZTS              Health Care      NaN       2.150

    [500 rows x 3 columns]
```

Deleting columns in a DataFrame

Columns can be deleted from a DataFrame by using the del keyword, the pop(column) method of the DataFrame, or by calling the drop() method of the DataFrame.

The behavior of each of these differs slightly:

- `del` will simply delete the `Series` from the `DataFrame` (in-place)
- `pop()` will both delete the `Series` and return the `Series` as a result (also in-place)
- `drop(labels, axis=1)` will return a new `DataFrame` with the column(s) removed (the original `DataFrame` object is not modified)

The following code demonstrates using `del` to delete the `BookValue` column from a copy of the `sp500` data:

```
In [60]:
    # Example of using del to delete a column
    # make a copy of a subset of the data frame
    copy = sp500[:2].copy()
    copy
```

```
Out[60]:
             Sector     Price   BookValue
    Symbol
    MMM      Industrials  141.14     26.668
    ABT      Health Care   39.60     15.573
```

```
In [61]:
    # delete the BookValue column
    # deletion is in-place
    del copy['BookValue']
    copy
```

```
Out[61]:
             Sector     Price
    Symbol
    MMM      Industrials  141.14
    ABT      Health Care   39.60
```

The following code demonstrates using the .pop() method to remove a column:

```
In [62]:
    # Example of using pop to remove a column from a DataFrame
    # first make a copy of a subset of the data frame
    # pop works in-place
    copy = sp500[:2].copy()
    # this will remove Sector and return it as a series
    popped = copy.pop('Sector')
    # Sector column removed in-place
    copy

Out[62]:
            Price    BookValue
    Symbol
    MMM     141.14   26.668
    ABT     39.60    15.573

In [63]:
    # and we have the Sector column as the result of the pop
    popped

Out[63]:
    Symbol
    MMM         Industrials
    ABT         Health Care
    Name: Sector, dtype: object
```

The .drop() method can be used to remove both rows and columns. To use it to remove a column, specify axis=1:

```
In [64]:
    # Example of using drop to remove a column
    # make a copy of a subset of the DataFrame
    copy = sp500[:2].copy()
    # this will return a new DataFrame with 'Sector' removed
    # the copy DataFrame is not modified
    afterdrop = copy.drop(['Sector'], axis = 1)
```

```
afterdrop
```

```
Out[64]:
          Price   BookValue
   Symbol
   MMM     141.14    26.668
   ABT      39.60    15.573
```

Adding rows to a DataFrame

Rows can be added to a DataFrame object via several different operations:

- Appending a DataFrame to another
- Concatenation of two DataFrame objects
- Setting with enlargement

Appending rows with .append()

Appending is performed using the .append() method of the DataFrame. The process of appending returns a new DataFrame with the data from the original DataFrame added first, and the rows from the second. Appending does not perform alignment and can result in duplicate index values.

The following code demonstrates appending two DataFrame objects extracted from the sp500 data. The first DataFrame consists of rows 0, 1 and 2, and the second consists of rows 10, 11 and 2. Row 2 (with label ABBV) is included in both to demonstrate creation of duplicate index labels. The code is as follows:

```
In [65]:
    # copy the first three rows of sp500
    df1 = sp500.iloc[0:3].copy()
    # copy 10th and 11th rows
    df2 = sp500.iloc[[10, 11, 2]]
    # append df1 and df2
    appended = df1.append(df2)
    # the result is the rows of the first followed by
    # those of the second
    appended
```

```
Out[65]:
```

```
              Sector    Price    BookValue
Symbol
MMM        Industrials   141.14      26.668
ABT        Health Care    39.60      15.573
ABBV       Health Care    53.95       2.954
A          Health Care    56.18      16.928
GAS          Utilities    52.98      32.462
ABBV       Health Care    53.95       2.954
```

The set of columns of the DataFrame objects being appended do not need to be the same. The resulting DataFrame will consist of the union of the columns in both and where either did not have a column, NaN will be used as the value. The following code demonstrates this by creating a third DataFrame using the same index as df1, but having a single column with a unique column name:

```
In [66]:
    # DataFrame using df1.index and just a PER column
    # also a good example of using a scalar value
    # to initialize multiple rows
    df3 = pd.DataFrame(0.0,
                       index=df1.index,
                       columns=['PER'])
    df3
```

```
Out[66]:
          PER
Symbol
MMM        0
ABT        0
ABBV       0
```

```
In [67]:
    # append df1 and df3
    # each has three rows, so 6 rows is the result
    # df1 had no PER column, so NaN for those rows
    # df3 had no BookValue, Price or Sector, so NaN values
```

```
df1.append(df3)
```

Out[67]:

	BookValue	PER	Price	Sector
Symbol				
MMM	26.668	NaN	141.14	Industrials
ABT	15.573	NaN	39.60	Health Care
ABBV	2.954	NaN	53.95	Health Care
MMM	NaN	0	NaN	NaN
ABT	NaN	0	NaN	NaN
ABBV	NaN	0	NaN	NaN

To append without forcing the index to be taken from either DataFrame, you can use the ignore_index=True parameter. This is useful when the index values are not of significant meaning, and you just want concatenated data with sequentially increasing integers as indexes:

In [68]:

```
# ignore index labels, create default index
df1.append(df3, ignore_index=True)
```

Out[68]:

	BookValue	PER	Price	Sector
0	26.668	NaN	141.14	Industrials
1	15.573	NaN	39.60	Health Care
2	2.954	NaN	53.95	Health Care
3	NaN	0	NaN	NaN
4	NaN	0	NaN	NaN
5	NaN	0	NaN	NaN

Concatenating DataFrame objects with pd.concat()

A DataFrame can be concatenated to another using the pd.concat() function. This function functions similarly to the .append() method, but also adds the ability to specify an axis (appending can be row or column based), as well as being able to perform several join operations between the objects. Also, the function takes a list of pandas objects to concatenate, so you can concatenate more than two objects in a single call.

The default operation of `pd.concat()` on two `DataFrame` objects operates in the same way as the `.append()` method. This can be demonstrated by reconstructing the two datasets from the earlier example and concatenating them. This is shown in the following example:

```
In [69]:
    # copy the first three rows of sp500
    df1 = sp500.iloc[0:3].copy()
    # copy 10th and 11th rows
    df2 = sp500.iloc[[10, 11, 2]]
    # pass them as a list
    pd.concat([df1, df2])
```

```
Out[69]:
                Sector    Price   BookValue
    Symbol
    MMM        Industrials  141.14    26.668
    ABT        Health Care   39.60    15.573
    ABBV       Health Care   53.95     2.954
    A          Health Care   56.18    16.928
    GAS          Utilities   52.98    32.462
    ABBV       Health Care   53.95     2.954
```

Actually, pandas calculates the sorted union of distinct column names across all supplied objects and uses those as the columns, and then appends data along the rows for each object in the order given in the list.

A slight variant of this example adds an additional column to one of the `DataFrame` objects and then performs the concatenation:

```
In [70]:
    # copy df2
    df2_2 = df2.copy()
    # add a column to df2_2 that is not in df1
    df2_2.insert(3, 'Foo', pd.Series(0, index=df2.index))
    # see what it looks like
    df2_2
```

```
Out[70]:
```

```
          Sector   Price  BookValue   Foo
Symbol
A        Health Care  56.18     16.928    0
GAS        Utilities  52.98     32.462    0
ABBV     Health Care  53.95      2.954    0
```

In [71]:

```
# now concatenate
pd.concat([df1, df2_2])
```

Out[71]:

```
        BookValue  Foo   Price        Sector
Symbol
MMM        26.668  NaN  141.14   Industrials
ABT        15.573  NaN   39.60   Health Care
ABBV        2.954  NaN   53.95   Health Care
A          16.928    0   56.18   Health Care
GAS        32.462    0   52.98     Utilities
ABBV        2.954    0   53.95   Health Care
```

Duplicate index labels still result, as the rows are copied verbatim from the source objects. However, note the NaN values in the rows originating from df1, since it does not have a Foo column.

Using the keys parameter, it is possible to differentiate the pandas objects from which the rows originated. The following code adds a level to the index which represents the source object:

In [72]:

```
# specify keys
r = pd.concat([df1, df2_2], keys=['df1', 'df2'])
r
```

Out[72]:

```
           BookValue  Foo   Price        Sector
     Symbol
df1 MMM       26.668  NaN  141.14   Industrials
    ABT       15.573  NaN   39.60   Health Care
```

```
        ABBV          2.954  NaN   53.95   Health Care
df2 A                16.928    0   56.18   Health Care
        GAS          32.462    0   52.98     Utilities
        ABBV          2.954    0   53.95   Health Care
```

We can change the axis of the concatenation to work along the columns by specifying `axis=1`, which will calculate the sorted union of the distinct index labels from the rows and then append columns and their data from the specified objects.

To demonstrate, the following splits the sp500 data into two `DataFrame` objects, each with a different set of columns, and then concatenates along `axis=1`:

```
In [73]:
    # first three rows, columns 0 and 1
    df3 = sp500[:3][[0, 1]]
    df3

Out[73]:
                  Sector    Price
    Symbol
    MMM       Industrials   141.14
    ABT       Health Care    39.60
    ABBV      Health Care    53.95

In [74]:
    # first three rows, column 2
    df4 = sp500[:3][[2]]
    df4

Out[74]:
            BookValue
    Symbol
    MMM        26.668
    ABT        15.573
    ABBV        2.954

In [75]:
    # put them back together
```

```
pd.concat([df3, df4], axis=1)
```

Out[75]:

	Sector	Price	BookValue
Symbol			
MMM	Industrials	141.14	26.668
ABT	Health Care	39.60	15.573
ABBV	Health Care	53.95	2.954

We can further examine this operation by adding a column to the second DataFrame that has a duplicate name to a column in the first. The result will have duplicate columns, as the columns are blindly appended without regard to already existing columns:

In [76]:

```
# make a copy of df4
df4_2 = df4.copy()
# add a column to df4_2, that is also in df3
df4_2.insert(1, 'Sector', pd.Series(1, index=df4_2.index))
df4_2
```

Out[76]:

	BookValue	Sector
Symbol		
MMM	26.668	1
ABT	15.573	1
ABBV	2.954	1

In [77]:

```
# demonstrate duplicate columns
pd.concat([df3, df4_2], axis=1)
```

Out[77]:

	Sector	Price	BookValue	Sector
Symbol				
MMM	Industrials	141.14	26.668	1
ABT	Health Care	39.60	15.573	1
ABBV	Health Care	53.95	2.954	1

To be very specific, pandas is performing an outer join along the labels of the specified axis. An inner join can be specified using the `join='inner'` parameter, which changes the operation from being a sorted union of distinct labels to the distinct values of the intersection of the labels. To demonstrate, the following selects two subsets of the financial data with one row in common and performs an inner join:

```
In [78]:
    # first three rows and first two columns
    df5 = sp500[:3][[0, 1]]
    df5
```

```
Out[78]:
                Sector     Price
    Symbol
    MMM        Industrials  141.14
    ABT        Health Care   39.60
    ABBV       Health Care   53.95
```

```
In [79]:
    # row 2 through 4 and first two columns
    df6 = sp500[2:5][[0,1]]
    df6
```

```
Out[79]:
                          Sector    Price
    Symbol
    ABBV                Health Care   53.95
    ACN     Information Technology   79.79
    ACE                 Financials  102.91
```

```
In [80]:
    # inner join on index labels will return in only one row
    pd.concat([df5, df6], join='inner', axis=1)
```

```
Out[80]:
                Sector  Price       Sector  Price
    Symbol
    ABBV     Health Care  53.95  Health Care  53.95
```

Adding rows (and columns) via setting with enlargement

Rows can also be added to a DataFrame through the .loc property. This technique is referred to as setting with enlargement. The parameter for .loc specifies the index label where the row is to be placed. If the label does not exist, the values are appended to the DataFrame using the given index label. If it does exist, then the values in the specified row are replaced.

The following example takes a subset of sp500 and adds a row with the label FOO:

```
In [81]:
    # get a small subset of the sp500
    # make sure to copy the slice to make a copy
    ss = sp500[:3].copy()
    # create a new row with index label FOO
    # and assign some values to the columns via a list
    ss.loc['FOO'] = ['the sector', 100, 110]
    ss
```

```
Out[81]:
            Sector    Price  BookValue
    MMM    Industrials  141.14    26.668
    ABT    Health Care   39.60    15.573
    ABBV   Health Care   53.95     2.954
    FOO     the sector  100.00   110.000
```

Note that the change is made in place. If FOO already exists as an index label, then the column data would be replaced. This is one of the means of updating data in a DataFrame in-place, as .loc not only retrieves row(s), but also lets you modify the results that are returned.

It is also possible to add columns in this manner. The following code demonstrates by adding a new column to a subset of sp500 using .loc. Note that to accomplish this, we use the colon in the rows' position to select all rows to be included to add the new column and value:

```
In [82]:
    # copy of subset / slice
    ss = sp500[:3].copy()
    # add the new column initialized to 0
```

```
ss.loc[:,'PER'] = 0
# take a look at the results
ss
```

Out[82]:

	Sector	Price	BookValue	PER
Symbol				
MMM	Industrials	141.14	26.668	0
ABT	Health Care	39.60	15.573	0
ABBV	Health Care	53.95	2.954	0

Removing rows from a DataFrame

Removing rows from a DataFrame object is normally performed using one of three techniques:

- Using the .drop() method
- Boolean selection
- Selection using a slice

Technically, only the .drop() method removes rows in-place on the source object. The other techniques either create a copy without specific rows, or a view into the rows that are not to be dropped. Details of each are given in the following sections.

Removing rows using .drop()

To remove rows from a DataFrame by the index label, you can use the .drop() method of the DataFrame. The .drop() method takes a list of index labels and will return a copy of the DataFrame with the rows for the specified labels removed. The source DataFrame remains unmodified. The code is as follows:

In [83]:
```
# get a copy of the first 5 rows of sp500
ss = sp500[:5].copy()
ss
```

Out[83]:

	Sector	Price	BookValue
Symbol			
MMM	Industrials	141.14	26.668

```
ABT              Health Care     39.60        15.573
ABBV             Health Care     53.95         2.954
ACN     Information Technology   79.79         8.326
ACE                 Financials  102.91        86.897
```

In [84]:
```
# drop rows with labels ABT and ACN
afterdrop = ss.drop(['ABT', 'ACN'])
afterdrop
```

Out[84]:
```
            Sector    Price   BookValue
Symbol
MMM     Industrials   141.14     26.668
ABBV    Health Care    53.95      2.954
ACE      Financials   102.91     86.897
```

In [85]:
```
# note that ss is not modified
ss
```

Out[85]:
```
                        Sector    Price   BookValue
Symbol
MMM                Industrials   141.14     26.668
ABT                Health Care    39.60     15.573
ABBV               Health Care    53.95      2.954
ACN     Information Technology    79.79      8.326
ACE                 Financials   102.91     86.897
```

Removing rows using Boolean selection

Boolean selection can be used to remove rows from a `DataFrame` by creating a new `DataFrame` without the desired rows. Suppose we want to remove rows where `Price` is greater than `300`. The process to do this, is to first determine which rows match that criteria, and then to select the rows that do not. The following code selects those rows and lets us know how many of them there are:

```
In [86]:
    # determine the rows where Price > 300
    selection = sp500.Price > 300
    # to make the output shorter, report the # of rows returned (500),
    # and the sum of those where Price > 300 (which is 10)
    "{0} {1}".format(len(selection), selection.sum())
```

```
Out[86]:
    '500 10'
```

We now know both the rows that match this criteria (the `10` with `True` values) and those that do not (the other 490). To remove the rows now, select out the complement of the previous result. This gives us a new `DataFrame` containing only the rows where we had a `False` value from the previous selection:

```
In [87]:
    # select the complement
    withPriceLessThan300 = sp500[~selection]
    withPriceLessThan300
```

```
Out[87]:

                              Sector     Price   BookValue
    Symbol
    MMM                  Industrials    141.14      26.668
    ABT                  Health Care     39.60      15.573
    ABBV                 Health Care     53.95       2.954
    ACN       Information Technology     79.79       8.326
    ACE                   Financials    102.91      86.897
    ...                          ...       ...         ...
    YHOO      Information Technology     35.02      12.768
```

YUM	Consumer Discretionary	74.77	5.147
ZMH	Health Care	101.84	37.181
ZION	Financials	28.43	30.191
ZTS	Health Care	30.53	2.150

```
[490 rows x 3 columns]
```

Removing rows using a slice

Slicing is also often used to remove records from a DataFrame. It is a process similar to Boolean selection, where we select out all of the rows, except for the ones you want deleted.

Suppose we want to remove all but the first three records from sp500. The slice to perform this task is [:3]:

```
In [88]:
    # get only the first three rows
    onlyFirstThree = sp500[:3]
    onlyFirstThree
```

```
Out[88]:
              Sector    Price  BookValue
    Symbol
    MMM    Industrials  141.14    26.668
    ABT    Health Care   39.60    15.573
    ABBV   Health Care   53.95     2.954
```

Remember, that this result is a slice. Therefore, it is a view into the DataFrame. Data has not been removed from the sp500 object. Changes to these three rows will change the data in sp500. To prevent this from occurring, the proper action is to make a copy of the slice, as follows:

```
In [89]:
    # first three, but a copy of them
    onlyFirstThree = sp500[:3].copy()
    onlyFirstThree
```

```
Out[89]:
```

```
                Sector    Price   BookValue
    Symbol
    MMM         Industrials   141.14      26.668
    ABT         Health Care    39.60      15.573
    ABBV        Health Care    53.95       2.954
```

Changing scalar values in a DataFrame

Scalar values in a `DataFrame` can be changed by assignment of the new value to the result of the value lookup using the `.ix`, `.iloc` and `.loc` attributes. These three attributes can all be passed both a row and column selectors, and the result can be assigned a new value that will be made in the original `DataFrame`.

`.ix` can be used by passing either the index label of the row and the name of the column, or the integer location of the row and column. The following code makes a copy of the first three rows of `sp500` and then demonstrates changing the `Price` on the `MMM` and `ABBV` securities:

```
In [90]:
    # get a subset / copy of the data
    subset = sp500[:3].copy()
    subset
```

```
Out[90]:
                Sector    Price   BookValue
    Symbol
    MMM         Industrials   141.14      26.668
    ABT         Health Care    39.60      15.573
    ABBV        Health Care    53.95       2.954
```

```
In [91]:
    # change scalar by label on row and column
    subset.ix['MMM', 'Price'] = 0
    subset
```

```
Out[91]:
                Sector    Price   BookValue
```

```
Symbol
MMM        Industrials    0.00      26.668
ABT        Health Care   39.60      15.573
ABBV       Health Care   53.95       2.954
```

Using .ix is generally frowned upon when using production code, as it has performance issues over using the .loc and .iloc attributes, which have a higher performance, with .iloc being the highest performance of those two.

The following code replicates the .ix example, but uses .loc with the index and column labels and uses different values to differentiate the result slightly:

```
In [92]:
    subset = sp500[:3].copy()
    subset.loc['MMM', 'Price'] = 10
    subset.loc['ABBV', 'Price'] = 20
    subset
```

```
Out[92]:
                 Sector    Price   BookValue
    Symbol
    MMM        Industrials   10.0    26.668
    ABT        Health Care   39.6    15.573
    ABBV       Health Care   20.0     2.954
```

.loc may suffer from lower performance, as compared to .iloc, due to the possibility of needing to map the label values into locations. The following example gets the location of the specific row and column that is desired to be changed and then uses .iloc to execute the change (the examples only change one price for brevity):

```
In [93]:
    # subset of the first three rows
    subset = sp500[:3].copy()
    # get the location of the Price column
    price_loc = sp500.columns.get_loc('Price')
    # get the location of the MMM row
    abt_row_loc = sp500.index.get_loc('ABT')
    # change the price
    subset.iloc[abt_row_loc, price_loc] = 1000
```

```
subset
```

Out[93]:

	Sector	Price	BookValue
Symbol			
MMM	Industrials	141.14	26.668
ABT	Health Care	1000.00	15.573
ABBV	Health Care	53.95	2.954

This may be look like overkill for this small example. But if this is where code is being executed frequently, such as in a loop or in response to market changes, looking up the locations once and always using `.loc` with those values, will give significant performance gains over the other options.

Arithmetic on a DataFrame

Arithmetic operations using scalar values will be applied to every element of a `DataFrame`. To demonstrate, we will use a `DataFrame` object initialized with random values:

In [94]:

```
# set the seed to allow replicatable results
np.random.seed(123456)
# create the DataFrame
df = pd.DataFrame(np.random.randn(5, 4),
                  columns=['A', 'B', 'C', 'D'])
df
```

Out[94]:

	A	B	C	D
0	0.469112	-0.282863	-1.509059	-1.135632
1	1.212112	-0.173215	0.119209	-1.044236
2	-0.861849	-2.104569	-0.494929	1.071804
3	0.721555	-0.706771	-1.039575	0.271860
4	-0.424972	0.567020	0.276232	-1.087401

By default, any arithmetic operation will be applied across all rows and columns of a `DataFrame` and will return a new `DataFrame` with the results (leaving the original unchanged):

```
In [95]:
    # multiply everything by 2
    df * 2


Out[95]:
            A         B         C         D
    0   0.938225 -0.565727 -3.018117 -2.271265
    1   2.424224 -0.346429  0.238417 -2.088472
    2  -1.723698 -4.209138 -0.989859  2.143608
    3   1.443110 -1.413542 -2.079150  0.543720
    4  -0.849945  1.134041  0.552464 -2.174801
```

When performing an operation between a `DataFrame` and a `Series`, pandas will align the `Series` index along the `DataFrame` columns, performing what is referred to as a row-wise broadcast.

The following example retrieves the first row of the `DataFrame`, and then subtracts this from each row of the `DataFrame`. pandas is broadcasting the `Series` to each row of the `DataFrame`, which aligns each series item with the `DataFrame` item of the same index label and then applies the minus operator on the matched values:

```
In [96]:
    # get first row
    s = df.iloc[0]
    # subtract first row from every row of the DataFrame
    diff = df - s
    diff


Out[96]:
            A         B         C         D
    0   0.000000  0.000000  0.000000  0.000000
    1   0.743000  0.109649  1.628267  0.091396
    2  -1.330961 -1.821706  1.014129  2.207436
    3   0.252443 -0.423908  0.469484  1.407492
    4  -0.894085  0.849884  1.785291  0.048232
```

This also works when reversing the order by subtracting the `DataFrame` to the `Series` object:

```
In [97]:
    # subtract DataFrame from Series
    diff2 = s - df
    diff2
```

```
Out[97]:
            A          B          C          D
0    0.000000   0.000000   0.000000   0.000000
1   -0.743000  -0.109649  -1.628267  -0.091396
2    1.330961   1.821706  -1.014129  -2.207436
3   -0.252443   0.423908  -0.469484  -1.407492
4    0.894085  -0.849884  -1.785291  -0.048232
```

The set of columns returned will be the union of the labels in the index of both the series and the columns index of the `DataFrame` object. If a label representing the result column is not found in either the `Series` of the `DataFrame` object, then the values will be NaN filled. The following code demonstrates, by creating a `Series` with an index representing a subset of the column in the `DataFrame`, but also with an additional label:

```
In [98]:
    # B, C
    s2 = s[1:3]
    # add E
    s2['E'] = 0
    # see how alignment is applied in math
    df + s2
```

```
Out[98]:
        A          B          C    D    E
0  NaN  -0.565727  -3.018117  NaN  NaN
1  NaN  -0.456078  -1.389850  NaN  NaN
2  NaN  -2.387433  -2.003988  NaN  NaN
3  NaN  -0.989634  -2.548633  NaN  NaN
4  NaN   0.284157  -1.232826  NaN  NaN
```

pandas aligns the index labels of df with those of s2. Since s2 does not have an A or D label, the result contains NaN in those columns. Since df has no E label, it is also NaN.

An arithmetic operation between two DataFrame objects will align by both the column and index labels. The following extracts a small portion of df and subtracts it from df. The result demonstrates that the aligned values subtract to 0, while the others are set to NaN:

```
In [99]:
    # get rows 1 through three, and only B, C columns
    subframe = df[1:4][['B', 'C']]
    # we have extracted a little square in the middle of the df
    subframe

Out[99]:
            B          C
    1 -0.173215   0.119209
    2 -2.104569  -0.494929
    1 -0.706771  -1.039575
```

```
In [100]:
    # demonstrate the alignment of the subtraction
    df - subframe

Out[100]:
         A    B    C    D
    0  NaN  NaN  NaN  NaN
    1  NaN    0    0  NaN
    2  NaN    0    0  NaN
    3  NaN    0    0  NaN
    2  NaN  NaN  NaN  NaN
```

Additional control of an arithmetic operation can be gained using the arithmetic methods provided by the `DataFrame` object. These methods provide the specification of a specific axis. The following demonstrates performing subtraction along a column axis by using the `DataFrame` objects `.sub()` method, subtracting the A column from every column:

```
In [101]:
    # get the A column
    a_col = df['A']
    df.sub(a_col, axis=0)
```

```
Out[101]:
        A         B         C         D
    0   0 -0.751976 -1.978171 -1.604745
    1   0 -1.385327 -1.092903 -2.256348
    2   0 -1.242720  0.366920  1.933653
    3   0 -1.428326 -1.761130 -0.449695
    4   0  0.991993  0.701204 -0.662428
```

Resetting and reindexing

A `DataFrame` can have its index reset by using the `.reset_index()`. A common use of this, is to move the contents of a `DataFrame` object's index into one or more columns. The following code moves the symbols in the index of sp500 into a column and replaces the index with a default integer index. The result is a new `DataFrame`, not an in-place update. The code is as follows:

```
In [102]:
    # reset the index, moving it into a column
    reset_sp500 = sp500.reset_index()
    reset_sp500
```

```
Out[102]:
       Symbol                 Sector   Price  BookValue
    0     MMM            Industrials  141.14     26.668
    1     ABT            Health Care   39.60     15.573
    2    ABBV            Health Care   53.95      2.954
    3     ACN Information Technology   79.79      8.326
    4     ACE             Financials  102.91     86.897
```

..	...		...	...	...
495	YHOO	Information Technology	35.02	12.768	
496	YUM	Consumer Discretionary	74.77	5.147	
497	ZMH	Health Care	101.84	37.181	
498	ZION	Financials	28.43	30.191	
499	ZTS	Health Care	30.53	2.150	

```
[500 rows x 4 columns]
```

One or more columns can also be moved into the index. Another common scenario is exhibited by the reset variable we just created, as this may have been data read in from a file with the symbols in a column when we really would like it in the index. To do this, we can utilize the `.set_index()` method. The following code moves Symbol into the index of a new `DataFrame`:

```
In [103]:
    # move the Symbol column into the index
    reset_sp500.set_index('Symbol')

Out[103]:
```

Symbol	Sector	Price	BookValue
MMM	Industrials	141.14	26.668
ABT	Health Care	39.60	15.573
ABBV	Health Care	53.95	2.954
ACN	Information Technology	79.79	8.326
ACE	Financials	102.91	86.897
...	...	...	...
YHOO	Information Technology	35.02	12.768
YUM	Consumer Discretionary	74.77	5.147
ZMH	Health Care	101.84	37.181
ZION	Financials	28.43	30.191
ZTS	Health Care	30.53	2.150

```
[500 rows x 4 columns]
```

An index can be explicitly set using the `.set_index()` method. This method, given a list of values representing the new index, will create a new `DataFrame` using the specified values, and then align the data from the target in the new object. The following code demonstrates this, by using a subset of `sp500` and assigning a new index that contains a subset of those indexes and an additional label `FOO`:

```
In [104]:
    # get first four rows
    subset = sp500[:4].copy()
    subset
```

```
Out[104]:
                           Sector    Price   BookValue
    Symbol
    MMM                Industrials   141.14     26.668
    ABT                Health Care    39.60     15.573
    ABBV               Health Care    53.95      2.954
    ACN      Information Technology    79.79      8.326
```

```
In [105]:
    # reindex to have MMM, ABBV, and FOO index labels
    reindexed = subset.reindex(index=['MMM', 'ABBV', 'FOO'])
    # note that ABT and ACN are dropped and FOO has NaN values
    reindexed
```

```
Out[105]:
                 Sector   Price   BookValue
    Symbol
    MMM     Industrials   141.14     26.668
    ABBV    Health Care    53.95      2.954
    FOO             NaN     NaN        NaN
```

Reindexing can also be done upon the columns. The following reindexes the columns of `subset`:

```
In [106]:
    # reindex columns
    subset.reindex(columns=['Price',
                            'Book Value',
```

```
                                 'NewCol'])
```

Out[106]:

	Price	Book Value	NewCol
Symbol			
MMM	141.14	NaN	NaN
ABT	39.60	NaN	NaN
ABBV	53.95	NaN	NaN
ACN	79.79	NaN	NaN

This result is created by pandas by creating a new DataFrame with the specified columns, and then aligning the data for those columns from the subset into the new object. Because subset did not have a NewCol column, the values are filled with NaN.

Finally, a DataFrame can also be reindexed on rows and columns at the same time, but that will be left as an exercise for you.

Hierarchical indexing

Hierarchical indexing is a feature of pandas that allows specifying two or more index levels on an axis. The specification of multiple levels in an index allows for efficient selection of subsets of data. A pandas index that has multiple levels of hierarchy is referred to as a MultiIndex.

We can demonstrate creating a MultiIndex using the sp500 data. Suppose we want to organize this data by both the Sector and Symbol. We can accomplish this with the following code:

In [107]:

```
# first, push symbol into a column
reindexed = sp500.reset_index()
# and now index sp500 by sector and symbol
multi_fi = reindexed.set_index(['Sector', 'Symbol'])
multi_fi
```

Out[107]:

Sector	Symbol	Price	BookValue
Industrials	MMM	141.14	26.668
Health Care	ABT	39.60	15.573

```
                            ABBV        53.95          2.954
       Information Technology ACN        79.79          8.326
       Financials             ACE       102.91         86.897
       ...                               ...            ...
       Information Technology YHOO       35.02          12.768
       Consumer Discretionary YUM        74.77          5.147
       Health Care            ZMH       101.84         37.181
       Financials             ZION       28.43          30.191
       Health Care            ZTS        30.53          2.150

       [500 rows x 2 columns]
```

We can now examine the `.index` property and check whether it is a `MultiIndex` object:

```
In [108]:
    # the index is a MultiIndex
    type(multi_fi.index)
```

```
Out[108]:
    pandas.core.index.MultiIndex
```

Then, examine the index itself:

```
In [109]:
    # examine the index
    print (multi_fi.index)
```

```
Out[109]:
    Sector                      Symbol
    Industrials                 MMM
    Health Care                 ABT
                                ABBV
    Information Technology       ACN
                        ...
    Information Technology       YHOO
    Consumer Discretionary       YUM
    Health Care                 ZMH
    Financials                  ZION
    Health Care                 ZTS
```

A `MultiIndex` contains two or more levels:

```
In [110]:
    # this has two levels
    len(multi_fi.index.levels)
```

```
Out[110]:
    2
```

Also, each level is a distinct `Index` object:

```
In [111]:
    # each index level is an index
    multi_fi.index.levels[0]
```

```
Out[111]:
    Index([u'Consumer Discretionary', u'Consumer Discretionary ',
    u'Consumer Staples', u'Consumer Staples ', u'Energy', u'Financials',
    u'Health Care', u'Industrials', u'Industries', u'Information
    Technology', u'Materials', u'Telecommunications Services',
    u'Utilities'], dtype='object')
```

```
In [112]:
    # each index level is an index
    multi_fi.index.levels[1]
```

```
Out[112]:
    Index([u'A', u'AA', u'AAPL', u'ABBV', u'ABC', u'ABT', u'ACE', u'ACN',
    u'ACT', u'ADBE', u'ADI', u'ADM', u'ADP', u'ADS', u'ADSK', u'ADT',
    u'AEE', u'AEP', u'AES', u'AET', u'AFL', u'AGN', u'AIG', u'AIV',
    u'AIZ', u'AKAM', u'ALL', u'ALLE', u'ALTR', u'ALXN', u'AMAT', u'AME',
    u'AMGN', u'AMP', u'AMT', u'AMZN', u'AN', u'AON', u'APA', u'APC',
    u'APD', u'APH', u'ARG', u'ATI', u'AVB', u'AVP', u'AVY', u'AXP',
    u'AZO', u'BA', u'BAC', u'BAX', u'BBBY', u'BBT', u'BBY', u'BCR',
    u'BDX', u'BEAM', u'BEN', u'BF-B', u'BHI', u'BIIB', u'BK', u'BLK',
    u'BLL', u'BMS', u'BMY', u'BRCM', u'BRK-B', u'BSX', u'BTU', u'BWA',
    u'BXP', u'C', u'CA', u'CAG', u'CAH', u'CAM', u'CAT', u'CB', u'CBG',
    u'CBS', u'CCE', u'CCI', u'CCL', u'CELG', u'CERN', u'CF', u'CFN',
    u'CHK', u'CHRW', u'CI', u'CINF', u'CL', u'CLF', u'CLX', u'CMA',
    u'CMCSA', u'CME', u'CMG', ...], dtype='object')
```

Values of the index, at a specific level for every row, can be retrieved by the
`.get_level_values()` method:

```
In [113]:
    # values of the index level 0
    multi_fi.index.get_level_values(0)
```

```
Out[113]:
    Index([u'Industrials', u'Health Care', u'Health Care', u'Information
    Technology', u'Financials', u'Health Care', u'Information Technology',
    u'Utilities', u'Health Care', u'Financials', u'Health Care',
    u'Utilities', u'Materials', u'Materials', u'Information Technology',
    u'Materials', u'Health Care', u'Materials', u'Industrials', u'Health
    Care', u'Information Technology', u'Financials', u'Information
    Technology', u'Consumer Staples', u'Consumer Discretionary',
    u'Utilities', u'Utilities', u'Financials', u'Financials',
    u'Financials', u'Financials', u'Health Care', u'Information
    Technology', u'Health Care', u'Industrials', u'Energy', u'Information
    Technology', u'Financials', u'Energy', u'Financials', u'Information
    Technology', u'Information Technology', u'Consumer Staples',
    u'Financials', u'Telecommunications Services', u'Information
    Technology', u'Information Technology', u'Consumer Discretionary',
    u'Consumer Discretionary', u'Financials', u'Industrials', u'Consumer
    Staples', u'Energy', u'Materials', u'Financials', u'Health Care',
    u'Health Care', u'Financials', u'Consumer Discretionary', u'Health
    Care', u'Consumer Discretionary', u'Materials', u'Financials',
    u'Consumer Discretionary', u'Health Care', u'Financials', u'Consumer
    Discretionary', u'Industrials', u'Consumer Discretionary',
    u'Financials', u'Health Care', u'Health Care', u'Information
    Technology', u'Consumer Staples', u'Information Technology',
    u'Consumer Discretionary', u'Energy', u'Energy', u'Consumer Staples',
    u'Financials', u'Health Care', u'Health Care', u'Consumer
    Discretionary', u'Consumer Discretionary', u'Industrials',
    u'Financials', u'Consumer Discretionary', u'Health Care',
    u'Utilities', u'Telecommunications Services', u'Health Care',
    u'Materials', u'Industrials', u'Energy', u'Energy', u'Consumer
    Discretionary', u'Financials', u'Health Care', u'Financials',
    u'Industrials', ...], dtype='object')
```

Access of elements via a hierarchical index is performed using the `.xs()` method.
This method works similar to the `.ix` attribute but provides parameters to specify
multidimensionality of the index.

The following code selects all items with a level 0 index value of `Industrials`:

```
In [114]:
    # get all stocks that are Industrials
    # note the result drops level 0 of the index
```

```
multi_fi.xs('Industrials')
```

Out[114]:

	Price	BookValue
Symbol		
MMM	141.14	26.668
ALLE	52.46	0.000
APH	95.71	18.315
AVY	48.20	15.616
BA	132.41	19.870
...	...	...
UNP	196.26	46.957
UPS	102.73	6.790
UTX	115.54	35.252
WM	43.37	12.330
XYL	38.42	12.127

```
[64 rows x 2 columns]
```

To select the rows with a specific value of the index at level 1, use the level parameter. The following code selects rows where the Symbol component of the index is ALLE.

In [115]:

```
# select rows where level 1 (Symbol) is ALLE
# note that the Sector level is dropped from the result
multi_fi.xs('ALLE', level=1)
```

Out[115]:

	Price	BookValue
Sector		
Industrials	52.46	0

To prevent levels from being dropped, you can use the drop_levels=False option:

In [116]:

```
# Industrials, without dropping the level
multi_fi.xs('Industrials', drop_level=False)
```

Out[116]:

```
                  Price   BookValue

Sector        Symbol

Industrials   MMM     141.14      26.668

              ALLE     52.46       0.000

              APH      95.71      18.315

              AVY      48.20      15.616

              BA      132.41      19.870

...                     ...         ...

              UNP     196.26      46.957

              UPS     102.73       6.790

              UTX     115.54      35.252

              WM       43.37      12.330

              XYL      38.42      12.127


[64 rows x 2 columns]
```

To select from a hierarchy of indexes you can chain .xs() calls with different levels together. The following code selects the row with Industrials at level 0 and UPS at level 1:

```
In [117]:
    # drill through the levels
    multi_fi.xs('Industrials').xs('UPS')

Out[117]:
    Price       102.73
    BookValue     6.79
    Name: UPS, dtype: float64
```

An alternate syntax is to pass the values of each level of the hierarchical index as a tuple:

```
In [118]:
    # drill through using tuples
    multi_fi.xs(('Industrials', 'UPS'))

Out[118]:
    Price       102.73
    BookValue     6.79
    Name: (Industrials, UPS), dtype: float64
```

Note that .xs() can only be used for getting, not setting, values.

 One of the things I'd like to point out about indexing in pandas, is that a pandas index is its own set of data, not references to data in the Series or DataFrame. This is different from how indexes are used in SQL databases, where the index is built upon the actual data in the table. The values in a pandas index can be completely different from the data in the row that it references, and it can be changed as needed to support much more interactive analysis than can be done with SQL.

Summarized data and descriptive statistics

pandas provides several classes of statistical operations that can be applied to a Series or DataFrame object. These reductive methods, when applied to a Series, result in a single value. When applied to a DataFrame, an axis can be specified and the method will then be either applied to each column or row and results in a Series.

The average value is calculated using .mean(). The following calculates the average of the prices for AAPL and MSFT:

```
In [119]:
    # calc the mean of the values in each column
    one_mon_hist.mean()

Out[119]:
    MSFT        47.493182
    AAPL       112.411364
    dtype: float64
```

pandas has taken each column and independently calculated the mean for each and returned the results as values in a Series that is indexed with the column names.

The default is to apply the method on axis=0, applying the function to each column. The following code calculates the mean across axis=1:

```
In [120]:
    # calc the mean of the values in each row
    one_mon_hist.mean(axis=1)

Out[120]:
```

```
0     81.845
1     81.545
2     82.005
...
19    80.680
20    79.770
21    78.415
Length: 22, dtype: float64
```

Variance is calculated using the .var() method. The following code calculates the variance of the price for both stocks during the period represented in the DataFrame object:

```
In [121]:
    # calc the variance of the values in each column
    one_mon_hist.var()
```

```
Out[121]:
    MSFT    0.870632
    AAPL    5.706231
    dtype: float64
```

The median of the values is determined using the .median() method:

```
In [122]:
    # calc the median of the values in each column
    one_mon_hist.median()

    Out[122]:
    MSFT     47.625
    AAPL    112.530
    dtype: float64
```

Although not a reductive calculation, the minimum and maximum values can be found with the .min() and .max() methods:

```
In [123]:
    # location of min price for both stocks
```

```
one_mon_hist[['MSFT', 'AAPL']].min()
```

Out[123]:
```
    MSFT      45.16
    AAPL     106.75
    dtype: float64
```

In [124]:
```
    # and location of the max
    one_mon_hist[['MSFT', 'AAPL']].max()
```

Out[124]:
```
    MSFT      48.84
    AAPL     115.93
    dtype: float64
```

Some pandas statistical methods are referred to as indirect statistics, for example, `.idxmin()` and `.idxmax()` return the index location where the minimum and maximum values exist, respectively. The following code determines the location of the minimum prices for both stocks:

In [125]:
```
    # location of the min price for both stocks
    one_mon_hist[['MSFT', 'AAPL']].idxmin()
```

Out[125]:
```
    MSFT     11
    AAPL     11
    dtype: int64
```

In [126]:
```
    # and location of the max
    one_mon_hist[['MSFT', 'AAPL']].idxmax()
```

Out[126]:
```
    MSFT     3
    AAPL     2
    dtype: int64
```

The most common value of a `Series`, the mode, can be determined with `.mode()`. Determining the mode is best demonstrated with data different from `sp500`. The following code determines the mode of the given `Series`:

```
In [127]:
    # find the mode of this Series
    s = pd.Series([1, 2, 3, 3, 5])
    s.mode()
```

```
Out[127]:
    0    3
    dtype: int64
```

This has not returned a scalar value representing the mode, but a `Series`. This is because there can be more than one value for the mode of a `Series`, as demonstrated in the following sample:

```
In [128]:
    # there can be more than one mode
    s = pd.Series([1, 2, 3, 3, 5, 1])
    s.mode()
```

```
Out[128]:
    0    1
    1    3
    dtype: int64
```

Accumulations in pandas are statistical methods that determine a value, by continuously applying the next value in a `Series` to the current result. Good examples are the cumulative product and cumulative sum of a `Series`. To demonstrate, we can use the following `DataFrame` that calculates both on a simple `Series` of data:

```
In [129]:
    # calculate a cumulative product
    pd.Series([1, 2, 3, 4]).cumprod()
```

```
Out[129]:
    0    1
    1    2
    2    6
```

```
3      24
dtype: int64
```

In [130]:

```
# calculate a cumulative sum
pd.Series([1, 2, 3, 4]).cumsum()
```

Out[130]:

```
0     1
1     3
2     6
3    10
dtype: int64
```

Note that these do not reduce to a single value, but represent the cumulative value at each location across the Series.

The .describe() returns a simple set of summary statistics about a Series or DataFrame. The values returned are, themselves, a Series where the index label contains the name of the specific statistics that are computed. This function is handy if you want to get a quick and easy overview of the important statistics of a Series or DataFrame.

The following code returns summary statistics on the monthly stock data, including the count of items that are not part of NaN; the mean and standard deviation; minimum and maximum values; and the values of the 25, 50, and 75 percentiles. The code is as follows:

In [131]:

```
# summary statistics
one_mon_hist.describe()
```

Out[131]:

	MSFT	AAPL
count	22.000000	22.000000
mean	47.493182	112.411364
std	0.933077	2.388772
min	45.160000	106.750000

```
25%    46.967500   111.660000
50%    47.625000   112.530000
75%    48.125000   114.087500
max    48.840000   115.930000
```

Non-numerical data will result in a slightly different set of summary statistics:

```
In [132]:
    # get summary stats on non-numeric data
    s = pd.Series(['a', 'a', 'b', 'c', np.NaN])
    s.describe()
```

```
Out[132]:
    count      4
    unique     3
    top        a
    freq       2
    dtype: object
```

This has given us the count variable of items that are not part of NaN, the number of unique items that are not part of NaN, the most common item (top), and the number of times the most frequent item occurred (freq).

This example leads into a category of descriptive methods that assist in determining counts of items or unique values. The .count() method will return the number of values that are not part of NaN values in a Series or on a specific axis of a DataFrame:

```
In [133]:
    # get summary stats on non-numeric data
    s.count()
```

```
Out[133]:
    4
```

A list of unique items can be obtained using the .unique() method:

```
In [134]:
    # return a list of unique items
    s.unique()
```

```
Out[134]:
    array(['a', 'b', 'c', nan], dtype=object)
```

The number of occurrences of each unique (value that is not part of NaN) value can be determined with the .value_counts() method:

```
In [135]:
    # number of occurrences of each unique value
    s.value_counts()

Out[135]:
    a    2
    b    1
    c    1
    dtype: int64
```

There are quite a few more built-in statistical functions, but the focus of this chapter (and book) is not on statistical analysis and their discovery will be left to you.

Summary

In this chapter, you learned about the pandas DataFrame object. We covered various means of creating DataFrame objects; and investigated, many techniques of manipulating the structure and contents of data held within.

Even with the extensive coverage that we have had in this chapter, the focus has been on the basic mechanics of manipulating DataFrame objects, and there are many concepts which were excluded at this point, but which we will investigate in upcoming chapters. These include working with missing data, identifying and removing duplicate data, as well as pivoting, merging, sorting, and grouping data.

However, before we get into those details, in the next chapter we will look into how to populate the data in a DataFrame object from sources outside of your application.

6
Accessing Data

pandas is a tool that is used to manipulate and analyze data. But where does this data come from? It is almost universal that any pandas application will start by loading data from an outside source. As pandas is built on Python, you can use any means available in Python to retrieve data from outside the application. This really makes the possibility of the data that can be accessed unlimited, including files, excel spreadsheets, web sites and services, databases, and cloud services.

However, using Python to load data will require you to convert Python objects into pandas `Series` or `DataFrame` objects, increasing the complexity of your code. Fortunately, over the evolution of pandas, it has become apparent that there is a frequently used set of data access patterns, as well as data formats that were so commonly used, that direct support for them was added into the core of pandas. These often make retrieving data from outside sources, directly as a pandas `Series` or `DataFrame` objects, as simple as a single line of code.

This chapter will introduce you to these capabilities that are part of the pandas framework. Specifically, in this chapter, we will cover:

- Reading and writing pandas data from files
- Working with data in CSV, JSON, HTML, Excel, and HDF5 formats
- Accessing data on the web and in the cloud
- Reading and writing from/to SQL databases
- Reading data from remote web data services

Setting up the IPython notebook

We will, as usual, start with some imports and set up options for pandas that facilitate the examples:

```
In [1]:
    # import pandas and numpy
    import numpy as np
    import pandas as pd

    # Set some pandas options for controlling output
    pd.set_option('display.notebook_repr_html', False)
    pd.set_option('display.max_columns', 10)
    pd.set_option('display.max_rows', 10)
```

CSV and Text/Tabular format

It is a pretty safe bet to say that **Comma Separated Values (CSV)** is likely to be the most common format of data that you will deal with in pandas. Many web-based services provide data in a CSV format, as well as many information systems within an enterprise. It is an easy format to use and is commonly used as an export format for spreadsheet applications, such as Excel.

CSV is a file consisting of multiple lines of text-based data with values separated by commas. It can be thought of as a table of data similar to a single sheet in a spreadsheet program. Each row of the data is in its own line in the file, and each column for each row is stored in the text format, with a comma separating the data in each column. For more detail on the specifics of CSV files, feel free to visit http://en.wikipedia.org/wiki/Comma-separated_values.

As CSV is so common and easily understood, we will spend most of the time describing how to read and write pandas data in this format. Lessons learned from CSV methods will apply to the other formats as well and allow a little more expediency when covering these other formats.

The sample CSV data set

We will start by reading a simple CSV file, data/msft.csv (in the book's source data folder). This file is a snapshot of Yahoo! Finance data for the MSFT ticker. Conveniently, Yahoo! Finance happens to be one of the financial web services that offers its data in a CSV format, and this data was simply retrieved and saved to a file.

The first several lines of this file can be examined using the `!head` command (on a Windows system, use the `type` command):

```
In [2]:
    # view the first five lines of data/msft.csv
    !head -n 5 data/msft.csv # osx or Linux
    # !type data\msft.csv # on windows, but shows the entire file

    Date,Open,High,Low,Close,Volume,Adj Close
    2014-07-21,83.46,83.53,81.81,81.93,2359300,81.93
    2014-07-18,83.30,83.40,82.52,83.35,4020800,83.35
    2014-07-17,84.35,84.63,83.33,83.63,1974000,83.63
    2014-07-16,83.77,84.91,83.66,84.91,1755600,84.91
```

The first row of the file contains the names of all of the columns represented in the data, separated with a comma. For a specific day (the first column), each remaining row represents the open, high, low, close, volume, and adjusted close values for MSFT on that date.

Reading a CSV file into a DataFrame

The data in `data/MSFT.CSV` is perfect to read into `DataFrame`. All of its data is complete and has column names in the first row. All that we need to do to read this data into a `DataFrame` is use the pandas `pd.read_csv()` function:

```
In [3]:
    # read in msft.csv into a DataFrame
    msft = pd.read_csv("data/msft.csv")
    msft.head()
```

```
Out[3]:
        Date        Open    High    Low     Close   Volume   Adj Close
    0   2014-07-21  83.46   83.53   81.81   81.93   2359300     81.93
    1   2014-07-18  83.30   83.40   82.52   83.35   4020800     83.35
    2   2014-07-17  84.35   84.63   83.33   83.63   1974000     83.63
    3   2014-07-16  83.77   84.91   83.66   84.91   1755600     84.91
    4   2014-07-15  84.30   84.38   83.20   83.58   1874700     83.58
```

Wow, that was easy! pandas has realized that the first line of the file contains the names of the columns and bulk read in the data to `DataFrame`.

Specifying the index column when reading a CSV file

In the result of the previous example, the index is a numerical starting from 0, instead of by date. This is because pandas does not assume that any specific column should be the index. To help this situation, you can specify which column(s) should be the index in the call to `read_csv()` using the `index_col` parameter by assigning it the zero-based position of the column to be used as the index.

The following reads the data and tells pandas to use the column at position 0 in the file as the index (the Date column):

```
In [4]:
    # use column 0 as the index
    msft = pd.read_csv("data/msft.csv", index_col=0)
    msft.head()
```

```
Out[4]:
               Open    High    Low    Close    Volume   Adj Close
    Date
    2014-07-21  83.46   83.53   81.81  81.93    2359300     81.93
    2014-07-18  83.30   83.40   82.52  83.35    4020800     83.35
    2014-07-17  84.35   84.63   83.33  83.63    1974000     83.63
    2014-07-16  83.77   84.91   83.66  84.91    1755600     84.91
    2014-07-15  84.30   84.38   83.20  83.58    1874700     83.58
```

The date field is now the index. However, because of this, it is also not column data. If you want to use the date as a column, you will need to create a new column and assign the index labels to that column.

Data type inference and specification

An examination of the types of each column shows that pandas has attempted to infer the types of the columns from their content:

```
In [5]:
    # examine the types of the columns in this DataFrame
    msft.dtypes
```

```
Out[5]:
    Open           float64
```

```
High              float64
Low               float64
Close             float64
Volume              int64
Adj Close         float64
dtype: object
```

To force the types of columns, use the `dtypes` parameter of `pd.read_csv()`. The following forces the `Volume` column to also be `float64`:

```
In [6]:
    # specify that the Volume column should be a float64
    msft = pd.read_csv("data/msft.csv",
                       dtype = { 'Volume' : np.float64})
    msft.dtypes
```

```
Out[6]:
    Date              object
    Open             float64
    High             float64
    Low              float64
    Close            float64
    Volume           float64
    Adj Close        float64
    dtype: object
```

Specifying column names

It is also possible to specify the column names at the time of reading the data using the `names` parameter:

```
In [7]:
    # specify a new set of names for the columns
    # all lower case, remove space in Adj Close
    # also, header=0 skips the header row
    df = pd.read_csv("data/msft.csv",
                     header=0,
                     names=['open', 'high', 'low',
                            'close', 'volume', 'adjclose'])
```

```
df.head()
```

Out[7]:

	open	high	low	close	volume	adjclose
2014-07-21	83.46	83.53	81.81	81.93	2359300	81.93
2014-07-18	83.30	83.40	82.52	83.35	4020800	83.35
2014-07-17	84.35	84.63	83.33	83.63	1974000	83.63
2014-07-16	83.77	84.91	83.66	84.91	1755600	84.91
2014-07-15	84.30	84.38	83.20	83.58	1874700	83.58

Note that because we specified the names of the columns, we need to skip over the column names' row in the file, which was performed with `header=0`. If not, pandas will assume the first row is part of the data, which will cause some issues later in processing.

Specifying specific columns to load

It is also possible to specify which columns to load when reading the file. This can be useful if you have a lot of columns in the file and some are of no interest to your analysis and you want to save the time and memory required to read and store them. Specifying which columns to read is accomplished with the `usecols` parameter, which can be passed a list of column names or column offsets.

The following reads only the `Date` and `Close` columns and uses `Date` as the index:

```
In [8]:
    # read in data only in the Date and Close columns
    # and index by the Date column
    df2 = pd.read_csv("data/msft.csv",
                    usecols=['Date', 'Close'],
                    index_col=['Date'])
    df2.head()
```

Out[8]:

	Close
Date	
2014-07-21	81.93
2014-07-18	83.35
2014-07-17	83.63
2014-07-16	84.91
2014-07-15	83.58

Saving DataFrame to a CSV file

CSV files can be saved from DataFrame using the .to_csv() method. To demonstrate saving data to a CSV file, we will save the df2 object with the revised column names to a new file named data/msft_modified.csv:

In [9]:

```
# save df2 to a new csv file
# also specify naming the index as date
df2.to_csv("data/msft_modified.csv", index_label='date')
```

It was necessary to tell the method that the index label should be saved with a column name of date using index_label=date. Otherwise, the index does not have a name added to the first row of the file, which makes it difficult to read back properly.

To examine that this worked properly, we can explore the new file to view some of its content using !head command (and if on a Windows system use the !type command):

In [10]:

```
# view the start of the file just saved
!head data/msft_modified.csv # Linux or osx
# !type data\msft_modified.csv # windows


date,Close
2014-07-21,81.93
2014-07-18,83.35
2014-07-17,83.63
2014-07-16,84.91
2014-07-15,83.58
2014-07-14,84.4
2014-07-11,83.35
2014-07-10,83.42
2014-07-09,85.5
```

General field-delimited data

CSV is actually a specific implementation of what is referred to as field-delimited data. In field-delimited data, items in each row are separated by a specific symbol. In the case of CSV, it happens to be a comma. However, other symbols are common, such as the | (pipe) symbol. When using a | character, the data is often called pipe-delimited data.

To facilitate reading field-delimited data, pandas provides the pd.read_table() function. The following example uses this function to read the data/MSFT.CSV file by specifying a comma as the value to the sep parameter:

```
In [11]:
    # use read_table with sep=',' to read a CSV
    df = pd.read_table("data/msft.csv", sep=',')
    df.head()
```

```
Out[11]:
            Date   Open   High    Low  Close    Volume  Adj Close
    0  2014-07-21  83.46  83.53  81.81  81.93   2359300      81.93
    1  2014-07-18  83.30  83.40  82.52  83.35   4020800      83.35
    2  2014-07-17  84.35  84.63  83.33  83.63   1974000      83.63
    3  2014-07-16  83.77  84.91  83.66  84.91   1755600      84.91
    4  2014-07-15  84.30  84.38  83.20  83.58   1874700      83.58
```

pandas does not provide a .to_table() method as an analogous write method to .to_csv(). However, the .to_csv() method can be used to write field-delimited data using a different delimiter than a comma. As an example, the following writes a pipe-delimited version of the data in DataFrame:

```
In [12]:
    # save as pipe delimited
    df.to_csv("data/msft_piped.txt", sep='|')
    # check that it worked
    !head -n 5 data/msft_piped.txt # osx or linux
    # !type data\msft_piped.txt # on windows

    |Date|Open|High|Low|Close|Volume|Adj Close
    0|2014-07-21|83.46|83.53|81.81|81.93|2359300|81.93
    1|2014-07-18|83.3|83.4|82.52|83.35|4020800|83.35
```

```
2|2014-07-17|84.35|84.63|83.33|83.63|1974000|83.63
3|2014-07-16|83.77|84.91|83.66|84.91|1755600|84.91
```

Handling noise rows in field-delimited data

Sometimes, data in a field-delimited file may contain extraneous headers and footers.
Examples can be company information at the top, such as in an invoice number,
addresses, and summary footers. Sometimes, I have even seen where data is stored
on every other line. These situations will cause errors when loading the data like this.
So, to handle these scenarios, the pandas `pd.read_csv()` and `pd.read_table()`
methods have some useful parameters to help out.

To demonstrate, take the following variation on the MSFT stock data, which has
extra rows of what could be referred to as noise information:

```
In [13]:
    # messy file
    !head data/msft2.csv # osx or Linux
    #!type data\msft2.csv # windows


    This is fun because the data does not start on the first line
    Date,Open,High,Low,Close,Volume,Adj Close

    And there is space between the header row and data
    2014-07-21,83.46,83.53,81.81,81.93,2359300,81.93
    2014-07-18,83.30,83.40,82.52,83.35,4020800,83.35
    2014-07-17,84.35,84.63,83.33,83.63,1974000,83.63
    2014-07-16,83.77,84.91,83.66,84.91,1755600,84.91
    2014-07-15,84.30,84.38,83.20,83.58,1874700,83.58
    2014-07-14,83.66,84.64,83.11,84.40,1432100,84.40
```

This situation can be handled using the `skiprows` parameter, informing pandas to
skip rows 0, 2, and 3:

```
In [14]:
    # read, but skip rows 0, 2 and 3
    df = pd.read_csv("data/msft2.csv", skiprows=[0, 2, 3])
    df

Out[14]:
```

	Date	Open	High	Low	Close	Volume	Adj Close
0	NaN	NaN	NaN	NaN	NaN	NaN	NaN
1	2014-07-21	83.46	83.53	81.81	81.93	2359300	81.93
2	2014-07-18	83.30	83.40	82.52	83.35	4020800	83.35
3	2014-07-17	84.35	84.63	83.33	83.63	1974000	83.63
4	2014-07-16	83.77	84.91	83.66	84.91	1755600	84.91
5	2014-07-15	84.30	84.38	83.20	83.58	1874700	83.58
6	2014-07-14	83.66	84.64	83.11	84.40	1432100	84.40
7	2014-07-11	83.55	83.98	82.85	83.35	2001400	83.35
8	2014-07-10	85.20	85.57	83.36	83.42	2713300	83.42
9	2014-07-09	84.83	85.79	84.76	85.50	1540700	85.50

Another common situation is where a file has content at the end of the file, which should be ignored to prevent an error, such as the following.

In [15]:

```
# another messy file, with the mess at the end
!cat data/msft_with_footer.csv # osx or Linux
# !type data\msft_with_footer.csv # windows

Date,Open,High,Low,Close,Volume,Adj Close
2014-07-21,83.46,83.53,81.81,81.93,2359300,81.93
2014-07-18,83.30,83.40,82.52,83.35,4020800,83.35

Uh oh, there is stuff at the end.
```

This will cause an exception during reading, but it can be handled using the skip_footer parameter, which specifies how many lines at the end of the file to ignore:

In [16]:

```
# skip only two lines at the end
df = pd.read_csv("data/msft_with_footer.csv",
                 skip_footer=2,
                 engine = 'python')
df
```

Out[16]:

	Date	Open	High	Low	Close	Volume	Adj Close
0	2014-07-21	83.46	83.53	81.81	81.93	2359300	81.93
1	2014-07-18	83.30	83.40	82.52	83.35	4020800	83.35

Note that I had to specify `engine = 'python'`. At least with Anaconda, `skip_footer`, without this option, gives a warning, as this option is not implemented by the default underlying C implementation. This forces it to use a Python implementation.

Suppose the file is large and you only want to read the first few rows, as you only want the data at the start of the file and do not want to read it all into the memory. This can be handled with the `nrows` parameter:

```
In [17]:
    # only process the first three rows
    pd.read_csv("data/msft.csv", nrows=3)
```

```
Out[17]:
           Date   Open   High    Low  Close   Volume  Adj Close
    0  2014-07-21  83.46  83.53  81.81  81.93  2359300      81.93
    1  2014-07-18  83.30  83.40  82.52  83.35  4020800      83.35
    2  2014-07-17  84.35  84.63  83.33  83.63  1974000      83.63
```

If you want, you can skip a specific number of rows at the start of a file and read to the end, or you can read just a few lines once you get to that point in the file. To do this, use the `skiprows` parameter. The following example skips `100` rows and then reads in the next `5`:

```
In [18]:
    # skip 100 lines, then only process the next five
    pd.read_csv("data/msft.csv", skiprows=100, nrows=5,
                header=0,
                names=['open', 'high', 'low', 'close', 'vol',
                       'adjclose'])
```

```
Out[18]:
                 open   high    low  close      vol  adjclose
    2014-03-03  80.35  81.31  79.91  79.97  5004100     77.40
    2014-02-28  82.40  83.42  82.17  83.42  2853200     80.74
    2014-02-27  84.06  84.63  81.63  82.00  3676800     79.36
    2014-02-26  82.92  84.03  82.43  83.81  2623600     81.12
    2014-02-25  83.80  83.80  81.72  83.08  3579100     80.41
```

Note that the preceding example also skipped reading the header line, so it was necessary to inform the process to not look for a header and use the specified names.

Reading and writing data in an Excel format

pandas supports reading data in Excel 2003 and newer formats using the pd.read_ excel() function or via the ExcelFile class. Internally, both techniques use either the XLRD or OpenPyXL packages, so you will need to ensure that either is installed first in your Python environment.

For demonstration, a data/stocks.xlsx file is provided with the sample data. If you open it in Excel, you will see something similar to what is shown in the following:

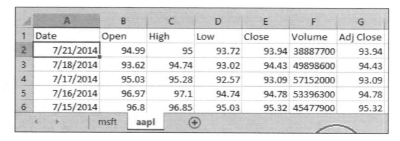

The workbook contains two sheets, msft and aapl, which hold the stock data for each respective stock.

The following reads the data/stocks.xlsx file into DataFrame:

```
In [19]:
    # read excel file
    # only reads first sheet (msft in this case)
    df = pd.read_excel("data/stocks.xlsx")
    df.head()

Out[19]:
          Date   Open   High    Low  Close   Volume  Adj Close
0  2014-07-21  83.46  83.53  81.81  81.93  2359300      81.93
1  2014-07-18  83.30  83.40  82.52  83.35  4020800      83.35
2  2014-07-17  84.35  84.63  83.33  83.63  1974000      83.63
3  2014-07-16  83.77  84.91  83.66  84.91  1755600      84.91
4  2014-07-15  84.30  84.38  83.20  83.58  1874700      83.58
```

This has read only content from the first worksheet in the Excel file (the msft worksheet) and used the contents of the first row as column names. To read the other worksheet, you can pass the name of the worksheet using the `sheetname` parameter:

```
In [20]:
    # read from the aapl worksheet
    aapl = pd.read_excel("data/stocks.xlsx", sheetname='aapl')
    aapl.head()
```

```
Out[20]:
          Date    Open    High     Low   Close     Volume  Adj Close
0   2014-07-21   94.99   95.00   93.72   93.94   38887700      93.94
1   2014-07-18   93.62   94.74   93.02   94.43   49898600      94.43
2   2014-07-17   95.03   95.28   92.57   93.09   57152000      93.09
3   2014-07-16   96.97   97.10   94.74   94.78   53396300      94.78
4   2014-07-15   96.80   96.85   95.03   95.32   45477900      95.32
```

Like with `pd.read_csv()`, many assumptions are made about column names, data types, and indexes. All of the options explained for `pd.read_csv()` to specify this information also apply to the `pd.read_excel()` function.

Excel files can be written using the `.to_excel()` method of `DataFrame`. Writing to the XLS format requires the inclusion of the XLWT package, so make sure it is loaded in your Python environment.

The following writes the data we just acquired to `stocks2.xls`. The default is to store `DataFrame` in the `Sheet1` worksheet:

```
In [21]:
    # save to an .XLS file, in worksheet 'Sheet1'
    df.to_excel("data/stocks2.xls")
```

Opening this in Excel shows you the following:

	A	B	C	D	E	F	G	H
1		Date	Open	High	Low	Close	Volume	Adj Close
2	0	2014-07-21 00:00:00	83.46	83.53	81.81	81.93	2359300	81.93
3	1	2014-07-18 00:00:00	83.3	83.4	82.52	83.35	4020800	83.35
4	2	2014-07-17 00:00:00	84.35	84.63	83.33	83.63	1974000	83.63
5	3	2014-07-16 00:00:00	83.77	84.91	83.66	84.91	1755600	84.91
6	4	2014-07-15 00:00:00	84.3	84.38	83.2	83.58	1874700	83.58
7	5	2014-07-14 00:00:00	83.66	84.64	83.11	84.4	1432100	84.4

Sheet1

You can specify the name of the worksheet using the `sheet_name` parameter:

```
In [22]:
    # write making the worksheet name MSFT
    df.to_excel("data/stocks_msft.xls", sheet_name='MSFT')
```

In Excel, we can see that the sheet has been named MSFT.

	A	B	C	D	E	F	G	H
1		Date	Open	High	Low	Close	Volume	Adj Close
2	0	2014-07-21 00:00:00	83.46	83.53	81.81	81.93	2359300	81.93
3	1	2014-07-18 00:00:00	83.3	83.4	82.52	83.35	4020800	83.35
4	2	2014-07-17 00:00:00	84.35	84.63	83.33	83.63	1974000	83.63
5	3	2014-07-16 00:00:00	83.77	84.91	83.66	84.91	1755600	84.91
6	4	2014-07-15 00:00:00	84.3	84.38	83.2	83.58	1874700	83.58
7	5	2014-07-14 00:00:00	83.66	84.64	83.11	84.4	1432100	84.4

MSFT

To write more than one `DataFrame` to a single Excel file and each `DataFrame` object on a separate worksheet, use the `ExcelWriter` object, along with the `with` keyword. `ExcelWriter` is part of pandas, but you will need to make sure it is imported, as it is not in the top level namespace of pandas. The following writes two DataFrame objects to two different worksheets in one Excel file:

```
In [23]:
    # write multiple sheets
    # requires use of the ExcelWriter class
    from pandas import ExcelWriter
    with ExcelWriter("data/all_stocks.xls") as writer:
        aapl.to_excel(writer, sheet_name='AAPL')
        df.to_excel(writer, sheet_name='MSFT')
```

We can see that there are two worksheets in the Excel file:

	A	B	C	D	E	F	G	H
1		Date	Open	High	Low	Close	Volume	Adj Close
2	0	2014-07-21 00:00:00	94.99	95	93.72	93.94	38887700	93.94
3	1	2014-07-18 00:00:00	93.62	94.74	93.02	94.43	49898600	94.43
4	2	2014-07-17 00:00:00	95.03	95.28	92.57	93.09	57152000	93.09
5	3	2014-07-16 00:00:00	96.97	97.1	94.74	94.78	53396300	94.78
6	4	2014-07-15 00:00:00	96.8	96.85	95.03	95.32	45477900	95.32
7	5	2014-07-14 00:00:00	95.86	96.89	95.65	96.45	42731000	96.45

AAPL   MSFT

Writing to XLSX files uses the same function but specifies .XLSX through the file extension:

```
In [24]:
    # write to xlsx
    df.to_excel("data/msft2.xlsx")
```

When writing an XLSX file, pandas will use the openpyxl or xlsxwriter packages, so make sure one is installed.

Reading and writing JSON files

pandas can read and write data stored in the **JavaScript Object Notation (JSON)** format. This is one of my favorites due to its ability to be used across platforms and with many programming languages.

To demonstrate saving as JSON, we will save the Excel data we just read in to a JSON file and then take a look at the contents:

```
In [25]:
    # write the excel data to a JSON file
    df.head().to_json("data/stocks.json")
    !cat data/stocks.json # osx or Linux
    # !type data\stocks.json # windows
```

```
{"Date":{"0":1405900800000,"1":1405641600000,"2":
1405555200000,"3":1405468800000,"4":1405382400000},
"Open":{"0":83.46,"1":83.3,"2":84.35,"3":83.77,"4":84.3},
"High":{"0":83.53,"1":83.4,"2":84.63,"3":84.91,"4":84.38},
"Low":{"0":81.81,"1":82.52,"2":83.33,"3":83.66,"4":83.2},
"Close":{"0":81.93,"1":83.35,"2":83.63,"3":84.91,"4":83.58},
"Volume":{"0":2359300,"1":4020800,"2":1974000,"3":1755600,"4":1874700},
"Adj Close":{"0":81.93,"1":83.35,"2":83.63,"3":84.91,"4":83.58}}
```

JSON-based data can be read with the `pd.read_json()` function:

```
In [26]:
    # read data in from JSON
    df_from_json = pd.read_json("data/stocks.json")
    df_from_json.head(5)
```

```
Out[26]:
        Adj Close    Close        Date      High      Low      Open      Volume
```

0	81.93	81.93	2014-07-21	83.53	81.81	83.46	2359300
1	83.35	83.35	2014-07-18	83.40	82.52	83.30	4020800
2	83.63	83.63	2014-07-17	84.63	83.33	84.35	1974000
3	84.91	84.91	2014-07-16	84.91	83.66	83.77	1755600
4	83.58	83.58	2014-07-15	84.38	83.20	84.30	1874700

Notice two slight differences here caused by the reading/writing of data from JSON. First, the columns have been reordered alphabetically. Second, the index for `DataFrame`, although containing content, is sorted as a string. These issues can be fixed easily, but they will not be covered here.

Reading HTML data from the Web

pandas has very nice support for reading data from HTML files (or HTML from URLs). Underneath the covers, pandas makes use of the LXML, Html5Lib, and BeautifulSoup4 packages, which provide some very impressive capabilities for reading and writing HTML tables.

The `pd.read_html()` function will read HTML from a file (or URL) and parse all HTML tables found in the content into one or more pandas `DataFrame` object. The function always returns a list of `DataFrame` objects (actually, zero or more, depending on the number of tables found in the HTML).

To demonstrate, we will read table data from the FDIC failed bank list located at `https://www.fdic.gov/bank/individual/failed/banklist.html`. Viewing the page, you can see there is a list of quite a few failed banks.

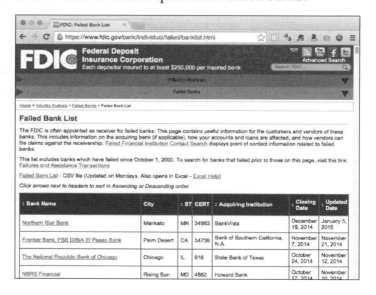

This data is actually very simple to read with pandas and its `pd.read_html()` function. The following reads from this URL and reports the findings:

```
In [27]:
    # the URL to read
    url = "http://www.fdic.gov/bank/individual/failed/banklist.html"
    # read it
    banks = pd.read_html(url)
    # examine a subset of the first table read
    banks[0][0:5].ix[:,0:4]
```

```
Out[27]:
                          Bank Name          City  ST   CERT
    0                Doral BankEn Espanol  San Juan  PR  32102
    1   Capitol City Bank & Trust Company   Atlanta  GA  33938
    2              Highland Community Bank   Chicago  IL  20290
    3   First National Bank of Crestview  Crestview  FL  17557
    4                  Northern Star Bank   Mankato  MN  34983
```

Again, that was almost too easy!

`DataFrame` can be written to an HTML file with the `.to_html()` method. The method creates a file containing the table tag for the data (not the entire HTML document). The following writes the stock data we read earlier to an HTML file:

```
In [28]:
    # read the stock data
    df = pd.read_excel("data/stocks.xlsx")
    # write the first two rows to HTML
    df.head(2).to_html("data/stocks.html")
    # check the first 28 lines of the output
    !head -n 28 data/stocks.html # max or linux
    # !type data\stocks.html # window, but prints the entire file

    <table border="1" class="dataframe">
      <thead>
        <tr style="text-align: right;">
          <th></th>
          <th>Date</th>
```

```
        <th>Open</th>
        <th>High</th>
        <th>Low</th>
        <th>Close</th>
        <th>Volume</th>
        <th>Adj Close</th>
      </tr>
    </thead>
    <tbody>
      <tr>
        <th>0</th>
        <td>2014-07-21</td>
        <td> 83.46</td>
        <td> 83.53</td>
        <td> 81.81</td>
        <td> 81.93</td>
        <td> 2359300</td>
        <td> 81.93</td>
      </tr>
      <tr>
        <th>1</th>
        <td>2014-07-18</td>
        <td> 83.30</td>
```

Viewing this in the browser looks like what is shown in the following:

	Date	Open	High	Low	Close	Volume	Adj Close
0	2014-07-21	83.46	83.53	81.81	81.93	2359300	81.93
1	2014-07-18	83.30	83.40	82.52	83.35	4020800	83.35

This is useful, as you can use pandas to write HTML fragments to be included in websites, updating them when needed and therefore, having the new data available to the site statically, instead of through a more complicated data query or service call.

Reading and writing HDF5 format files

HDF5 is a data model, library, and file format to store and manage data. It is commonly used in scientific computing environments. It supports an unlimited variety of data types and is designed for flexible and efficient I/O and for high volume and complex data.

HDF5 is portable and is extensible, allowing applications to evolve in their use of HDF5. The HDF5 Technology suite includes tools and applications to manage, manipulate, view, and analyze data in the HDF5 format. HDF5 is:

- A versatile data model that can represent very complex data objects and a wide variety of metadata
- A completely portable file format with no limit on the number or size of data objects in the collection
- A software library that runs on a range of computational platforms, from laptops to massively parallel systems, and implements a high-level API with C, C++, Fortran 90, and Java interfaces
- A rich set of integrated performance features that allow for access time and storage space optimizations
- Tools and applications to manage, manipulate, view, and analyze the data in the collection

HDFStore is a hierarchical, dictionary-like object that reads and writes pandas objects to the HDF5 format. Under the covers, HDFStore uses the PyTables library, so make sure that it is installed if you want to use this format.

The following demonstrates writing DataFrame into an HDF5 format. The output shows you that the HDF5 store has a root level object named df, which is a frame and whose shape is eight rows of three columns:

```
In [29]:
    # seed for replication
    np.random.seed(123456)
    # create a DataFrame of dates and random numbers in three columns
    df = pd.DataFrame(np.random.randn(8, 3),
                      index=pd.date_range('1/1/2000', periods=8),
                      columns=['A', 'B', 'C'])

    # create HDF5 store
    store = pd.HDFStore('data/store.h5')
```

```
store['df'] = df # persisting happened here
store
```

Out[29]:

```
<class 'pandas.io.pytables.HDFStore'>
File path: data/store.h5
/df                frame          (shape->[8,3])
```

The following reads the HDF5 store and retrieves `DataFrame`:

In [30]:

```
# read in data from HDF5
store = pd.HDFStore("data/store.h5")
df = store['df']
df
```

Out[30]:

```
                    A          B          C
2000-01-01   0.469112  -0.282863  -1.509059
2000-01-02  -1.135632   1.212112  -0.173215
2000-01-03   0.119209  -1.044236  -0.861849
2000-01-04  -2.104569  -0.494929   1.071804
2000-01-05   0.721555  -0.706771  -1.039575
2000-01-06   0.271860  -0.424972   0.567020
2000-01-07   0.276232  -1.087401  -0.673690
2000-01-08   0.113648  -1.478427   0.524988
```

`DataFrame` is written to the HDF5 file at the point it is assigned to the store object. Changes to `DataFrame` made after that point are not persisted, at least not until the object is assigned to the data store object again. The following demonstrates this by making a change to `DataFrame` and then reassigning it to the HDF5 store, thereby updating the data store:

In [31]:

```
# this changes the DataFrame, but did not persist
df.ix[0].A = 1

# to persist the change, assign the DataFrame to the
# HDF5 store object
```

```
store['df'] = df
# it is now persisted


# the following loads the store and
# shows the first two rows, demonstrating
# the the persisting was done
pd.HDFStore("data/store.h5")['df'].head(2) # it's now in there
```

Out[31]:

```
                  A          B          C
2000-01-01   1.000000  -0.282863  -1.509059
2000-01-02  -1.135632   1.212112  -0.173215
```

Accessing data on the web and in the cloud

It is quite common to read data off the web and from the cloud. pandas makes it extremely easy to read data from the web and cloud. All of the pandas functions we have examined can also be given an HTTP URL, FTP address, or S3 address instead of a local file path, and all work just the same as they work with a local file.

The following demonstrates how easy it is to directly make HTTP requests using the existing pd.read_csv() function. The following retrieves the daily stock data for Microsoft in June 2014 directly from the Yahoo! Finance web service via its HTTP query string model:

In [32]:

```
# read csv directly from Yahoo! Finance from a URL
df = pd.read_csv("http://ichart.yahoo.com/table.csv?s=MSFT&" +
                "a=5&b=1&c=2014&" +
                "d=5&e=30&f=2014&" +
                "g=d&ignore=.csv")
df[:5]
```

Out[32]:

```
            Date   Open   High    Low  Close    Volume  Adj Close
0     2014-06-30  42.17  42.21  41.70  41.70  30805500      40.89
1     2014-06-27  41.61  42.29  41.51  42.25  74640000      41.43
```

2	2014-06-26	41.93	41.94	41.43	41.72	23604400	40.91
3	2014-06-25	41.70	42.05	41.46	42.03	20049100	41.21
4	2014-06-24	41.83	41.94	41.56	41.75	26509100	40.94

Reading and writing from/to SQL databases

pandas can read data from any SQL databases that support Python data adapters, that respect the Python DB-API. Reading is performed using the `pandas.io.sql.read_sql()` function and writing to SQL databases using the `.to_sql()` method of `DataFrame`.

As an example of writing, the following reads the stock data from `msft.csv` and `aapl.csv`. It then makes a connection to a SQLite3 database file. If the file does not exist, it creates it on the fly. It then writes the MSFT data to a table named `STOCK_DATA`. If the table did not exist, it is created. If it exists, all the data is replaced with the MSFT data. It then appends the `AAPL` stock data to that table:

```
In [33]:
    # reference SQLite
    import sqlite3

    # read in the stock data from CSV
    msft = pd.read_csv("data/msft.csv")
    msft["Symbol"]="MSFT"
    aapl = pd.read_csv("data/aapl.csv")
    aapl["Symbol"]="AAPL"

    # create connection
    connection = sqlite3.connect("data/stocks.sqlite")
    # .to_sql() will create SQL to store the DataFrame
    # in the specified table.  if_exists specifies
    # what to do if the table already exists
    msft.to_sql("STOCK_DATA", connection, if_exists="replace")
    aapl.to_sql("STOCK_DATA", connection, if_exists="append")

    # commit the SQL and close the connection
    connection.commit()
    connection.close()
```

To demonstrate that this data was created, you can open the database file with a tool such as SQLite Data Browser (available at `http://sourceforge.net/projects/sqlitebrowser/`). The following shows you a few rows of the data in the database file:

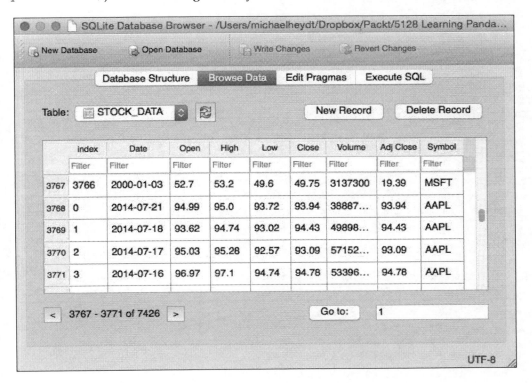

Data can be read using SQL from the database using the `pd.io.sql.read_sql()` function. The following queries the data from `stocks.sqlite` using SQL and reports it to the user:

```
In [34]:
    # connect to the database file
    connection = sqlite3.connect("data/stocks.sqlite")

    # query all records in STOCK_DATA
    # returns a DataFrame
    # inde_col specifies which column to make the DataFrame index
    stocks = pd.io.sql.read_sql("SELECT * FROM STOCK_DATA;",
```

```
                                    connection, index_col='index')

    # close the connection
    connection.close()

    # report the head of the data retrieved
    stocks.head()

Out[34]:

            Date   Open   High    Low Close   Volume Adj Close Symbol
    index
    0       2014-07-21 83.46 83.53 81.81 81.93 2359300      81.93    MSFT
    1       2014-07-18 83.30 83.40 82.52 83.35 4020800      83.35    MSFT
    2       2014-07-17 84.35 84.63 83.33 83.63 1974000      83.63    MSFT
    3       2014-07-16 83.77 84.91 83.66 84.91 1755600      84.91    MSFT
    4       2014-07-15 84.30 84.38 83.20 83.58 1874700      83.58    MSFT
```

It is also possible to use the WHERE clause in the SQL, as well as to select columns. To demonstrate, the following selects the records where MSFT's volume is greater than 29200100:

```
In [35]:
    # open the connection
    connection = sqlite3.connect("data/stocks.sqlite")

    # construct the query string
    query = "SELECT * FROM STOCK_DATA WHERE Volume>29200100 AND \
    Symbol='MSFT';"

    # execute and close connection
    items = pd.io.sql.read_sql(query, connection, index_col='index')
    connection.close()

    # report the query result
    Items

Out[35]:
            Date   Open   High    Low Close   Volume Adj Close Symbol
```

```
index
1081    2010-05-21  42.22  42.35  40.99  42.00  33610800    36.48    MSFT
1097    2010-04-29  46.80  46.95  44.65  45.92  47076200    38.41    MSFT
1826    2007-06-15  89.80  92.10  89.55  92.04  30656400    35.87    MSFT
3455    2001-03-16  47.00  47.80  46.10  45.33  40806400    17.66    MSFT
3712    2000-03-17  49.50  50.00  48.29  50.00  50860500    19.48    MSFT
```

A final point, is that most of the code of these examples was SQLite3 code. The only pandas part of these examples is the use of the `.to_sql()` and `.read_sql()` methods. As these functions take a connection object, which can be any Python DB-API-ompatible data adapter, you can more or less work with any supported database data by simply creating an appropriate connection object. The code at the pandas level should remain the same for any supported database.

Reading data from remote data services

pandas has direct support for various web-based data source classes in the `pandas. io.data` namespace. The primary class of interest is `pandas.io.data.DataReader`, which is implemented to read data from various supported sources and return it to the application directly as `DataFrame`.

Currently, support exists for the following sources via the `DataReader` class:

- Daily historical prices' stock from either Yahoo! and Google Finance
- Yahoo! Options
- The Federal Reserve Economic Data library
- Kenneth French's Data Library
- The World Bank

The specific source of data is specified via the `DataReader` object's `data_source` parameter. The specific items to be retrieved are specified using the `name` parameter. If the data source supports selecting data between a range of dates, these dates can be specified with the `start` and `end` parameters. We will now take a look at reading data from each of these sources.

Reading stock data from Yahoo! and Google Finance

Yahoo! Finance is specified by passing `'yahoo'` as the `data_source` parameter. The following retrieves data from Yahoo! Finance, specifically, the data for MSFT between 2012-01-01 and 2014-01-27:

```
In [36]:
    # import pandas.io.data namespace, alias as web
    import pandas.io.data as web
    # and datetime for the dates
    import datetime

    # start end end dates
    start = datetime.datetime(2012, 1, 1)
    end = datetime.datetime(2014, 1, 27)

    # read the MSFT stock data from yahoo! and view the head
    yahoo = web.DataReader('MSFT', 'yahoo', start, end)
    yahoo.head()
```

```
Out[36]:
             Open   High    Low    Close    Volume   Adj Close
    Date
    2012-01-03  26.55  26.96  26.39   26.77   64731500     24.42
    2012-01-04  26.82  27.47  26.78   27.40   80516100     25.00
    2012-01-05  27.38  27.73  27.29   27.68   56081400     25.25
    2012-01-06  27.53  28.19  27.53   28.11   99455500     25.64
    2012-01-09  28.05  28.10  27.72   27.74   59706800     25.31
```

The source of the data can be changed to Google Finance with a change of the `data_source` parameter to `'google'`:

```
In [37]:
    # read from google and display the head of the data
    goog = web.DataReader("MSFT", 'google', start, end)
```

```
goog.head()
```

Out[37]:

	Open	High	Low	Close	Volume
Date					
2012-01-03	26.55	26.96	26.39	26.76	64735391
2012-01-04	26.82	27.47	26.78	27.40	80519402
2012-01-05	27.38	27.73	27.29	27.68	56082205
2012-01-06	27.53	28.19	27.52	28.10	99459469
2012-01-09	28.05	28.10	27.72	27.74	59708266

Notice that the result of the Google query has different columns than the Yahoo! data; specifically, Google Finance does not provide an `Adjusted Close` value.

Retrieving data from Yahoo! Finance Options

pandas provides experimental support for Yahoo! Finance Options data to be retrieved via the `pandas.io.data.Options` class. In the following example, the `.get_all_data()` method is used to download options data for `AAPL` from `yahoo`:

In [38]:

```
# specify we want all yahoo options data for AAPL
# this can take a little time...
aapl = pd.io.data.Options('AAPL', 'yahoo')
# read all the data
data = aapl.get_all_data()
# examine the first six rows and four columns
data.iloc[0:6, 0:4]
```

Out[38]:

Strike	Expiry	Type	Symbol	Last	Bid	Ask	Chg
27.86	2015-01-17	call	AAPL150117C00027860	82.74	79.50	79.85	0
		put	AAPL150117P00027860	0.02	0.00	0.01	0
28.57	2015-01-17	call	AAPL150117C00028570	82.02	78.80	79.10	0
		put	AAPL150117P00028570	0.01	0.00	0.01	0
29.29	2015-01-17	call	AAPL150117C00029290	84.75	78.05	78.40	0
		put	AAPL150117P00029290	0.01	0.00	0.01	0

The resulting `DataFrame` object contains a hierarchical index, which can be used to easily extract specific subsets of data. To demonstrate, look at several examples of slicing by the values in the index.

The following code will return all `put` options at a Strike price of $80. Using `slice(None)` as one of the values in the tuple used to select by index will include all `Expiry` dates:

```
In [39]:
    # get all puts at strike price of $80 (first four columns only)
    data.loc[(80, slice(None), 'put'), :].iloc[0:5, 0:4]
```

```
Out[39]:
```

				Last	Bid	Ask	Chg
Strike	Expiry	Type	Symbol				
80	2015-01-09	put	AAPL150109P00080000	0.01	0.00	0.01	0
	2015-01-17	put	AAPL150117P00080000	0.01	0.01	0.02	0
	2015-01-23	put	AAPL150123P00080000	0.06	0.01	0.04	0
	2015-01-30	put	AAPL150130P00080000	0.12	0.07	0.12	0
	2015-02-20	put	AAPL150220P00080000	0.22	0.22	0.24	0

As another example, we can narrow the date range by specifying a date slice instead of `slice(None)`. The following narrows the result down to those where `Expiry` date is between 2015-01-17 and 2015-04-17:

```
In [40]:
    # put options at strike of $80, between 2015-01-17 and 2015-04-17
    data.loc[(80, slice('20150117','20150417'),
             'put'), :].iloc[:, 0:4]
```

```
Out[40]:
```

				Last	Bid	Ask	Chg
Strike	Expiry	Type	Symbol				
80	2015-01-17	put	AAPL150117P00080000	0.01	0.01	0.02	0.00
	2015-01-23	put	AAPL150123P00080000	0.06	0.01	0.04	0.00
	2015-01-30	put	AAPL150130P00080000	0.12	0.07	0.12	0.00
	2015-02-20	put	AAPL150220P00080000	0.22	0.22	0.24	0.00
	2015-03-20	put	AAPL150320P00080000	0.40	0.39	0.43	-0.06
	2015-04-17	put	AAPL150417P00080000	0.64	0.61	0.66	0.00

If you do not want to download all of the data (which can take a few minutes), then you can use other methods, such as `.get_call_data()` and `.get_put_data()`, which will only download the data for the call or puts, respectively, and for a specific expiry date. To demonstrate, the following loads all call data for MSFT with the expiry date of 2015-01-05:

```
In [41]:
    # msft calls expiring on 2015-01-05
    expiry = datetime.date(2015, 1, 5)
    msft_calls = pd.io.data.Options('MSFT', 'yahoo').get_call_data(
                                              expiry=expiry)
    msft_calls.iloc[0:5, 0:5]
```

```
Out[41]:
```

				Last	Bid	Ask	Chg	PctChg
Strike	Expiry	Type	Symbol					
35.5	2015-03-13	call	MSFT150313C00035500	6.20	5.55	7.20	0	0.00%
36.5	2015-03-13	call	MSFT150313C00036500	7.60	5.65	5.95	0	0.00%
37.5	2015-03-13	call	MSFT150313C00037500	5.10	4.65	5.25	0	0.00%
38.0	2015-03-13	call	MSFT150313C00038000	3.10	4.15	4.45	0	0.00%
39.0	2015-03-13	call	MSFT150313C00039000	3.15	3.15	3.45	0	0.00%

The `.get_all_data()` method will load data for all expiry months and cache that data. The cache will be automatically used to make subsequent calls return much more quickly if the data is present in the cache. As an example, the following example will return calls quickly, as the data has already been cached by the previous `.get_all_data()` call for appl call options:

```
In [42]:
    # msft calls expiring on 2015-01-17
    expiry = datetime.date(2015, 1, 17)
    aapl_calls = aapl.get_call_data(expiry=expiry)
    aapl_calls.iloc[0:5, 0:4]
```

```
Out[42]:
```

```
                                           Last    Bid    Ask  Chg

Strike  Expiry      Type  Symbol

27.86   2015-01-17  call  AAPL150117C00027860  82.74  79.50  79.85    0

28.57   2015-01-17  call  AAPL150117C00028570  82.02  78.80  79.10    0

29.29   2015-01-17  call  AAPL150117C00029290  84.75  78.05  78.40    0

30.00   2015-01-17  call  AAPL150117C00030000  81.20  77.35  77.70    0

30.71   2015-01-17  call  AAPL150117C00030710  83.20  76.65  77.00    0
```

Reading economic data from the Federal Reserve Bank of St. Louis

The **Federal Reserve Economic Data (FRED)** of St. Louis (`http://research.stlouisfed.org/fred2/`) provides downloads of over 240,000 US and International time series from over 76 data sources, and it is constantly growing.

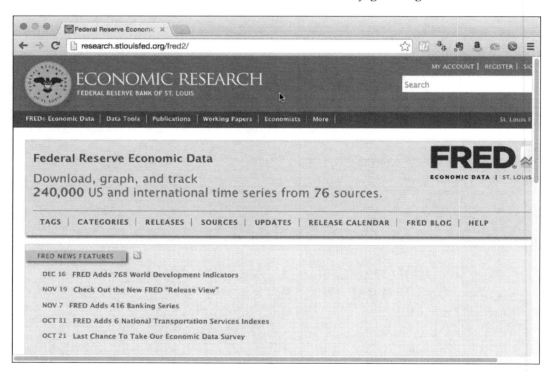

FRED data can be specified by `data_source="fred"`, passing the specific series tag as the `name` parameter. A specific data series can be specified using the series ID in the first parameter. As an example, the following retrieves GDP information between the two specified dates:

```
In [43]:
    # read GDP data from FRED
    gdp = web.DataReader("GDP", "fred",
                        datetime.date(2012, 1, 1),
                        datetime.date(2014, 1, 27))
    gdp

Out[43]:
                    GDP
    DATE
    2012-01-01  15956.5
    2012-04-01  16094.7
    2012-07-01  16268.9
    2012-10-01  16332.5
    2013-01-01  16502.4
    2013-04-01  16619.2
    2013-07-01  16872.3
    2013-10-01  17078.3
    2014-01-01  17044.0
```

To select another series, simply specify the series identifier in the first parameter. The site can be conveniently navigated through series and data visualized directly on the site. For example, the following screenshot shows you the series **Compensation of employees: Wages and salaries**:

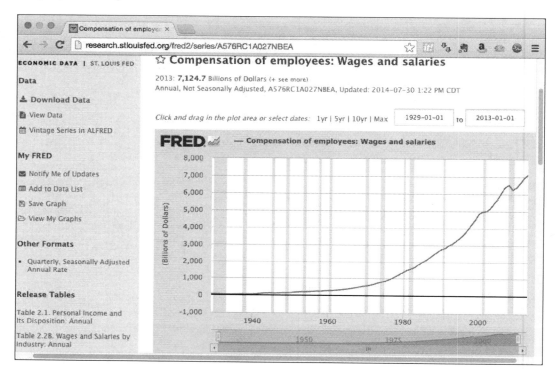

This data series is represented by the A576RC1A027NBEA ID and we can download it with the following code:

```
In [44]:

    # Get Compensation of employees: Wages and salaries
    web.DataReader("A576RC1A027NBEA",
                "fred",
                datetime.date(1929, 1, 1),
                datetime.date(2013, 1, 1))

Out[44]:

            A576RC1A027NBEA
    DATE
    1929-01-01              50.5
```

```
1930-01-01              46.2
1931-01-01              39.2
1932-01-01              30.5
1933-01-01              29.0
   ...                  ...
2009-01-01            6251.4
2010-01-01            6377.5
2011-01-01            6633.2
2012-01-01            6932.1
2013-01-01            7124.7


[85 rows x 1 columns]
```

Accessing Kenneth French's data

Kenneth R. French is a professor of finance at the Tuck School of Business at Dartmouth University. He has created an extensive library of economic data, which is available for download over the Web. The website for his data is at `http://mba.tuck.dartmouth.edu/pages/faculty/ken.french/data_library.html`, and it contains a detailed description of the datasets.

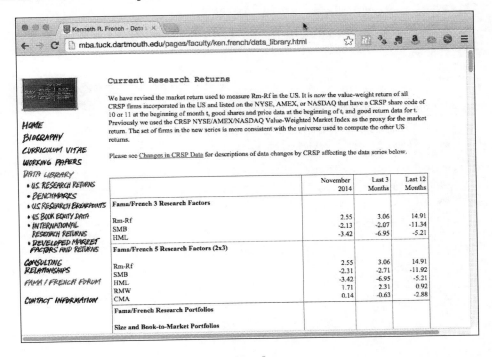

The data available at the site is downloadable in zip files and can be read directly into DataFrame by specifying the dataset's filename (without .zip) as the first parameter of DataReader and using data_source="famafrench":

As an example, the following reads the Global Factors data:

```
In [45]:
    # read from Kenneth French fama global factors data set
    factors = web.DataReader("Global_Factors", "famafrench")
    factors
```

```
Out[45]:
    {3:        1 Mkt-RF   2 SMB   3 HML   4 WML   5 RF
     199007       0.79     0.07    0.24  -99.99   0.68
     199008     -10.76    -1.56    0.42  -99.99   0.66
     199009     -12.24     1.68    0.34  -99.99   0.60
     199010       9.58    -8.11   -3.29  -99.99   0.68
     199011      -3.87     1.62    0.68   -0.32   0.57
     ...           ...      ...     ...     ...    ...
     201409      -3.05    -2.63   -1.05    1.07   0.00
     201410       0.34    -0.23   -2.98   -0.46   0.00
     201411       1.67    -2.14   -1.92    0.65   0.00
     201412      -1.45     1.89   -0.33    1.06   0.00
     201501      -1.75     0.04   -2.78    4.50   0.00

     [295 rows x 5 columns]}
```

Reading from the World Bank

Thousands of data feeds are available from the World Bank and can be read directly into pandas DataFrame objects. The World Bank data catalog can be explored at http://www.worldbank.org/.

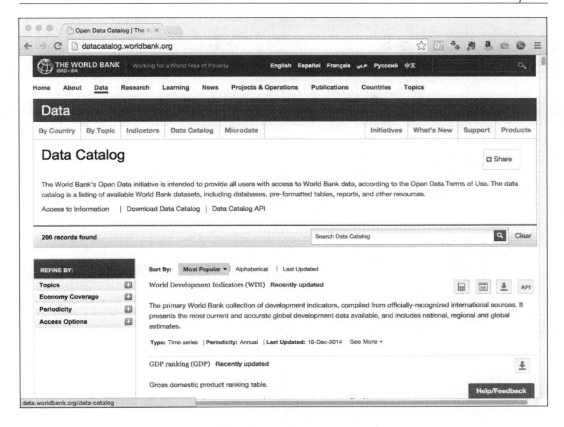

World Bank datasets are identified using indicators, a text code that represents each dataset. A full list of indicators can be retrieved using the pandas.io.wb.get_ indicators() function. At the time of writing this, there were 13079 indicators:

```
In [46]:
    # make referencing pandas.io.wb a little less typing
    import pandas.io.wb as wb
    # get all indicators
    all_indicators = wb.get_indicators()
```

```
In [47]:
    # examine some of the indicators
    all_indicators.ix[:,0:1]
```

```
Out[47]:
                                    id
```

```
0                      1.0.HCount.1.25usd
1                       1.0.HCount.10usd
2                       1.0.HCount.2.5usd
3                      1.0.HCount.Mid10to50
4                         1.0.HCount.Ofcl
...                              ...
13074        per_sionl.overlap_pop_urb
13075        per_sionl.overlap_q1_preT_tot
13076        per_sionl.overlap_q1_rur
13077        per_sionl.overlap_q1_tot
13078        per_sionl.overlap_q1_urb


[13079 rows x 1 columns]
```

These indicators can be investigated using the World Bank website, but if you have an idea of the indicator you would like to sample, you can perform a search. As an example, the following uses the `pandas.io.wb.search()` function to search for indicators with data related to life expectancy:

In [48]:

```
# search of life expectancy indicators
le_indicators = wb.search("life expectancy")
# report first three rows, first two columns
le_indicators.iloc[:3,:2]
```

Out[48]:

```
                     id                                name
7785    SP.DYN.LE00.FE.IN    Life expectancy at birth, female (years)
7786       SP.DYN.LE00.IN    Life expectancy at birth, total (years)
7787    SP.DYN.LE00.MA.IN    Life expectancy at birth, male (years)
```

Each indicator is broken down into various countries. A full list of country data can be retrieved using the `pandas.io.wb.get_countries()` function, as demonstrated here:

In [49]:

```
# get countries and show the 3 digit code and name
countries = wb.get_countries()
# show a subset of the country data
```

```
countries.iloc[0:10].ix[:,['name', 'capitalCity', 'iso2c']]
```

Out[49]:

	name	capitalCity	iso2c
0	Aruba	Oranjestad	AW
1	Afghanistan	Kabul	AF
2	Africa		A9
3	Angola	Luanda	AO
4	Albania	Tirane	AL
5	Andorra	Andorra la Vella	AD
6	Andean Region		L5
7	Arab World		1A
8	United Arab Emirates	Abu Dhabi	AE
9	Argentina	Buenos Aires	AR

Data for an indicator can be downloaded using the `pandas.io.wb.download()` function, specifying the dataset using the `indicator` parameter. The following downloads the life expectancy data for countries from 1980 through 2012:

In [50]:

```
# get life expectancy at birth for all countries from 1980 to 2014
le_data_all = wb.download(indicator="SP.DYN.LE00.IN",
                          start='1980',
                          end='2014')
le_data_all
```

Out[50]:

		SP.DYN.LE00.IN
country	year	
Canada	2014	NaN
	2013	NaN
	2012	81.238049
	2011	81.068317
	2010	80.893488
...		...
United States	1984	74.563415
	1983	74.463415

```
        1982            74.360976
        1981            74.007317
        1980            73.658537
```

```
[105 rows x 1 columns]
```

By default, data is only returned for the United States, Canada, and Mexico. This can be seen by examining the index of the result of the previous query:

```
In [51]:
    # only US, CAN, and MEX are returned by default
    le_data_all.index.levels[0]
```

```
Out[51]:
    Index([u'Canada', u'Mexico', u'United States'], dtype='object')
```

To get the data for more countries, specify them explicitly using the country parameter. The following gets the data for all known countries:

```
In [52]:
    # retrieve life expectancy at birth for all countries
    # from 1980 to 2014
    le_data_all = wb.download(indicator="SP.DYN.LE00.IN",
                              country = countries['iso2c'],
                              start='1980',
                              end='2012')
    le_data_all
```

```
Out[52]:
                          SP.DYN.LE00.IN
    country     year
    Aruba       2012          75.206756
                2011          75.080390
                2010          74.952024
                2009          74.816146
                2008          74.674220
    ...                            ...
    Zimbabwe    1984          61.217561
                1983          60.902854
```

```
1982        60.466171
1981        59.944951
1980        59.377610
```

[8151 rows x 1 columns]

We can do some interesting things with this data. The example we will look at, determines which country has the lowest life expectancy for each year. To do this, we first need to pivot this data, so that the index is the country name and the year is the column. We will look at pivoting in more detail in later chapters, but for now, just know that the following reorganized the data into the country along the index and the year across the columns. Also, each value is the life expectancy for each country for that specific year:

```
In [53]:
#le_data_all.pivot(index='country', columns='year')
le_data = le_data_all.reset_index().pivot(index='country',
                                          columns='year')

# examine pivoted data
le_data.ix[:,0:3]
```

```
Out[53]:
                   SP.DYN.LE00.IN
year                    1980          1981          1982
country
Afghanistan        41.233659     41.760634     42.335610
Albania            70.235976     70.454463     70.685122
Algeria            58.164024     59.486756     60.786341
American Samoa           NaN           NaN           NaN
Andorra                  NaN           NaN           NaN
...                      ...           ...           ...
West Bank and Gaza       NaN           NaN           NaN
World              63.186868     63.494118     63.798264
Yemen, Rep.        50.559537     51.541341     52.492707
Zambia             51.148951     50.817707     50.350805
Zimbabwe           59.377610     59.944951     60.466171
```

[247 rows x 3 columns]

With the data in this format, we can perform and determine which country has the lowest life expectancy for each year using `.idxmin(axis=0)`:

```
In [54]:
    # ask what is the name of the country for each year
    # with the least life expectancy
    country_with_least_expectancy = le_data.idxmin(axis=0)
    country_with_least_expectancy
```

```
Out[54]:
                    year
    SP.DYN.LE00.IN  1980        Cambodia
                    1981        Cambodia
                    1982     Timor-Leste
    ...
    SP.DYN.LE00.IN  2010    Sierra Leone
                    2011    Sierra Leone
                    2012    Sierra Leone
    Length: 33, dtype: object
```

The actual minimum value for each year can be retrieved using `.min(axis=0)`:

```
In [55]:
    # and what is the minimum life expectancy for each year
    expectancy_for_least_country = le_data.min(axis=0)
    expectancy_for_least_country
```

```
Out[55]:
                    year
    SP.DYN.LE00.IN  1980        29.613537
                    1981        35.856341
                    1982        38.176220
    ...
    SP.DYN.LE00.IN  2010        44.838951
                    2011        45.102585
                    2012        45.329049
    Length: 33, dtype: float64
```

These two results can then be combined into a new `DataFrame` that tells us which country had the least life expectancy for each year and what that value is:

```
In [56]:
    # this merges the two frames together and gives us
    # year, country and expectancy where there minimum exists
    least = pd.DataFrame(
        data = {'Country': country_with_least_expectancy.values,
                'Expectancy': expectancy_for_least_country.values},
        index = country_with_least_expectancy.index.levels[1])
    least
```

```
Out[56]:
                Country   Expectancy
    year
    1980        Cambodia  29.613537
    1981        Cambodia  35.856341
    1982     Timor-Leste  38.176220
    1983     South Sudan  39.676488
    1984     South Sudan  40.011024
    ...             ...          ...
    2008    Sierra Leone  44.067463
    2009    Sierra Leone  44.501439
    2010    Sierra Leone  44.838951
    2011    Sierra Leone  45.102585
    2012    Sierra Leone  45.329049

    [33 rows x 2 columns]
```

Summary

In this chapter, we examined how pandas makes it simple to access data in various locations and formats, providing automatic mapping of data in these formats into `DataFrame` objects. We started with learning how to read and write data from local files in CSV, HTML, JSON, HDF5, and Excel formats, reading into, and writing directly, from DataFrame objects without having to worry about the details of mapping the contained data into these various formats.

We then examined how to access data from remote sources. First, we saw that the functions and methods that work with local files can also read from web and cloud data sources. We then looked at pandas support for accessing various forms of web and web-service-based data, such as Yahoo! Finance and the World Bank.

Now that we are able to load the data, the next step in using that data is to perform the cleaning of the data. Often, the data that is loaded has missing information and ill-formed content. The next chapter will focus on these issues of tidying the data that is loaded into your application.

7
Tidying Up Your Data

Data analysis typically flows in a processing pipeline that starts with retrieving data from one or more sources. Upon receipt of this data, it is often the case that it can be in a raw form and can be difficult to use for data analysis. This can be for a multitude of reasons such as data is not recorded, it is lost, or it is just in a different format than what you require.

Therefore, one of the most common things you will do with pandas involves **tidying** your data, which is the process of preparing raw data for analysis. Showing you how to use various features of pandas to get raw data into a tidy form is the focus of this chapter.

In this chapter, you will learn:

- The concept of tidy data
- How pandas represents unknown values
- How to find NaN values in data
- How to filter (drop) data
- What pandas does with unknown values in calculations
- How to find, filter and fix unknown values
- How to identify and remove duplicate data
- How to transform values using replace, map, and apply

What is tidying your data?

Tidy data is a term that was created in what many refer to as a famous data science paper, "Tidy Data" by Hadley Wickham, which I highly recommend that you read and it can be downloaded at `http://vita.had.co.nz/papers/tidy-data.pdf`. The paper covers many details of the process that he calls tidying data, with the result of the process being that you now have tidy data; data that is ready for analysis.

This chapter will introduce and briefly demonstrate many of the capabilities of pandas. We will not get into all of the details of the paper, but as an opening to what we will cover, I would like to create a brief summary of the reasons why you need to tidy data and what are the characteristics of tidy data, so that you know you have completed the task and are ready to move on to analysis.

Tidying of data is required for many reasons including these:

- The names of the variables are different from what you require
- There is *missing* data
- Values are not in the units that you require
- The period of sampling of records is not what you need
- Variables are categorical and you need quantitative values
- There is *noise* in the data,
- Information is of an incorrect type
- Data is organized around incorrect axes
- Data is at the wrong level of normalization
- Data is duplicated

This is quite a list, and it is very likely that I have missed a few points. In working with data, I have seen all of these issues at one time or another, or many of them at once. Fixing these can often be very difficult in programming languages, such as Java or C#, and often cause exceptions at the worst times (such as in production of a high-volume trading system).

Moving away from a list of problems with data that needs to be addressed, there are several characteristics of data that can be considered good, tidy, and ready for analysis, which are as follows:

- Each variable is in one column
- Each observation of the variable is in a different row
- There should be one table for each kind of variable

- If multiple tables, they should be relatable
- Qualitative and categorical variables have mappings to values useful for analysis

Fortunately, pandas has been designed to make dealing with all of these issues as painless as possible and you will learn how to address most of these issues in the remainder of this chapter.

Setting up the IPython notebook

To utilize the examples in this chapter, we will need to include the following imports and settings:

```
In [1]:
    # import pandas, numpy and datetime
    import numpy as np
    import pandas as pd
    import datetime

    # Set some pandas options for controlling output
    pd.set_option('display.notebook_repr_html', False)
    pd.set_option('display.max_columns', 10)
    pd.set_option('display.max_rows', 10)
```

Working with missing data

Data is "missing" in pandas when it has a value of NaN (also seen as np.nan—the form from NumPy). The NaN value represents that in a particular Series that there is not a value specified for the particular index label.

In pandas, there are a number of reasons why a value can be NaN:

- A join of two sets of data does not have matched values
- Data that you retrieved from an external source is incomplete
- The NaN value is not known at a given point in time and will be filled in later
- There is a data collection error retrieving a value, but the event must still be recorded in the index

- Reindexing of data has resulted in an index that does not have a value
- The shape of data has changed and there are now additional rows or columns, which at the time of reshaping could not be determined

There are likely more reasons, but the general point is that they occur and you, as a pandas programmer, will need to work with them effectively to be able to perform correct data analysis. Fortunately, pandas provides you with several tools to identify missing values and to substitute them with values that facilitate your analysis.

To demonstrate handling missing data, we will use the following `DataFrame` object, which exhibits various patterns of missing data:

```
In [2]:
    # create a DataFrame with 5 rows and 3 columns
    df = pd.DataFrame(np.arange(0, 15).reshape(5, 3),
                 index=['a', 'b', 'c', 'd', 'e'],
                 columns=['c1', 'c2', 'c3'])
    df
```

```
Out[2]:
      c1  c2  c3
  a    0   1   2
  b    3   4   5
  c    6   7   8
  d    9  10  11
  e   12  13  14
```

There is no missing data at this point, so let's add some:

```
In [3]:
    # add some columns and rows to the DataFrame
    # column c4 with NaN values
    df['c4'] = np.nan
    # row 'f' with 15 through 18
    df.loc['f'] = np.arange(15, 19)
    # row 'g' will all NaN
    df.loc['g'] = np.nan
    # column 'C5' with NaN's
    df['c5'] = np.nan
    # change value in col 'c4' row 'a'
```

```
df['c4']['a'] = 20
df
```

Out[3]:

	c1	c2	c3	c4	c5
a	0	1	2	20	NaN
b	3	4	5	NaN	NaN
c	6	7	8	NaN	NaN
d	9	10	11	NaN	NaN
e	12	13	14	NaN	NaN
f	15	16	17	18	NaN
g	NaN	NaN	NaN	NaN	NaN

This DataFrame object exhibits the following characteristics that will support most of the examples that follow in this section:

- One row consisting only of NaN values
- One column is consisiting only of NaN values
- Several rows and columns consisting of both numeric values and NaN values

Determining NaN values in Series and DataFrame objects

The NaN values in a DataFrame object can be identified using the .isnull() method. Any True value means that the item is a NaN value:

```
In [4]:
    # which items are NaN?
    df.isnull()
```

Out[4]:

	c1	c2	c3	c4	c5
a	False	False	False	False	True
b	False	False	False	True	True
c	False	False	False	True	True
d	False	False	False	True	True
e	False	False	False	True	True
f	False	False	False	False	True
g	True	True	True	True	True

We can use the fact that the `.sum()` method treats `True` as 1 and `False` as 0 to determine the number of NaN values in a `DataFrame` object. By applying `.sum()` on the result of `.isnull()`, we will get a total for the number of `True` values (representing NaN values) in each column:

```
In [5]:
    # count the number of NaN values in each column
    df.isnull().sum()
```

```
Out[5]:
    c1    1
    c2    1
    c3    1
    c4    5
    c5    7
    dtype: int64
```

Applying `.sum()` to the resulting series gives the total number of NaN values in the original `DataFrame` object.

```
In [6]:
    # total count of NaN values
    df.isnull().sum().sum()
```

```
Out[6]:
    15
```

Another way to determine this is to use the `.count()` method of a `Series` object and `DataFrame`. For a `Series` method, this method will return the number of non-NaN values. For a `DataFrame` object, it will count the number of non-NaN values in each column:

```
In [7]:
    # number of non-NaN values in each column
    df.count()
```

```
Out[7]:
    c1    6
    c2    6
    c3    6
```

```
c4     2
c5     0
dtype: int64
```

This then needs to be flipped around to sum the number of NaN values, which can be calculated as follows:

In [8]:

```
# and this counts the number of NaN values too
(len(df) - df.count()).sum()
```

Out[8]:

```
15
```

We can also determine whether an item is not NaN using the .notnull() method, which returns True if the value is not a NaN value, otherwise it returns False:

In [9]:

```
# which items are not null?
df.notnull()
```

Out[9]:

	c1	c2	c3	c4	c5
a	True	True	True	True	False
b	True	True	True	False	False
c	True	True	True	False	False
d	True	True	True	False	False
e	True	True	True	False	False
f	True	True	True	True	False
g	False	False	False	False	False

Selecting out or dropping missing data

One technique of handling missing data, is to simply remove it from your dataset. A scenario for this would be where data is sampled at regular intervals, but devices are offline and do not receive a reading, but you only need the actual periodic values.

The pandas library makes this possible using several techniques; one is through Boolean selection using the results of .isnull() and .notnull() to retrieve the values that are NaN or not NaN out of a Series object. To demonstrate, the following example selects all non-NaN values from the c4 column of DataFrame:

```
In [10]:
    # select the non-NaN items in column c4
    df.c4[df.c4.notnull()]
```

```
Out[10]:
    a    20
    f    18
    Name: c4, dtype: float64
```

pandas also provides a convenience function .dropna(), which will drop the items in a Series where the value is NaN, involving less typing than the previous example.

```
In [11]:
    # .dropna will also return non NaN values
    # this gets all non NaN items in column c4
    df.c4.dropna()
```

```
Out[11]:
    a    20
    f    18
    Name: c4, dtype: float64
```

Note that .dropna() has actually returned a copy of DataFrame without the rows. The original DataFrame is not changed:

```
In [12]:
    # dropna returns a copy with the values dropped
    # the source DataFrame / column is not changed
    df.c4
```

```
Out[12]:
    a    20
    b    NaN
    c    NaN
    d    NaN
```

```
e   NaN
f    18
g   NaN
Name: c4, dtype: float64
```

When applied to a `DataFrame` object, `.dropna()` will drop all rows from a `DataFrame` object that have at least one `NaN` value. The following code demonstrates this in action, and since each row has at least one `NaN` value, there are no rows in the result:

```
In [13]:
    # on a DataFrame this will drop entire rows
    # where there is at least one NaN
    # in this case, that is all rows
    df.dropna()
```

```
Out[13]:
    Empty DataFrame
    Columns: [c1, c2, c3, c4, c5]
    Index: []
```

If you want to only drop rows where all values are `NaN`, you can use the `how='all'` parameter. The following code only drops the g row since it has all `NaN` values:

```
In [14]:
    # using how='all', only rows that have all values
    # as NaN will be dropped
    df.dropna(how = 'all')
```

```
Out[14]:
       c1  c2  c3  c4   c5
    a   0   1   2  20  NaN
    b   3   4   5 NaN  NaN
    c   6   7   8 NaN  NaN
    d   9  10  11 NaN  NaN
    e  12  13  14 NaN  NaN
    f  15  16  17  18  NaN
```

This can also be applied to the columns instead of the rows, by changing the axis parameter to `axis=1`. The following code drops the `c5` column as it is the only one with all `NaN` values:

```
In [15]:
    # flip to drop columns instead of rows
    df.dropna(how='all', axis=1) # say goodbye to c5
```

```
Out[15]:
        c1   c2   c3   c4
    a    0    1    2   20
    b    3    4    5  NaN
    c    6    7    8  NaN
    d    9   10   11  NaN
    e   12   13   14  NaN
    f   15   16   17   18
    g  NaN  NaN  NaN  NaN
```

We can also examine this process using a slightly different `DataFrame` object that has columns `c1` and `c3` with all values that are not `NaN`. In this case, all columns except `c1` and `c3` will be dropped:

```
In [16]:
    # make a copy of df
    df2 = df.copy()

    # replace two NaN cells with values
    df2.ix['g'].c1 = 0
    df2.ix['g'].c3 = 0
    df2
```

```
Out[16]:
        c1   c2   c3   c4   c5
    a    0    1    2   20  NaN
    b    3    4    5  NaN  NaN
    c    6    7    8  NaN  NaN
    d    9   10   11  NaN  NaN
    e   12   13   14  NaN  NaN
```

```
f   15   16   17   18 NaN

g    0  NaN    0 NaN NaN
```

In [17]:

```
# now drop columns with any NaN values
df2.dropna(how='any', axis=1)
```

Out[17]:

	c1	c3
a	0	2
b	3	5
c	6	8
d	9	11
e	12	14
f	15	17
g	0	0

The .dropna() methods also has a parameter, thresh, which when given an integer value specifies the minimum number of NaN values that must exist before the drop is performed. The following code drops all columns with at least five NaN values; these are the c4 and c5 columns:

In [18]:

```
# only drop columns with at least 5 NaN values
df.dropna(thresh=5, axis=1)
```

Out[18]:

	c1	c2	c3
a	0	1	2
b	3	4	5
c	6	7	8
d	9	10	11
e	12	13	14
f	15	16	17
g	NaN	NaN	NaN

Note that the .dropna() method (and the Boolean selection) returns a copy of the DataFrame object, and the data is dropped from that copy. If you want to drop the data in the actual DataFrame, use the inplace=True parameter.

How pandas handles NaN values in mathematical operations

The NaN values are handled differently in pandas than in NumPy. This is demonstrated using the following example:

```
In [19]:
    # create a NumPy array with one NaN value
    a = np.array([1, 2, np.nan, 3])
    # create a Series from the array
    s = pd.Series(a)
    # the mean of each is different
    a.mean(), s.mean()
```

```
Out[19]:
    (nan, 2.0)
```

NumPy functions, when encountering a NaN value, will return NaN. pandas functions and will typically ignore the NaN values and continue processing the function as though the values were not part of the Series object.

 Note that the mean of the preceding series was calculated as (1+2+3)/3 = 2, not (1+2+3)/4, or (1+2+0+4)/4. This verifies that NaN is totally ignored and not even counted as an item in the Series.

More specifically, the way that pandas handles NaN values is as follows:

- Summing of data treats NaN as 0
- If all values are NaN, the result is NaN
- Methods like .cumsum() and .cumprod() ignore NaN values, but preserve them in the resulting arrays

The following code demonstrates all of these concepts:

```
In [20]:
    # demonstrate sum, mean and cumsum handling of NaN
    # get one column
    s = df.c4
```

```
    s.sum()  # NaN values treated as 0
```

Out[20]:

```
    (38.0,)
```

In [21]:

```
    s.mean()  # NaN also treated as 0
```

Out[21]:

```
    19.0
```

In [22]:

```
    # as 0 in the cumsum, but NaN values preserved in result Series
    s.cumsum()
```

Out[22]:

```
    a     20
    b    NaN
    c    NaN
    d    NaN
    e    NaN
    f     38
    g    NaN
    Name: c4, dtype: float64
```

When using traditional mathematical operators, NaN is propagated through to the result.

In [23]:

```
    # in arithmetic, a NaN value will result in NaN
    df.c4 + 1
```

Out[23]:

```
    a     21
    b    NaN
    c    NaN
    d    NaN
    e    NaN
```

```
f    19
g    NaN
Name: c4, dtype: float64
```

Filling in missing data

If you prefer to replace the NaN values with a specific value, instead of having them propagated or flat out ignored, you can use the .fillna() method. The following code fills the NaN values with 0:

```
In [24]:
    # return a new DataFrame with NaN values filled with 0
    filled = df.fillna(0)
    filled
```

```
Out[24]:
       c1   c2   c3   c4   c5
    a   0    1    2   20    0
    b   3    4    5    0    0
    c   6    7    8    0    0
    d   9   10   11    0    0
    e  12   13   14    0    0
    f  15   16   17   18    0
    g   0    0    0    0    0
```

Be aware that this causes differences in the resulting values. As an example, the following code shows the result of applying the .mean() method to the DataFrame object with the NaN values, as compared to the DataFrame that has its NaN values filled with 0:

```
In [25]:
    # NaNs don't count as an item in calculating
    # the means
    df.mean()
```

```
Out[25]:
    c1    7.5
    c2    8.5
    c3    9.5
```

```
c4      19.0
c5       NaN
dtype: float64
```

In [26]:

```
# having replaced NaN with 0 can make
# operations such as mean have different results
filled.mean()
```

Out[26]:

```
c1      6.428571
c2      7.285714
c3      8.142857
c4      5.428571
c5      0.000000
dtype: float64
```

It is also possible to limit the number of times that the data will be filled using the limit parameter. Each time the NaN values are identified, pandas will fill the NaN values with the previous value up to the limit times in each group of NaN values.

In [27]:

```
# only fills the first two NaN values in each row with 0
df.fillna(0, limit=2)
```

Out[27]:

	c1	c2	c3	c4	c5
a	0	1	2	20	0
b	3	4	5	0	0
c	6	7	8	0	NaN
d	9	10	11	NaN	NaN
e	12	13	14	NaN	NaN
f	15	16	17	18	NaN
g	0	0	0	NaN	NaN

Forward and backward filling of missing values

Gaps in data can be filled by propagating non-NaN values forward or backward along a `Series`. To demonstrate this, the following example will "fill forward" the c4 column of `DataFrame`:

```
In [28]:
    # extract the c4 column and fill NaNs forward
    df.c4.fillna(method="ffill")
```

```
Out[28]:
    a     20
    b     20
    c     20
    d     20
    e     20
    f     18
    g     18
    Name: c4, dtype: float64
```

> When working with time series data, this technique of filling is often referred to as the "last known value".

The direction of the fill can be reversed using `method='bfill'`:

```
In [29]:
    # perform a backwards fill
    df.c4.fillna(method="bfill")
```

```
Out[29]:
    a     20
    b     18
    c     18
    d     18
    e     18
    f     18
    g    NaN
    Name: c4, dtype: float64
```

To save a little typing, pandas also has global level functions `pd.ffill()` and `pd.bfill()`, which are equivalent to `.fillna(method="ffill")` and `.fillna(method="bfill")`.

Filling using index labels

Data can be filled using the labels of a `Series` or keys of a Python dictionary. This allows you to specify different fill values for different elements based upon the value of the index label:

```
In [30]:
    # create a new Series of values to be
    # used to fill NaN values where the index label matches
    fill_values = pd.Series([100, 101, 102], index=['a', 'e', 'g'])
    fill_values

Out[30]:
    a    100
    e    101
    g    102
    dtype: int64
```

```
In [31]:
    # using c4, fill using fill_values
    # a, e and g will be filled with matching values
    df.c4.fillna(fill_values)

Out[31]:
    a     20
    b    NaN
    c    NaN
    d    NaN
    e    101
    f     18
    g    102
    Name: c4, dtype: float64
```

Only values of NaN will be filled. Notice that the values with label a are not changed.

Another common scenario, is to fill all the NaN values in a column with the mean of the column:

```
In [32]:
    # fill NaN values in each column with the
    # mean of the values in that column
    df.fillna(df.mean())
```

```
Out[32]:
         c1     c2     c3   c4  c5
    a    0.0    1.0    2.0   20 NaN
    b    3.0    4.0    5.0   19 NaN
    c    6.0    7.0    8.0   19 NaN
    d    9.0   10.0   11.0   19 NaN
    e   12.0   13.0   14.0   19 NaN
    f   15.0   16.0   17.0   18 NaN
    g    7.5    8.5    9.5   19 NaN
```

Interpolation of missing values

Both DataFrame and Series have an .interpolate() method that will, by default, perform a linear interpolation of missing values:

```
In [33]:
    # linear interpolate the NaN values from 1 through 2
    s = pd.Series([1, np.nan, np.nan, np.nan, 2])
    s.interpolate()
```

```
Out[33]:
    0    1.00
    1    1.25
    2    1.50
    3    1.75
    4    2.00
    dtype: float64
```

The value of the interpolation is calculated by taking the first value before and after any sequence of NaN values and then incrementally adding that value from the start and substituting NaN values. In this case, 2.0 and 1.0 are the surrounding values, resulting in (2.0 – 1.0)/(5-1) = 0.25, which is then added incrementally through all the NaN values.

The interpolation method also has the ability to specify a specific method of interpolation. One of the common methods is to use time-based interpolation. Consider the following Series of dates and values:

In [34]:

```
# create a time series, but missing one date in the Series
ts = pd.Series([1, np.nan, 2],
            index=[datetime.datetime(2014, 1, 1),
                   datetime.datetime(2014, 2, 1),
                   datetime.datetime(2014, 4, 1)])
ts
```

Out[34]:

```
2014-01-01      1
2014-02-01    NaN
2014-04-01      2
dtype: float64
```

Normal interpolation results are as shown in the following example:

In [35]:

```
# linear interpolate based on the number of items in the Series
ts.interpolate()
```

Out[35]:

```
2014-01-01    1.0
2014-02-01    1.5
2014-04-01    2.0
dtype: float64
```

The value for 2014-02-01 is calculated as 1.0 + (2.0-1.0)/2 = 1.5, since there is one NaN value between the values 2.0 and 1.0.

The important thing to note is that the series is missing an entry for 2014-03-01. If we were expecting to interpolate daily values, there would be two values calculated, one for 2014-02-01 and another for 2014-03-01, resulting in one more value in the numerator of the interpolation.

This can be corrected by specifying the method of interpolation as "time":

```
In [36]:
    # this accounts for the fact that we don't have
    # an entry for 2014-03-01
    ts.interpolate(method="time")
```

```
Out[36]:
    2014-01-01    1.000000
    2014-02-01    1.344444
    2014-04-01    2.000000
    dtype: float64
```

This is the correct interpolation for 2014-02-01 based upon dates. Also note that the index label and value for 2014-03-01 is not added to the Series, it is just factored into the interpolation.

Interpolation can also be specified to calculate values relative to the index values when using numeric index labels. To demonstrate this, we will use the following Series:

```
In [37]:
    # a Series to demonstrate index label based interpolation
    s = pd.Series([0, np.nan, 100], index=[0, 1, 10])
    s
```

```
Out[37]:
    0          0
    1        NaN
    10       100
    dtype: float64
```

If we perform a linear interpolation, we get the following value for label 1, which is correct for a linear interpolation:

```
In [38]:
    # linear interpolate
    s.interpolate()
```

```
Out[38]:
    0        0
    1       50
    10     100
    dtype: float64
```

However, what if we want to interpolate the value to be relative to the index value? To do this, we can use method="values":

```
In [39]:
    # interpolate based upon the values in the index
    s.interpolate(method="values")
```

```
Out[39]:
    0        0
    1       10
    10     100
    dtype: float64
```

Now, the value calculated for NaN is interpolated using relative positioning based upon the labels in the index. The NaN value has a label of 1, which is one tenth of the way between 0 and 10, so the interpolated value will be 0 + (100-0)/10, or 10.

Handling duplicate data

The data in your sample can often contain duplicate rows. This is just a reality of dealing with data collected automatically, or even a situation created in manually collecting data. Often, it is considered best to err on the side of having duplicates instead of missing data, especially if the data can be considered to be idempotent. However, duplicate data can increase the size of the dataset, and if it is not idempotent, then it would not be appropriate to process the duplicates.

To facilitate finding duplicate data, pandas provides a `.duplicates()` method that returns a Boolean `Series` where each entry represents whether or not the row is a duplicate. A `True` value represents that the specific row has appeared earlier in the `DataFrame` object with all column values being identical.

To demonstrate this, the following code creates a `DataFrame` object with duplicate rows:

```
In [40]:
    # a DataFrame with lots of duplicate data
    data = pd.DataFrame({'a': ['x'] * 3 + ['y'] * 4,
                         'b': [1, 1, 2, 3, 3, 4, 4]})
    data


Out[40]:
       a   b
    0  x   1
    1  x   1
    2  x   2
    3  y   3
    4  y   3
    5  y   4
    6  y   4
```

A `DataFrame` object with duplicate rows which were created by the preceding code can be analyzed using `.duplicated()` method. This method determines that a row is a duplicate if the values in all columns were seen already in a row earlier in the `DataFrame` object:

```
In [41]:
    # reports which rows are duplicates based upon
    # if the data in all columns was seen before
    data.duplicated()


Out[41]:
    0       False
    1        True
    2       False
    3       False
```

```
4        True
5        False
6        True
dtype: bool
```

Duplicate rows can be dropped from a DataFrame using the .drop_duplicates() method. This method will return a copy of the DataFrame object with the duplicate rows removed.

Duplicate rows can be dropped from a DataFrame by using the .drop_duplicates() method. This method will return a copy of the DataFrame with the duplicate rows removed.

It is also possible to use the inplace=True parameter to remove the rows without making a copy:

```
In [42]:
    # drop duplicate rows retaining first row of the duplicates
    data.drop_duplicates()


Out[42]:
        a   b
    0   x   1
    2   x   2
    3   y   3
    5   y   4
```

Note that there is a ramification to which indexes remain when dropping duplicates. The duplicate records may have different index labels (labels are not taken into account in calculating a duplicate). So, which row is kept can affect the set of labels in the resulting DataFrame object.

The default operation is to keep the first row of the duplicates. If you want to keep the last row of duplicates, you can use the take_last=True parameter. The following code demonstrates how the result differs using this parameter:

```
In [43]:
    # drop duplicate rows, only keeping the first
    # instance of any data
    data.drop_duplicates(take_last=True)


Out[43]:
```

```
      a  b
  1   x  1
  2   x  2
  4   y  3
  6   y  4
```

If you want to check for duplicates based on a smaller set of columns, you can specify a list of columns names:

In [44]:

```
# add a column c with values 0..6
# this makes .duplicated() report no duplicate rows
data['c'] = range(7)
data.duplicated()
```

Out[44]:

```
0      False
1      False
2      False
3      False
4      False
5      False
6      False
dtype: bool
```

In [45]:

```
# but if we specify duplicates to be dropped only in columns a & b
# they will be dropped
data.drop_duplicates(['a', 'b'])
```

Out[45]:

```
     a  b  c
  0  x  1  0
  2  x  2  2
  3  y  3  3
  5  y  4  5
```

Transforming Data

Another part of tidying data involves transforming existing data into another presentation. This may be needed for the following reasons:

- Values are not in the correct units
- Values are qualitative and need to be converted to appropriate numeric values
- There is extraneous data that either wastes memory and processing time, or can affect results simply by being included

To address these situations, we can take one or more of the following actions:

- Map values to other values using a table lookup process
- Explicitly replace certain values with other values (or even another type of data)
- Apply methods to transform the values based on an algorithm
- Simply remove extraneous columns and rows

We have already seen how to delete rows and columns with several techniques, so we will not reiterate those here. We will cover the facilities provided by pandas for mapping, replacing, and applying functions to transform data based upon its content.

Mapping

One of the basic tasks in data transformations is mapping of a set of values to another set. pandas provides a generic ability to map values using a lookup table (via a Python dictionary or a pandas `Series`) using the `.map()` method. This method performs the mapping by matching the values of the outer `Series` with the index labels of the inner `Series`, and returning a new `Series` with the index labels of the outer `Series` but the values from the inner `Series`:

```
In [46]:
    # create two Series objects to demonstrate mapping
    x = pd.Series({"one": 1, "two": 2, "three": 3})
    y = pd.Series({1: "a", 2: "b", 3: "c"})
    x

Out[46]:
    one      1
    three    3
    two      2
```

```
dtype: int64
```

In [47]:

```
y
```

Out[47]:

```
1    a
2    b
3    c
dtype: object
```

In [48]:

```
# map values in x to values in y
x.map(y)
```

Out[48]:

```
one      a
three    c
two      b
dtype: object
```

Like with other alignment operations, if pandas does not find a map between the value of the outer `Series` and an index label of the inner `Series`, it will fill the value with `NaN`. To demonstrate this, the following code removes the 3 key from the outer `Series`, therefore causing the alignment to fail for that record, and the result is that a `NaN` value is introduced:

In [49]:

```
# three in x will not align / map to a value in y
x = pd.Series({"one": 1, "two": 2, "three": 3})
y = pd.Series({1: "a", 2: "b"})
x.map(y)
```

Out[49]:

```
one      a
three    NaN
two      b
dtype: object
```

Replacing values

We previously saw how the .fillna() method can be used to replace the NaN values with a value of your own decision. The .fillna() method can actually be thought of as an implementation of the .map() method that maps a single value, NaN, to a specific value.

Even more generically, the .fillna() method itself can be considered a specialization of a more general replacement that is provided by the .replace() method, which provides more flexibility by being able to replace any value (not just NaN) with another value.

The most basic use of the .replace() method replaces an individual value with another:

```
In [50]:
    # create a Series to demonstrate replace
    s = pd.Series([0., 1., 2., 3., 2., 4.])
    s
```

```
Out[50]:
    0    0
    1    1
    2    2
    3    3
    4    2
    5    4
    dtype: float64
```

```
In [51]:
    # replace all items with index label 2 with value 5
    s.replace(2, 5)
```

```
Out[51]:
    0    0
    1    1
    2    5
    3    3
    4    5
    5    4
    dtype: float64
```

It is also possible to specify multiple items to replace and also specify their substitute values by passing two lists:

```
In [52]:
    # replace all items with new values
    s.replace([0, 1, 2, 3, 4], [4, 3, 2, 1, 0])
```

```
Out[52]:
    0    4
    1    3
    2    2
    3    1
    4    2
    5    0
    dtype: float64
```

Replacement can also be performed by specifying a dictionary for lookup (a variant of the map process in the previous section):

```
In [53]:
    # replace using entries in a dictionary
    s.replace({0: 10, 1: 100})
```

```
Out[53]:
    0     10
    1    100
    2      2
    3      3
    4      2
    5      4
    dtype: float64
```

If using .replace() on a DataFrame, it is possible to specify different replacement values for each column. This is performed by passing a Python dictionary to the .replace() method, where the keys of the dictionary represent the names of the columns where replacement is to occur and the values of the dictionary are values that you want to replace. The second parameter to the method is the value that will be replaced where any matches are found.

The following code demonstrates by creating a `DataFrame` object and then replacing specific values in each of the columns with 100:

```
In [54]:
    # DataFrame with two columns
    df = pd.DataFrame({'a': [0, 1, 2, 3, 4], 'b': [5, 6, 7, 8, 9]})
    df
```

```
Out[54]:
      a  b
   0  0  5
   1  1  6
   2  2  7
   3  3  8
   4  4  9
```

```
In [55]:
    # specify different replacement values for each column
    df.replace({'a': 1, 'b': 8}, 100)
```

```
Out[55]:
        a    b
   0    0    5
   1  100    6
   2    2    7
   3    3  100
   4    4    9
```

Replacing specific values in each of the columns is very convenient, as it provides a shorthand for what otherwise would require coding a loop through all the columns.

It is also possible to replace items at specific index positions as though they are missing values. The following code demonstrates by forward filling the value at index position 0 into locations 1, 2, and 3:

```
In [56]:
    # demonstrate replacement with pad method
    # set first item to 10, to have a distinct replacement value
    s[0] = 10
```

```
s
```

Out[56]:

```
0    10
1     1
2     2
3     3
4     2
5     4
dtype: float64
```

In [57]:

```
# replace items with index label 1, 2, 3, using fill from the
# most recent value prior to the specified labels (10)
s.replace([1, 2, 3], method='pad')
```

Out[57]:

```
0    10
1    10
2    10
3    10
4    10
5     4
dtype: float64
```

Applying functions to transform data

In situations where a direct mapping or substitution will not suffice, it is possible to apply a function to the data to perform an algorithm on the data. pandas provides the ability to apply functions to individual items, entire columns, or entire rows, providing incredible flexibility in transformation.

Functions can be applied using the conveniently named .apply() method, which given a Python function, will iteratively call the function passing in each value from a Series, or each Series representing a DataFrame column, or a list of values representing each row in a DataFrame. The choice of technique to be used depends on whether the object is a Series or a DataFrame object, and when a DataFrame object, depending upon which axis is specified.

To begin demonstrations, the following code applies a lambda function to each item of a Series:

```
In [58]:
    # demonstrate applying a function to every item of a Series
    s = pd.Series(np.arange(0, 5))
    s.apply(lambda v: v * 2)
```

```
Out[58]:
    0    0
    1    2
    2    4
    3    6
    4    8
    dtype: int64
```

When applying a function to items in a Series, only the value for each Series item is passed to the function, not the index label and the value.

When a function is applied to a DataFrame, the default is to apply the method to each column. pandas will iterate through all columns passing each as a Series to your function. The result will be a Series object with index labels matching column names and with the result of the function applied to the column:

```
In [59]:
    # demonstrate applying a sum on each column
    df = pd.DataFrame(np.arange(12).reshape(4, 3),
                      columns=['a', 'b', 'c'])
    df
```

```
Out[59]:
       a   b   c
    0  0   1   2
    1  3   4   5
    2  6   7   8
    3  9  10  11
```

```
In [60]:
    # calculate cumulative sum of items in each column
```

```
df.apply(lambda col: col.sum())
```

Out[60]:

```
a    18
b    22
c    26
dtype: int64
```

Application of the function can be switched to the values from each row by specifying `axis=1`:

In [61]:

```
# calculate the sum of items in each row
df.apply(lambda row: row.sum(), axis=1)
```

Out[61]:

```
0     3
1    12
2    21
3    30
dtype: int64
```

A common practice is to take the result of an apply operation and add it as a new column of the `DataFrame`. This is convenient as you can add onto the DataFrame the result of one or more successive calculations, providing yourself with progressive representations of the derivation of results through every step of the process.

The following code demonstrates this process. The first step will multiply column a by column b and create a new column named `interim`. The second step will add those values and column c, and create a `result` column with those values:

In [62]:

```
# create a new column 'interim' with a * b
df['interim'] = df.apply(lambda r: r.a * r.b, axis=1)
df
```

Out[62]:

```
    a    b    c    interim
```

```
0  0   1   2        0
1  3   4   5       12
2  6   7   8       42
3  9  10  11       90
```

In [63]:

```python
# and now a 'result' column with 'interim' + 'c'
df['result'] = df.apply(lambda r: r.interim + r.c, axis=1)
df
```

Out[63]:

```
   a   b   c  interim  result
0  0   1   2        0       2
1  3   4   5       12      17
2  6   7   8       42      50
3  9  10  11       90     101
```

If you would like to change the values in the existing column, simply assign the result to an already existing column. The following code changes the 'a' column values to be the sum of the values in the row:

In [64]:

```python
# replace column a with the sum of columns a, b and c
df.a = df.a + df.b + df.c
df
```

Out[64]:

```
    a   b   c  interim  result
0   3   1   2        0       2
1  12   4   5       12      17
2  21   7   8       42      50
3  30  10  11       90     101
```

As a matter of practice, replacing a column with completely new values is not the best way to do things and often leads to situations of temporary insanity trying to debug problems caused by data that is lost. In pandas, it is a common practice to just add new rows or columns (or totally new objects), and if memory or performance becomes a problem later on, do the optimizations as required.

Another point to note, is that a pandas `DataFrame` is not a spreadsheet where cells are assigned formulas and can be recalculated when cells that are referenced by the formula change. If you desire this to happen, you will need to execute the formulas whenever the dependent data changes. On the flip side, this is more efficient than with spreadsheets as every little change does not cause a cascade of operations to occur.

The `.apply()` method will always apply to the provided function to all of the items, or rows or columns. If you want to apply the function to a subset of these, then first perform a Boolean selection to filter the items you do not want process.

To demonstrate this, the following code creates a `DataFrame` of values and inserts one `NaN` value into the second row. It then applies a function to only the rows where all values are not `NaN`:

```
In [65]:
    # create a 3x5 DataFrame
    # only second row has a NaN
    df = pd.DataFrame(np.arange(0, 15).reshape(3,5))
    df.loc[1, 2] = np.nan
    df
```

```
Out[65]:
        0    1    2    3    4
    0    0    1    2    3    4
    1    5    6  NaN    8    9
    2   10   11   12   13   14
```

```
In [66]:
    # demonstrate applying a function to only rows having
    # a count of 0 NaN values
    df.dropna().apply(lambda x: x.sum(), axis=1)
```

```
Out[66]:
    0     10
    2     60
    dtype: float64
```

The last (but not least) method to apply functions that you will see in the next example is the .applymap() method of the DataFrame. The .apply() method was always passed an entire row or column. If you desire to apply a function to every individual item in the DataFrame one by one, then .applymap() is the method to use.

Here is a practical example of using .applymap() method to every item in a DataFrame, and specifically to format each value to a specified number of decimal points:

```
In [67]:
    # use applymap to format all items of the DataFrame
    df.applymap(lambda x: '%.2f' % x)
```

```
Out[67]:
            0       1       2       3       4
    0    0.00    1.00    2.00    3.00    4.00
    1    5.00    6.00     nan    8.00    9.00
    2   10.00   11.00   12.00   13.00   14.00
```

Summary

In this chapter, we have examined various techniques of tidying up data in Series or DataFrame. We've covered identifying missing data, replacing it with real data, or dropping it from the overall set of data. We also saw how to transform values into other values that may be better suited for further analysis.

However, the focus of this chapter was on working with individual values in Series or DataFrame, and made the assumption that the DataFrame is shaped properly for further usage, and can be aligned with data from other Series or DataFrame objects. In the next chapter, we will examine how to combine and restructure data in one or more DataFrame (and Series) objects through concatenation, merges, joins, and pivoting.

8
Combining and Reshaping Data

In *Chapter 7, Tidying Up Your Data* we examined how to clean up our data in order to get it ready for analysis. Everything that we did focused upon working within the data of a single `DataFrame` or `Series` object, and keeping the same structure of data within those objects. Once the data is tidied up, it will be likely that we will then need to use this data either to combine multiple sets of data, or to reorganize the structure of the data by moving data in and out of indexes.

This chapter has two general categories of topics: combination and reshaping of data. The first two sections will cover the capabilities provided by pandas to combine the data from multiple pandas objects together. Combination of data in pandas is performed by concatenating two sets of data, where data is combined simply along either axes but without regard to relationships in the data. Or data can be combined using relationships in the data by using a pandas capability referred to as merging, which provides join operations that are similar to those in many relational databases.

The remaining sections will examine the three primary means reshaping data in pandas. These will examine the processes of pivoting, stacking and unstacking, and melting of data. Pivoting allows us to restructure pandas data similarly to how spreadsheets pivot data by creating new index levels and moving data into columns based upon values (or vice-versa). Stacking and unstacking are similar to pivoting, but allow us to pivot data organized with multiple levels of indexes. And finally, melting allows us to restructure data into unique ID-variable-measurement combinations that are or required for many statistical analyses.

Specifically, in this chapter we will examine the following concepts of combining and reshaping pandas data:

- Concatenation
- Merging and joining
- Pivots
- Stacking/unstacking
- Melting
- The potential performance benefits of stacked data

Setting up the IPython notebook

To utilize the examples in this chapter we will need to include the following imports and settings.

```
In [1]:
    # import pandas, numpy and datetime
    import numpy as np
    import pandas as pd
    import datetime

    # Set some pandas options for controlling output
    pd.set_option('display.notebook_repr_html', False)
    pd.set_option('display.max_columns', 10)
    pd.set_option('display.max_rows', 10)
```

Concatenating data

Concatenation in pandas is the process of either adding rows to the end of an existing `Series` or `DataFrame` object or adding additional columns to a `DataFrame`. In pandas, concatenation is performed via the pandas function `pd.concat()`. The function will perform the operation on a specific axis and as we will see, will also perform any required set logic involved in aligning along that axis.

The general syntax to concatenate data is to pass a list of objects to `pd.concat()`. The following performs a concatenation of two `Series` objects:

```
In [2]:
    # two Series objects to concatenate
    s1 = pd.Series(np.arange(0, 3))
    s2 = pd.Series(np.arange(5, 8))
    s1
```

```
Out[2]:
    0    0
    1    1
    2    2
    dtype: int64
```

```
In [3]:
    s2
```

```
Out[3]:
    0    5
    1    6
    2    7
    dtype: int64
```

```
In [4]:
    # concatenate them
    pd.concat([s1, s2])
```

```
Out[4]:
    0    0
    1    1
    2    2
    0    5
    1    6
    2    7
    dtype: int64
```

Two `DataFrame` objects can also be similarly concatenated.

```
In [5]:
    # create two DataFrame objects to concatenate
    # using the same index labels and column names,
    # but different values
    df1 = pd.DataFrame(np.arange(9).reshape(3, 3),
                       columns=['a', 'b', 'c'])
    #df2 has 9 .. 18
    df2 = pd.DataFrame(np.arange(9, 18).reshape(3, 3),
                       columns=['a', 'b', 'c'])
    df1
```

```
Out[5]:
     a  b  c
  0  0  1  2
  1  3  4  5
  2  6  7  8
```

```
In [6]:
    df2
```

```
Out[6]:
      a   b   c
  0   9  10  11
  1  12  13  14
  2  15  16  17
```

```
In [7]:
    # do the concat
    pd.concat([df1, df2])
```

```
Out[7]:
```

	a	b	c
0	0	1	2
1	3	4	5
2	6	7	8
0	9	10	11
1	12	13	14
2	15	16	17

The process of concatenating the two DataFrame objects will first identify the set of columns formed by aligning the labels in the columns, effectively determining the union of the column names. The resulting DataFrame object will then consist of that set of columns, and columns with identical names will not be duplicated.

Rows will be then be added to the result, in the order of the each of the objects passed to pd.concat(). If a column in the result does not exist in the object being copied, NaN values will be filled in those locations. Duplicate row index labels can occur.

The following demonstrates the alignment of two DataFrame objects during concatenation that both have columns in common (a and c) and also have distinct columns (b in df1, and d in df2):

```
In [8]:
    # demonstrate concatenating two DataFrame objects with
    # different columns
    df1 = pd.DataFrame(np.arange(9).reshape(3, 3),
                       columns=['a', 'b', 'c'])
    df2 = pd.DataFrame(np.arange(9, 18).reshape(3, 3),
                       columns=['a', 'c', 'd'])
    df1
```

```
Out[8]:
```

	a	b	c
0	0	1	2
1	3	4	5
2	6	7	8

```
In [9]:
```

```
    df2
```

```
Out[9]:
        a    c    d
    0    9   10   11
    1   12   13   14
    2   15   16   17
```

```
In [10]:
    # do the concat, NaN values will be filled in for
    # the d column for df1 and b column for df2
    pd.concat([df1, df2])
```

```
Out[10]:
        a    b    c    d
    0    0    1    2  NaN
    1    3    4    5  NaN
    2    6    7    8  NaN
    0    9  NaN   10   11
    1   12  NaN   13   14
    2   15  NaN   16   17
```

It is possible to give each group of data in the result its own name using the keys parameter. This creates a hierarchical index on the DataFrame object that lets you refer to each group of data independently via the DataFrame objects' .ix property. This is convenient if you later need to determine where data in the concatenated DataFrame object came from.

The following sample demonstrates this concept by assigning names to each original DataFrame object and then retrieving the rows that originated in the df2 object, which are keyed with the label 'df2'. The following code demonstrates this labeling and also retrieves just the rows that originated in df2:

```
In [11]:
    # concat the two objects, but create an index using the
    # given keys
    c = pd.concat([df1, df2], keys=['df1', 'df2'])
```

```
# note the labeling of the rows in the output
c
```

Out[11]:

		a	b	c	d
df1	0	0	1	2	NaN
	1	3	4	5	NaN
	2	6	7	8	NaN
df2	0	9	NaN	10	11
	1	12	NaN	13	14
	2	15	NaN	16	17

In [12]:

```
# we can extract the data originating from
# the first or second source DataFrame
c.ix['df2']
```

Out[12]:

	a	b	c	d
0	9	NaN	10	11
1	12	NaN	13	14
2	15	NaN	16	17

The pd.concat() function also allows you to specify the axis on which to apply the concatenation. The following concatenates the two DataFrame objects along the columns axis:

In [13]:

```
# concat df1 and df2 along columns
# aligns on row labels, has duplicate columns
pd.concat([df1, df2], axis=1)
```

Out[13]:

	a	b	c	a	c	d
0	0	1	2	9	10	11
1	3	4	5	12	13	14
2	6	7	8	15	16	17

Note that the result now contains duplicate columns. The concatenation first aligns by the row index labels of each `DataFrame` object, and then fills in the columns from the first `DataFrame` object and then the second. The columns are not aligned and result in duplicate values.

The same rules of alignment and filling of NaN values apply in this case, except that they are applied to the rows' index labels. The following demonstrates a concatenation along the columns axis with two `DataFrame` objects that have row index labels in common (2 and 3) along with disjoint rows (0 in df1 and 4 in df3). Additionally, some of the columns in df3 overlap with df1 (a) as well as being disjoint (d):

```
In [14]:
    # a new DataFrame to merge with df1
    # this has two common row labels (2, 3)
    # common columns (a) and one disjoint column
    # in each (b in df1 and d in df2)
    df3 = pd.DataFrame(np.arange(20, 26).reshape(3, 2),
                    columns=['a', 'd'],
                    index=[2, 3, 4])
    df3
```

```
Out [14]:
        a    d
    2   20   21
    3   22   23
    4   24   25
```

```
In [15]:
    # concat them. Alignment is along row labels
    # columns first from df1 and then df3, with duplicates.
    # NaN filled in where those columns do not exist in the source
    pd.concat([df1, df3], axis=1)
```

```
Out [15]:
        a   b   c   a    d
    0   0   1   2   NaN  NaN
    1   3   4   5   NaN  NaN
```

```
2   6   7   8  20  21
3 NaN NaN NaN  22  23
4 NaN NaN NaN  24  25
```

A concatenation of two or more `DataFrame` objects actually performs an outer join operation along the index labels on the axis opposite to the one specified. This makes the result of the concatenation similar to having performed a union of those index labels, and then data is filled based on the alignment of those labels to the source objects.

The type of join can be changed to an inner join and can be performed by specifying `join='inner'` as the parameter. The inner join then logically performs an intersection instead of a union. The following demonstrates this and results in a single row because `2` is the only row index label in common:

```
In [16]:
    # do an inner join instead of outer
    # results in one row
    pd.concat([df1, df3], axis=1, join='inner')
```

```
Out[16]:
      a   b   c   a   d
2     6   7   8  20  21
```

It is also possible to use label groups of data along the columns using the `keys` parameter when applying the concatenation along `axis=1`.

```
In [17]:
    # add keys to the columns
    df = pd.concat([df1, df2],
                   axis=1,
                   keys=['df1', 'df2'])
    df
```

```
Out[17]:
     df1        df2
     a   b   c   a    c    d
0    0   1   2   9   10   11
1    3   4   5  12   13   14
2    6   7   8  15   16   17
```

The different groups can be accessed using the .ix process and slicing:

```
In [18]:
    # retrieve the data that originated from the
    # DataFrame with key 'df2'
    df.ix[:, 'df2']
```

```
Out[18]:
        a    c    d
    0    9   10   11
    1   12   13   14
    2   15   16   17
```

A DataFrame (and Series) object also contains an .append() method, which will concatenate the two specified DataFrame objects along the row index labels.

```
In [19]:
    # append does a concatenate along axis=0
    # duplicate row index labels can result
    df1.append(df2)
```

```
Out[19]:
        a    b    c    d
    0    0    1    2  NaN
    1    3    4    5  NaN
    2    6    7    8  NaN
    0    9  NaN   10   11
    1   12  NaN   13   14
    2   15  NaN   16   17
```

As with a concatenation on axis=1, the index labels in the rows are copied without consideration of the creation of duplicates, and the columns labels are joined in a manner which ensures no duplicate column name is included in the result. If you would like to ensure that the resulting index does not have duplicates but preserves all of the rows, you can use the ignore_index=True parameter. This essentially returns the same result except with new Int64Index:

```
In [20]:
    # remove duplicates in the result index by ignoring the
    # index labels in the source DataFrame objects
```

```
df1.append(df2, ignore_index=True)
```

Out[20]:

	a	b	c	d
0	0	1	2	NaN
1	3	4	5	NaN
2	6	7	8	NaN
3	9	NaN	10	11
4	12	NaN	13	14
5	15	NaN	16	17

Merging and joining data

pandas allows the merging of pandas objects with database-like join operations using the pd.merge() function and the .merge() method of a DataFrame object. These joins are high performance and are performed in memory. A merge combines the data of two pandas objects by finding matching values in one or more columns or row indexes. It then returns a new object that represents a combination of the data from both based on relational-database-like join semantics applied to those values.

Merges are useful as they allow us to model a single DataFrame for each type of data (one of the rules of having tidy data) but to be able to relate data in different DataFrame objects using values existing in both sets of data.

An overview of merges

A practical and probably canonical example would be that of looking up customer names from orders. To demonstrate this in pandas, we will use the following two DataFrame objects, where one represents a list of customer details, and the other represents the orders made by customers and what day the order was made. They will be related to each other using the CustomerID columns in each:

In [21]:

```
# these are our customers
customers = {'CustomerID': [10, 11],
             'Name': ['Mike', 'Marcia'],
             'Address': ['Address for Mike',
                         'Address for Marcia']}
customers = pd.DataFrame(customers)
```

```
customers
```

Out[21]:

```
          Address   CustomerID    Name
0   Address for Mike          10    Mike
1   Address for Marcia        11    Marcia
```

In [22]:

```
# and these are the orders made by our customers
# they are related to customers by CustomerID
orders = {'CustomerID': [10, 11, 10],
         'OrderDate': [datetime.date(2014, 12, 1),
                       datetime.date(2014, 12, 1),
                       datetime.date(2014, 12, 1)]}
orders = pd.DataFrame(orders)
orders
```

Out[22]:

```
    CustomerID    OrderDate
0          10    2014-12-01
1          11    2014-12-01
2          10    2014-12-01
```

Now suppose we would like to ship the orders to the customers. We would need to merge the orders data with the customers detail data to determine the address for each order. In pandas, this can be easily performed with the following statement:

In [23]:

```
# merge customers and orders so we can ship the items
customers.merge(orders)
```

Out[23]:

```
          Address   CustomerID    Name    OrderDate
0   Address for Mike          10    Mike    2014-12-01
1   Address for Mike          10    Mike    2014-12-01
2   Address for Marcia        11    Marcia  2014-12-01
```

pandas has done something magical for us here by being able to accomplish this with such a simple piece of code. What pandas has done is realized that our `customers` and `orders` objects both have a column named `CustomerID`. With this knowledge, it uses common values found in that column of both `DataFrame` objects to relate the data in both and form the merged data based on inner join semantics.

To be even more detailed, what pandas has specifically done is the following:

1. Determines the columns in both `customers` and `orders` with common labels. These columns are treated as the keys to perform the join.

2. It creates a new `DataFrame` whose columns are the labels from the keys identified in step 1, followed by all of the non-key labels from both objects.

3. It matches values in the key columns of both `DataFrame` objects.

4. It then creates a row in the result for each set of matching labels.

5. It then copies the data from those matching rows from each source object into that respective row and columns of the result.

6. It assigns a new `Int64Index` to the result.

The join in a merge can use values from multiple columns. To demonstrate, the following creates two `DataFrame` objects and performs the merge where pandas decides to use the values in the `key1` and `key2` columns of both objects:

```
In [24]:
    # data to be used in the remainder of this section's examples
    left_data = {'key1': ['a', 'b', 'c'],
                 'key2': ['x', 'y', 'z'],
                 'lval1': [ 0, 1, 2]}
    right_data = {'key1': ['a', 'b', 'c'],
                  'key2': ['x', 'a', 'z'],
                  'rval1': [ 6, 7, 8 ]}
    left = pd.DataFrame(left_data, index=[0, 1, 2])
    right = pd.DataFrame(right_data, index=[1, 2, 3])
    left

Out[24]:
    key1 key2  lval1
 0    a    x       0
```

```
   1    b    y    1
   2    c    z    2
```

In [25]:

```
   right
```

Out[25]:

```
     key1 key2  rval1
   1    a    x      6
   2    b    a      7
   3    c    z      8
```

In [26]:

```
   # demonstrate merge without specifying columns to merge
   # this will implicitly merge on all common columns
   left.merge(right)
```

Out[26]:

```
     key1 key2  lval1  rval1
   0    a    x      0      6
   1    c    z      2      8
```

This merge identifies key1 and key2 columns in common in both DataFrame objects and hence uses them for the merge. The matching tuples of values in both DataFrame objects for these columns are (a, x) and (c, z) and therefore this results in two rows of values.

To explicitly specify which column use to relate the objects, use the on parameter. The following performs a merge using only the values in the key1 column of both DataFrame objects:

In [27]:

```
   # demonstrate merge using an explicit column
   # on needs the value to be in both DataFrame objects
   left.merge(right, on='key1')
```

Out[27]:

```
     key1 key2_x  lval1 key2_y  rval1
```

0	a	x	0	x	6
1	b	y	1	a	7
2	c	z	2	z	8

Comparing this result to the previous example, as only the values in the key1 column were used to relate the data in the two objects, the result now has three rows as there are matching a, b, and c values in that single column of both objects.

The on parameter can also be given a list of column names. The following reverts to using both the key1 and key2 columns, resulting in being identical the earlier example where those two columns where implicitly identified by pandas:

In [28]:
```
# merge explicitly using two columns
left.merge(right, on=['key1', 'key2'])
```

Out[28]:

	key1	key2	lval1	rval1
0	a	x	0	6
1	c	z	2	8

The columns specified with on need to exist in both DataFrame objects. If you would like to merge based on columns with different names in each object, you can use the left_on and right_on parameters, passing the name or names of columns to each respective parameter.

To perform a merge with the labels of the row indexes of the two DataFrame objects, use the left_index=True and right_index=True parameters (both need to be specified):

In [29]:
```
# join on the row indices of both matrices
pd.merge(left, right, left_index=True, right_index=True)
```

Out[29]:

	key1_x	key2_x	lval1	key1_y	key2_y	rval1
1	b	y	1	a	x	6
2	c	z	2	b	a	7

This has identified that the index labels in common are 1 and 2, so the resulting DataFrame has two rows with these values and labels in the index. pandas then creates a column in the result for every column in both objects and then copies the values.

As both `DataFrame` objects had a column with an identical name, `key`, the columns in the result have the _x and _y suffixes appended to them to identify the `DataFrame` they originated from. _x is for left and _y for right. You can specify these suffixes using the `suffixes` parameter and passing a two-item sequence.

Specifying the join semantics of a merge operation

The default type of join performed by `pd.merge()` is an `inner` join. To use another join method, the method of join to be used can be specified using the how parameter of the `pd.merge()` function (or the `.merge()` method). The valid options are:

- `inner`: This is the intersection of keys from both `DataFrame` objects
- `outer`: This is the union of keys from both `DataFrame` objects
- `left`: This only uses keys from the left `DataFrame`
- `right`: This only uses keys from the right `DataFrame`

As we have seen, an inner join is the default and will return a merge of the data from both `DataFrame` objects only where the values match.

An outer join contrasts, in that it will return both the merge of the matched rows and the unmatched values from both the left and right `DataFrame` objects, but with NaN filled in the unmatched portion. The following code demonstrates an outer join:

```
In [30]:
    # outer join, merges all matched data,
    # and fills unmatched items with NaN
    left.merge(right, how='outer')

Out[30]:
    key1 key2  lval1  rval1
  0   a    x      0      6
  1   b    y      1    NaN
  2   c    z      2      8
  3   b    a    NaN      7
```

A left join will return the merge of the rows that satisfy the join of the values in the specified columns, and also returns the unmatched rows from only `left`:

In [31]:

```
# left join, merges all matched data, and only fills unmatched
# items from the left dataframe with NaN filled for the
# unmatched items in the result
# rows with labels 0 and 2
# match on key1 and key2 the row with label 1 is from left

left.merge(right, how='left')
```

Out[31]:

	key1	key2	lval1	rval1
0	a	x	0	6
1	b	y	1	NaN
2	c	z	2	8

A right join will return the merge of the rows that satisfy the join of the values in the specified columns, and also returns the unmatched rows from only `right`:

In [32]:

```
# right join, merges all matched data, and only fills unmatched
# item from the right with NaN filled for the unmatched items
# in the result
# rows with labels 0 and 1 match on key1 and key2
# the row with label 2 is from right
left.merge(right, how='right')
```

Out[32]:

	key1	key2	lval1	rval1
0	a	x	0	6
1	c	z	2	8
2	b	a	NaN	7

The pandas library also provides a `.join()` method that can be used to perform a join using the index labels of the two `DataFrame` objects (instead of values in columns). Note that if the columns in the two `DataFrame` objects do not have unique column names, you must specify suffixes using the `lsuffix` and `rsuffix` parameters (automatic suffixing is not performed). The following code demonstrates both the join and specification of suffixes:

```
In [33]:
    # join left with right (default method is outer)
    # and since these DataFrame objects have duplicate column names
    # we just specify lsuffix and rsuffix
    left.join(right, lsuffix='_left', rsuffix='_right')
```

```
Out[33]:
    key1_left key2_left  lval1 key1_right key2_right   rval1
0           a         x      0        NaN        NaN     NaN
1           b         y      1          a          x       6
2           c         z      2          b          a       7
```

The default type of join performed is an outer join. Note that this differs from the default of the `.merge()` method, which defaults to inner. To change to an inner join, specify `how='inner'`, as is demonstrated in the following example:

```
In [34]:
    # join left with right with an inner join
    left.join(right, lsuffix='_left', rsuffix='_right', how='inner')
```

```
Out[34]:
    key1_left key2_left  lval1 key1_right key2_right   rval1
1           b         y      1          a          x       6
2           c         z      2          b          a       7
```

Notice that this is roughly equivalent to the earlier result from `In[29]` except with the result having columns with slightly different names.

It is also possible to perform right and left joins, but they lead to results similar to previous examples, so they will be omitted for brevity.

Pivoting

Data is often stored in a stacked format, which is also referred to as record format; this is common in databases, .csv files, and Excel spreadsheets. In a stacked format, the data is often not normalized and has repeated values in many columns, or values that should logically exists in other tables (violating another concept of tidy data).

Take the following data, which represents a stream of data from an accelerometer on a mobile device (provided with the data from the sample code):

```
In [35]:
    # read in accellerometer data
    sensor_readings = pd.read_csv("data/accel.csv")
    sensor_readings
```

```
Out[35]:
     interval  axis   reading
0           0    X       0.0
1           0    Y       0.5
2           0    Z       1.0
3           1    X       0.1
4           1    Y       0.4
..        ...  ...       ...
7           2    Y       0.3
8           2    Z       0.8
9           3    X       0.3
10          3    Y       0.2
11          3    Z       0.7

[12 rows x 3 columns]
```

An issue with this data as it is organized is: how does one go about determining the readings for a specific axis? This can be naively done with Boolean selections:

```
In [36]:
    # extract X-axis readings
    sensor_readings[sensor_readings['axis'] == 'X']
```

```
Out[36]:
     interval  axis   reading
```

0	0	X	0.0
3	1	X	0.1
6	2	X	0.2
9	3	X	0.3

An issue here is what if you want to know the values for all axes at a given time, not just the x axis? You can perform a selection for each value of the axis, but that is repetitive code and does not handle the scenario of new axis values being inserted into `DataFrame` without a change to the code.

A better representation would be where columns represent the unique variable values. To convert to this form, use the `DataFrame` objects' `.pivot()` function:

```
In [37]:
    # pivot the data.  Interval becomes the index, the columns are
    # the current axes values, and use the readings as values
    sensor_readings.pivot(index='interval',
                          columns='axis',
                          values='reading')
```

```
Out[37]:
    axis          X     Y     Z
    interval
    0            0.0   0.5   1.0
    1            0.1   0.4   0.9
    2            0.2   0.3   0.8
    3            0.3   0.2   0.7
```

This has taken all of the distinct values from the axis column, and pivoted them into columns on the new `DataFrame`, while filling in values for the new columns from the appropriate rows and columns of the original `DataFrame`. This new `DataFrame` demonstrates that it is now very easy to identify the X, Y and Z sensor readings at each time interval.

Stacking and unstacking

Similar to the pivot function are the `.stack()` and `.unstack()` methods that are part of both `Series` and `DataFrame` objects. The process of stacking pivots a level of column labels to the row index. Unstacking performs the opposite, pivoting a level of the row index into the column index.

One of the differences between stacking/unstacking and performing a pivot is that unlike pivots the stack and unstack functions will be able to pivot specific levels of a hierarchical index. Also, where a pivot retains the same number of levels on an index, a stack and unstack will always increase the levels on the index of one of the axes (columns for unstack and rows for stack) and decrease the levels on the other axis.

The reasons for stacking and unstacking are along the same lines as for performing pivots. Fundamentally it comes down to how you want your data organized for analysis. The organization can change the means and ease of retrieving data and deriving results. As will be demonstrated it also can have significant performance ramifications.

To understand the process of stacking and unstacking, we will first look at simpler cases using nonhierarchical indexes, with very simple data, and focus on stacking. We then progress to more complicated data using hierarchical indexes, revisiting the sensor data we saw previously in the chapter and focusing on unstacking.

Stacking using nonhierarchical indexes

To demonstrate stacking, we will look at several examples using a `DataFrame` object with nonhierarchical indexes. We will begin our examples using the following `DataFrame`:

```
In [38]:
    # simple DataFrame with one column
    df = pd.DataFrame({'a': [1, 2]}, index={'one', 'two'})
    df

Out[38]:
        a

    two  1
    one  2
```

Stacking will move one level of the columns index into a new level of the rows index. As our `DataFrame` only has one level, this collapses a `DataFrame` object into a `Series` object with a hierarchical row index:

```
In [39]:
    # push the column to another level of the index
    # the result is a Series where values are looked up through
    # a multi-index
    stacked1 = df.stack()
```

```
    stacked1
```

Out[39]:

```
    two   a    1
    one   a    2
    dtype: int64
```

To access values, we now need to pass a tuple to the indexer of the `Series` object, which does the lookup with just the index:

In [40]:

```
    # lookup one / a using just the index via a tuple
    stacked1[('one', 'a')]
```

Out[40]:

```
    2
```

If `DataFrame` contains multiple columns, then all of the columns are moved to the same additional level of the new `Series` object:

In [41]:

```
    # DataFrame with two columns
    df = pd.DataFrame({'a': [1, 2],
                       'b': [3, 4]},
                      index={'one', 'two'})
    df
```

Out[41]:

```
          a   b
    two   1   3
    one   2   4
```

In [42]:

```
    # push the two columns into a single level of the index
    stacked2 = df.stack()
    stacked2
```

Out[42]:

```
    two   a    1
```

```
        b    3
one     a    2
        b    4
dtype: int64
```

Values for what would have previously been different columns can now still be accessed using the tuple syntax with the index.

```
In [43]:
    # lookup value with index of one / b
    stacked2[('one', 'b')]
```

```
Out[43]:
    4
```

Unstacking will perform a similar operation in the opposite direction by moving a level of the row index into a level of the columns axis. We will examine this process in the next section as unstacking generally assumes that the index being unstacked is hierarchical.

Unstacking using hierarchical indexes

To demonstrate unstacking with hierarchical indexes we will revisit the sensor data we saw earlier in the chapter. However, we will add in an additional column to the measurement data that represents readings for multiple users and copy data for two users. The following sets up this data:

```
In [44]:
    # make two copies of the sensor data, one for each user
    user1 = sensor_readings.copy()
    user2 = sensor_readings.copy()
    # add names to the two copies
    user1['who'] = 'Mike'
    user2['who'] = 'Mikael'
    # for demonstration, let's scale user2's readings
    user2['reading'] *= 100
    # and reorganize this to have a hierarchical row index
    multi_user_sensor_data = pd.concat([user1, user2]) \
                .set_index(['who', 'interval', 'axis'])
```

```
multi_user_sensor_data
```

Out[44]:

```
                        reading
who     interval axis
Mike    0        X         0.0
                 Y         0.5
                 Z         1.0
        1        X         0.1
                 Y         0.4
...                        ...
Mikael  2        Y        30.0
                 Z        80.0
        3        X        30.0
                 Y        20.0
                 Z        70.0
```

```
[24 rows x 1 columns]
```

With this organization in the data we can do things such as examine all the readings for a specific person using just the index.

In [45]:

```
# look up user data for Mike using just the index
multi_user_sensor_data.ix['Mike']
```

Out[45]:

```
                reading
interval axis
0        X         0.0
         Y         0.5
         Z         1.0
1        X         0.1
         Y         0.4
...                ...
2        Y         0.3
         Z         0.8
```

```
3          X          0.3
           Y          0.2
           Z          0.7
```

```
[12 rows x 1 columns]
```

Or get all the readings of all axes and for all users at interval 1 using .xs().

In [46]:

```
# readings for all users and axes at interval 1
multi_user_sensor_data.xs(1, level='interval')
```

Out[46]:

```
              reading
who     axis
Mike    X          0.1
        Y          0.4
        Z          0.9
Mikael  X         10.0
        Y         40.0
        Z         90.0
```

Unstacking will move the last level of the row index into a new level of the columns index resulting in columns having MultiIndex. The following demonstrates the last level of this unstacking (the axis level of the index):

In [47]:

```
# unstack axis
multi_user_sensor_data.unstack()
```

Out[47]:

```
                  reading
axis                 X      Y       Z
who     interval
Mikael  0            0.0   50.0   100.0
        1           10.0   40.0    90.0
        2           20.0   30.0    80.0
        3           30.0   20.0    70.0
Mike    0            0.0    0.5     1.0
```

1	0.1	0.4	0.9
2	0.2	0.3	0.8
3	0.3	0.2	0.7

To unstack a different level use the `level` parameter. The following code unstacks the first level (`level=0`):

```
In [48]:
    # unstack at level=0
    multi_user_sensor_data.unstack(level=0)
```

```
Out[48]:
                    reading
    who             Mikael Mike

    interval axis
    0        X            0  0.0
             Y           50  0.5
             Z          100  1.0
    1        X           10  0.1
             Y           40  0.4
    ...                 ...  ...
    2        Y           30  0.3
             Z           80  0.8
    3        X           30  0.3
             Y           20  0.2
             Z           70  0.7

    [12 rows x 2 columns]
```

Multiple levels can be unstacked simultaneously by passing a list of the levels to `.unstack()`. Additionally, if the levels are named, they can be specified by name instead of location. The following unstacks the who and axis levels by name:

```
In [49]:
    # unstack who and axis levels
    unstacked = multi_user_sensor_data.unstack(['who', 'axis'])
```

```
unstacked
```

```
Out[49]:
```

	reading					
axis	X	Y	Z	X	Y	Z
who	Mike	Mike	Mike	Mikael	Mikael	Mikael
interval						
0	0.0	0.5	1.0	0	50	100
1	0.1	0.4	0.9	10	40	90
2	0.2	0.3	0.8	20	30	80
3	0.3	0.2	0.7	30	20	70

To be thorough, we can restack this data. The following code will stack the who level of the column back into the row index.

```
In [50]:
# and we can of course stack what we have unstacked
# this re-stacks who
unstacked.stack(level='who')
```

```
Out[50]:
```

		reading		
axis		X	Y	Z
interval	who			
0	Mikael	0.0	50.0	100.0
	Mike	0.0	0.5	1.0
1	Mikael	10.0	40.0	90.0
	Mike	0.1	0.4	0.9
2	Mikael	20.0	30.0	80.0
	Mike	0.2	0.3	0.8
3	Mikael	30.0	20.0	70.0
	Mike	0.3	0.2	0.7

There are a couple of things worth pointing out about this result. First, stacking and unstacking always move the levels into the last levels of the other index. Notice that the who level is now the last level of the row index, but started out earlier as the first level. This would have ramifications on the code to access elements via that index as it has changed to another level. If you want to put a level back into another position you will need to reorganize the indexes with other means than stacking and unstacking.

Second, with all this moving around of data, stacking and unstacking (as well as pivoting) do not lose any information. They simply change the means by which it is organized and accessed.

Melting

Melting is a type of unpivoting, and is often referred to as changing a DataFrame object from wide format to long format. This format is common in various statistical analyses, and data you read may be provided already in a melted form, or you may need to pass data in this format to other code that expects this organization.

Technically, melting is the process of reshaping a DataFrame into a format where two or more columns, referred to as variable and value, are created by unpivoting column labels in the variable column, and then moving the data from these columns into the appropriate location in the value column. All other columns are then made into identifier columns that assist in describing the data.

The concept of melting is often best understood using a simple example such as the following. In this example, we start with a DataFrame that represents measurements of two variables, each represented with its own column, Height and Weight, and for one or more people specified in the Name column:

```
In [51]:
    # we will demonstrate melting with this DataFrame
    data = pd.DataFrame({'Name' : ['Mike', 'Mikael'],
                         'Height' : [6.1, 6.0],
                         'Weight' : [220, 185]})
    data
```

```
Out [51]:
     Height    Name  Weight
  0     6.1    Mike     220
  1     6.0  Mikael     185
```

The following melts this `DataFrame`, using the `Name` column as the identifier column, and the `Height` and `Weight` columns as measured variables. The `Name` column remains, with the `Height` and `Weight` columns unpivoted into the `variable` column. Then the values from these two columns are rearranged into the `value` column, and ensured to align with the appropriate combination values of `Name` and `variable` that would have existed in the original data:

```
In [52]:
    # melt it, use Name as the id,
    # Height and Weight columns as the variables
    pd.melt(data,
            id_vars=['Name'],
            value_vars=['Height', 'Weight'])

Out[52]:
        Name variable  value
    0    Mike   Height    6.1
    1  Mikael   Height    6.0
    2    Mike   Weight  220.0
    3  Mikael   Weight  185.0
```

The data is now restructured so that it is easy to extract the value for any combination of `variable` and `Name`. Additionally, when in this format it is easier to add a new variable and measurement as the data can simply be added as a new row instead of requiring a change of structure to `DataFrame` by adding a new column.

Performance benefits of stacked data

Finally, we will examine a reason for which we would want to stack data like this. This is because it can be shown to be more efficient than using lookup through a single level index and then a column lookup, or even compared to an `.iloc` lookup, specifying the location of the row and column by location. The following demonstrates this:

```
In [53]:
    # stacked scalar access can be a lot faster than
```

```
# column access


# time the different methods
import timeit
t = timeit.Timer("stacked1[('one', 'a')]",
                 "from __main__ import stacked1, df")
r1 = timeit.timeit(lambda: stacked1.loc[('one', 'a')],
                   number=10000)
r2 = timeit.timeit(lambda: df.loc['one']['a'],
                   number=10000)
r3 = timeit.timeit(lambda: df.iloc[1, 0],
                   number=10000)


# and the results are...  Yes, it's the fastest of the three
r1, r2, r3
```

Out[53]:
```
(0.5598540306091309, 1.0486528873443604, 1.2129769325256348)
```

This can have extreme benefits for application performance if we need to repeatedly access a large number of scalar values out of a DataFrame.

Summary

In this chapter, we examined several techniques of combining and reshaping data in one or more DataFrame objects. We started the chapter by examining how to combine data from multiple pandas objects. We saw how to concatenate multiple DataFrame objects both along the row and column axes. We then examined how pandas can be used to perform database-like joins and merges of data based on values in multiple DataFrame objects.

We then examined how to reshape data in DataFrame using pivots, stacking, and melting. We saw how each of these processes provides several variations on how to move data around by changing the shape of the indexes by moving data in and out of indexes.

We then finished the chapter with a brief but important example of how stacking data in a particular fashion can be used to provide significant performance benefits when accessing scalar data.

Even with all of this, we have not yet seen how to actually group data in a manner that will allow us to perform aggregate calculations efficiently. This will be the focus of the next chapter, which will show us how to use the grouping capabilities provided by pandas.

9
Grouping and Aggregating Data

The pandas library provides a flexible and high-performance "groupby" facility that enables you to slice, dice, and summarize data sets. This process follows a pattern known as split-apply-combine. This pattern data is first categorized into groups based on a criteria such as the indexes or values within the columns. Each group is then processed with an aggregation or transformation function, returning a set of data with transformed values or a single aggregate summary for each group. pandas then combines all of these results and presents it in a single data structure.

We will start by seeing how pandas is used to split data. This will start with a demonstration of how to group data both using categorical values in the columns of a `DataFrame` object or using the levels in the index of a pandas object. Using the result from a grouping operation, we will examine how to access the data in each group, as well as retrieve various basic statistical values of the groups.

The next section will focus on the apply portion of the pattern. This involves providing summaries of the groups via aggregation functions, transforming each row in a group into a new series of data, and removing groups of data based upon various criteria to prevent it from being in the results.

The chapter will close with a look at performing discretization of data in pandas. Although not properly a grouping function of pandas, discretization allows for data to be grouped into buckets, based upon ranges of values or to evenly distribute data across a number of buckets.

Specifically, in this chapter, we will cover:

- An overview of the split, apply, and combine pattern for data analysis
- Grouping by column values
- Accessing the results of grouping
- Grouping using index levels
- Applying functions to groups to create aggregate results
- Transforming groups of data using filtering to selectively remove groups of data
- The discretization of continuous data into bins

Setting up the IPython notebook

To utilize the examples in this chapter, we will need to include the following imports and settings:

```
In [1]:
    # import pandas and numpy
    import numpy as np
    import pandas as pd

    # Set some pandas options for controlling output
    pd.set_option('display.notebook_repr_html', False)
    pd.set_option('display.max_columns', 10)
    pd.set_option('display.max_rows', 10)

    # inline graphics
    %matplotlib inline
```

The split, apply, and combine (SAC) pattern

Many data analysis problems utilize a pattern of processing data, known as split-apply-combine. In this pattern, three steps are taken to analyze data:

1. A data set is split into smaller pieces
2. Each of these pieces are operated upon independently
3. All of the results are combined back together and presented as a single unit

The following diagram demonstrates a simple split-apply-combine process to sum groups of numbers:

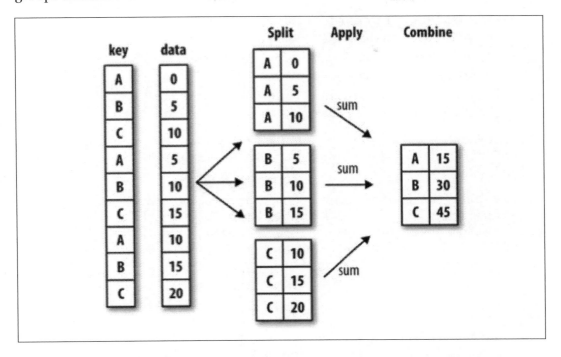

This process is actually very similar to the concepts in MapReduce. In MapReduce, massive sets of data, that are too big for a single computer, are divided into pieces and dispatched to many systems to spread the load in manageable pieces (split). Each system then performs analysis on the data and calculates a result (apply). The results are then collected from each system and used for decision making (combine).

Split-apply-combine, as implemented in pandas, differs in the scope of the data and processing. In pandas, all of the data is in memory of a single system. Because of this, it is limited to that single system's processing capabilities, but this also makes the data analysis for that scale of data faster and more interactive in nature.

Splitting in pandas is performed using the `.groupby()` method of a `Series` or `DataFrame` object, which given one or more index labels and/or column names, will divide the data based on the values present in the specified index labels and columns.

Once the data is split into groups, one or more of the following three broad classes of operations is applied:

- **Aggregation**: This calculates a summary statistic, such as group means or counts of the items in each group

- **Transformation**: This performs group- or item-specific calculations and returns a set of like-indexed results

- **Filtration**: This removes entire groups of data based on a group level computation

The combine stage of the pattern is performed automatically by pandas, which will collect the results of the apply stage on all of the groups and construct a single merged result.

For more information on split-apply-combine, there is a paper from the Journal of Statistical Software titled *The Split-Apply-Combine Strategy for Data Analysis*. This paper goes into more details of the pattern, and although it utilizes R in its examples, it is still a valuable read for someone learning pandas. You can get this paper at http://www.jstatsoft.org/v40/i01/paper.

Split

Our examination of splitting a pandas objects will be broken into several sections. We will first load data to use in the examples. Then, we will look at creating a grouping based on columns, examining properties of a grouping in the process. Next, will be an examination of accessing the results of the grouping. The last subsection will examine grouping using index labels, instead of content in columns.

Data for the examples

pandas' `Series` and `DataFrame` objects are split into groups using the `.groupby()` method. To demonstrate, we will use a variant of the accelerometer sensor data introduced in the previous chapter. This version of the data adds another column (sensor) that can be used to specify multiple sensors:

```
In [2]:
    # load the sensors data
    sensors = pd.read_csv("data/sensors.csv")
    sensors

Out[2]:
```

	interval	sensor	axis	reading
0	0	accel	Z	0.0
1	0	accel	Y	0.5
2	0	accel	X	1.0
3	1	accel	Z	0.1
4	1	accel	Y	0.4
..	...	...	...	...
19	2	orientation	Y	0.3
20	2	orientation	X	0.2
21	3	orientation	Z	0.0
22	3	orientation	Y	0.4
23	3	orientation	X	0.3

```
[24 rows x 4 columns]
```

Grouping by a single column's values

The sensor data consists of three categorical variables (sensor, interval, and axis) and one continuous variable (reading). In pandas, it is possible to group by any single categorical variable by passing its name to .groupby(). The following groups by the sensor column:

```
In [3]:
    # group this data by the sensor column / variable
    # returns a DataFrameGroupBy object
    grouped = sensors.groupby('sensor')
    grouped
```

```
Out[3]:
    <pandas.core.groupby.DataFrameGroupBy object at 0x106915f90>
```

The result of calling .groupby() on DataFrame is not the actual grouped data, but a DataFrameGroupBy object (SeriesGroupBy when grouping on Series). The actual process of grouping is a deferred/lazy process in pandas, and at this point, the grouping has not actually been performed. This object represents an interim description of the grouping to be performed. This allows pandas to first validate that the grouping description provided to it is valid, relative to the data before starting processing.

The .ngroups property will retrieve the number of groups that will be formed in the result:

```
In [4]:
    # get the number of groups that this will create
    grouped.ngroups
```

```
Out[4]:
    2
```

The .groups property will return a Python dictionary whose keys represent the names of each group (if multiple columns are specified, it is a tuple). The values in the dictionary are an array of the index labels contained within each respective group:

```
In [5]:
    # what are the groups that were found?
    grouped.groups
```

```
Out[5]:
    {'accel': [0, 1, 2, 3, 4, 5, 6, 7, 8, 9, 10, 11],
     'orientation': [12, 13, 14, 15, 16, 17, 18, 19, 20, 21, 22, 23]}
```

Accessing the results of grouping

The grouped variable can be thought of as a collection of named groups. We will use these properties, and the following function, to examine many of the results of groupings:

```
In [6]:
    # a helper function to print the contents of the groups
    def print_groups (groupobject):
        # loop over all groups, printing the group name
        # and group details
        for name, group in groupobject:
            print (name)
            print (group)
```

Using this method, we can see the results of the grouping we made a few steps back:

```
In [7]:
    # examine the content of the groups we created
    print_groups(grouped)
```

```
Out[7]:
    accel
```

	interval	sensor	axis	reading
0	0	accel	Z	0.0
1	0	accel	Y	0.5
2	0	accel	X	1.0
3	1	accel	Z	0.1
4	1	accel	Y	0.4
..	...	...	...	...
7	2	accel	Y	0.3
8	2	accel	X	0.8
9	3	accel	Z	0.3
10	3	accel	Y	0.2
11	3	accel	X	0.7

```
    [12 rows x 4 columns]
    orientation
```

	interval	sensor	axis	reading
12	0	orientation	Z	0.0
13	0	orientation	Y	0.1
14	0	orientation	X	0.0
15	1	orientation	Z	0.0
16	1	orientation	Y	0.2
..	...	...	...	...
19	2	orientation	Y	0.3
20	2	orientation	X	0.2
21	3	orientation	Z	0.0
22	3	orientation	Y	0.4
23	3	orientation	X	0.3

```
    [12 rows x 4 columns]
```

The examination of these results gives us some insight into how pandas has performed the split that we specified. A group has been created for each distinct value in the `sensors` column and has been named with that value. The group contains a DataFrame object whose content is the rows where the sensor value matched the name of the group.

We can use the `.size()` method to get a summary of the size of all the groups:

```
In [8]:
    # get how many items are in each group
    grouped.size()
```

```
Out[8]:
    sensor
    accel         12
    orientation   12
    dtype: int64
```

The `.count()` method will return the number of items in each column of every group:

```
In [9]:
    # get the count of items in each column of each group
    grouped.count()
```

```
Out[9]:
                  interval  axis  reading
    sensor
    accel             12    12      12
    orientation       12    12      12
```

Any specific group can be retrieved using the `.get_group()` property. The following retrieves the `accel` group:

```
In [10]:
    # get the data in one specific group
    grouped.get_group('accel')
```

```
Out[10]:
        interval sensor axis  reading
    0          0  accel   Z     0.0
```

1	0	accel	Y	0.5
2	0	accel	X	1.0
3	1	accel	Z	0.1
4	1	accel	Y	0.4
..	...	...	...	...
7	2	accel	Y	0.3
8	2	accel	X	0.8
9	3	accel	Z	0.3
10	3	accel	Y	0.2
11	3	accel	X	0.7

```
[12 rows x 4 columns]
```

The .head() and .tail() methods can be used to return the specified number of items in each group. The following code retrieved the first three rows in each group. There are six rows returned, as we requested the first three rows in each group, and there are two groups:

In [11]:

```
# get the first three items in each group
grouped.head(3)
```

Out[11]:

	interval	sensor	axis	reading
0	0	accel	Z	0.0
1	0	accel	Y	0.5
2	0	accel	X	1.0
12	0	orientation	Z	0.0
13	0	orientation	Y	0.1
14	0	orientation	X	0.0

The .nth() method will return the *n-th* item in each group. The following demonstrates how to use this to retrieve the first, the second, and then the third row of each group:

In [12]:

```
# get the first item in each group
```

```
grouped.nth(0)
```

Out[12]:

	interval	sensor	axis	reading
sensor				
accel	0	accel	Z	0
orientation	0	orientation	Z	0

In [13]:

```
# get the 2nd item in each group
grouped.nth(1)
```

Out[13]:

	interval	sensor	axis	reading
sensor				
accel	0	accel	Y	0.5
orientation	0	orientation	Y	0.1

In [14]:

```
# and so on...
grouped.nth(2)
```

Out[14]:

	interval	sensor	axis	reading
sensor				
accel	0	accel	X	1
orientation	0	orientation	X	0

Grouping can also be performed on multiple columns by passing a list of column names. The following groups the data by both sensor and axis variables:

In [15]:

```
# group by both sensor and axis values
mcg = sensors.groupby(['sensor', 'axis'])
print_groups(mcg)
```

Out[15]:

('accel', 'X')

	interval	sensor	axis	reading
2	0	accel	X	1.0
5	1	accel	X	0.9
8	2	accel	X	0.8
11	3	accel	X	0.7

('accel', 'Y')

	interval	sensor	axis	reading
1	0	accel	Y	0.5
4	1	accel	Y	0.4
7	2	accel	Y	0.3
10	3	accel	Y	0.2

('accel', 'Z')

	interval	sensor	axis	reading
0	0	accel	Z	0.0
3	1	accel	Z	0.1
6	2	accel	Z	0.2
9	3	accel	Z	0.3

('orientation', 'X')

	interval	sensor	axis	reading
14	0	orientation	X	0.0
17	1	orientation	X	0.1
20	2	orientation	X	0.2
23	3	orientation	X	0.3

('orientation', 'Y')

	interval	sensor	axis	reading
13	0	orientation	Y	0.1
16	1	orientation	Y	0.2
19	2	orientation	Y	0.3
22	3	orientation	Y	0.4

('orientation', 'Z')

	interval	sensor	axis	reading
12	0	orientation	Z	0
15	1	orientation	Z	0
18	2	orientation	Z	0
21	3	orientation	Z	0

Since multiple columns were specified, the name of each group is now a tuple with the value from both `sensor` and `axis`, which represents the group.

The `.describe()` method can be used to return descriptive statistics for each group:

```
In [16]:
    # get descriptive statistics for each
    mcg.describe()
```

```
Out[16]:
```

sensor	axis		interval	reading
accel	X	count	4.000000	4.000000
		mean	1.500000	0.850000
		std	1.290994	0.129099
		min	0.000000	0.700000
		25%	0.750000	0.775000
...			...	...
orientation	Z	min	0.000000	0.000000
		25%	0.750000	0.000000
		50%	1.500000	0.000000
		75%	2.250000	0.000000
		max	3.000000	0.000000

```
[48 rows x 2 columns]
```

By default, groups are sorted by their group name in an ascending order. This dataset already has them in an ascending order, but if you want to prevent sorting during grouping, use the `sort=False` option.

Grouping using index levels

The examples up to this point, have used `DataFrame` without any specific indexing (just the default sequential numerical index). This type of data would actually be very well suited for a hierarchical index. This can then be used directly to group the data based upon index label(s).

To demonstrate, the following script creates a new `DataFrame` object with `MultiIndex`, consisting of the original sensor and interval columns:

```
In [17]:
    # make a copy of the data and reindex the copy
    mi = sensors.copy()
    mi = mi.set_index(['sensor', 'axis'])
    mi
```

```
Out[17]:
                        interval   reading
    sensor       axis
    accel        Z            0       0.0
                 Y            0       0.5
                 X            0       1.0
                 Z            1       0.1
                 Y            1       0.4
    ...                     ...       ...
    orientation  Y            2       0.3
                 X            2       0.2
                 Z            3       0.0
                 Y            3       0.4
                 X            3       0.3

    [24 rows x 2 columns]
```

Grouping can now be performed using the levels of the hierarchical index. The following groups by index level 0 (the sensor names):

```
In [18]:
    # group by the first level of the index
    mig_l1 = mi.groupby(level=0)
    print_groups(mig_l1)
```

```
Out[18]:
    accel

                 interval   reading
    sensor axis
```

```
accel   Z                0          0.0
        Y                0          0.5
        X                0          1.0
        Z                1          0.1
        Y                1          0.4
...                     ...        ...
        Y                2          0.3
        X                2          0.8
        Z                3          0.3
        Y                3          0.2
        X                3          0.7

[12 rows x 2 columns]
orientation
                  interval   reading
sensor      axis
orientation Z            0          0.0
            Y            0          0.1
            X            0          0.0
            Z            1          0.0
            Y            1          0.2
...                     ...        ...
            Y            2          0.3
            X            2          0.2
            Z            3          0.0
            Y            3          0.4
            X            3          0.3

[12 rows x 2 columns]
```

Grouping by multiple levels can be performed by passing the levels in a list to `.groupby()`. Also, if `MultiIndex` has names specified for the levels, then these names can be used instead of integers. The following code groups the two levels of `MultiIndex` by their names:

```
In [19]:
    # group by multiple levels of the index
    mig_112 = mi.groupby(level=['sensor', 'axis'])
```

```
print_groups(mig_112)
```

Out[19]:

```
('accel', 'X')
             interval   reading
sensor axis
accel  X            0      1.0
       X            1      0.9
       X            2      0.8
       X            3      0.7
('accel', 'Y')
             interval   reading
sensor axis
accel  Y            0      0.5
       Y            1      0.4
       Y            2      0.3
       Y            3      0.2
('accel', 'Z')
             interval   reading
sensor axis
accel  Z            0      0.0
       Z            1      0.1
       Z            2      0.2
       Z            3      0.3
('orientation', 'X')
                 interval   reading
sensor      axis
orientation X           0      0.0
            X           1      0.1
            X           2      0.2
            X           3      0.3
('orientation', 'Y')
                 interval   reading
sensor      axis
orientation Y           0      0.1
            Y           1      0.2
```

```
        Y              2        0.3
        Y              3        0.4
('orientation', 'Z')
                    interval   reading
   sensor      axis
   orientation Z          0         0
               Z          1         0
               Z          2         0
               Z          3         0
```

Apply

After the grouping is performed, we have the ability to perform either aggregate calculations on each group of data resulting in a single value from each group, or to apply a transformation to each item in a group and return the combined result for each group. We can also filter groups based on results of expressions to exclude the groups from being included in the combined results.

Applying aggregation functions to groups

pandas allows the application of an aggregation function to each group of data. Aggregation is performed using the .aggregate() (or in short, .agg()) method of the GroupBy object. The parameter of .agg() is a reference to a function that is applied to each group. In the case of DataFrame, the function will be applied to each column.

As an example, the following code will calculate the mean of the values across each sensor and axis in the grouping mig_112:

```
In [20]:
    # calculate the mean for each sensor/axis
    mig_112.agg(np.mean)


Out[20]:
                    interval   reading
    sensor      axis
    accel       X        1.5      0.85
                Y        1.5      0.35
                Z        1.5      0.15
```

```
orientation X          1.5        0.15
            Y          1.5        0.25
            Z          1.5        0.00
```

As `.agg()` will apply the method to each column in each group, we also calculated the mean of the interval values (which is not of much interest).

The result of the aggregation will have an identically structured index as the original data. If you do not want this to happen, you can use the `as_index=False` option of the `.groupby()` method to specify not to duplicate the structure of the index:

In [21]:

```
# do not create an index matching the original object
sensors.groupby(['sensor', 'axis'],
            as_index=False).agg(np.mean)
```

Out[21]:

	sensor	axis	interval	reading
0	accel	X	1.5	0.85
1	accel	Y	1.5	0.35
2	accel	Z	1.5	0.15
3	orientation	X	1.5	0.15
4	orientation	Y	1.5	0.25
5	orientation	Z	1.5	0.00

This has derived the same results, but there is a slightly different organization.

 Aggregation functions can also be directly passed `level` parameters to specify which levels of the index to apply the function.

Many aggregation functions are built in directly to the `GroupBy` object to save you some more typing. Specifically, these functions are (prefixed by `gb.`):

gb.agg	gb.boxplot	gb.cummin	gb.describe	gb.filter
gb.get_group	gb.height	gb.last	gb.median	gb.ngroups
gb.plot	gb.rank	gb.std	gb.transform	
gb.aggregate	gb.count	gb.cumprod	gb.dtype	gb.first
gb.groups	gb.hist	gb.max	gb.min	gb.nth
gb.prod	gb.resample	gb.sum	gb.var	
gb.apply	gb.cummax	gb.cumsum	gb.fillna	gb.gender
gb.head	gb.indices	gb.mean	gb.name	gb.ohlc
gb.quantile	gb.size	gb.tail	gb.weight	

An equivalent to the previous `.agg(np.mean)` method is the following:

```
In [22]:
    # can simply apply the agg function to the group by object
    mig_112.mean()
```

```
Out[22]:
```

		interval	reading
sensor	**axis**		
accel	X	1.5	0.85
	Y	1.5	0.35
	Z	1.5	0.15
orientation	X	1.5	0.15
	Y	1.5	0.25
	Z	1.5	0.00

Multiple aggregation functions can be simultaneously applied to each group in a single call to `.agg()` by passing them in a list:

```
In [23]:
    # apply multiple aggregation functions at once
    mig_112.agg([np.sum, np.std])
```

```
Out[23]:
```

		interval		reading	
		sum	std	sum	std
sensor	**axis**				
accel	X	6	1.290994	3.4	0.129099
	Y	6	1.290994	1.4	0.129099
	Z	6	1.290994	0.6	0.129099
orientation	X	6	1.290994	0.6	0.129099
	Y	6	1.290994	1.0	0.129099
	Z	6	1.290994	0.0	0.000000

A different function can be applied to each column in each group by passing a Python dictionary to .agg(), where the keys of the dictionary represent the column name that the function is to be applied to, and the value is the function. The following demonstrates the mean of the reading column in each group by return, but for the interval, the column returns the length of the group:

```
In [24]:
    # apply a different function to each column
    mig_112.agg({'interval' : len,
                 'reading': np.mean})
```

```
Out[24]:
                     interval   reading

    sensor      axis
    accel       X           4      0.85

                Y           4      0.35

                Z           4      0.15

    orientation X           4      0.15

                Y           4      0.25

                Z           4      0.00
```

Aggregation can also be performed on specific columns using the [] operator on the GroupBy object. The following sums only the reading column:

```
In [25]:
    # calculate the mean of the reading column
    mig_112['reading'].mean()
```

```
Out[25]:
    sensor        axis
    accel         X       0.85

                  Y       0.35

                  Z       0.15

    orientation   X       0.15

                  Y       0.25

                  Z       0.00
    Name: reading, dtype: float64
```

The transformation of group data

Transformation is one of the more mysterious capabilities of pandas. I have personally found the operation of the `.transform()` method to be difficult for many to grasp (including myself) when starting to first use it. This is easily verifiable with many Stack Overflow postings about not being able to get it to work the way you think it should.

Documentation is fuzzy on these difficulties, so I feel it worthwhile to give some good examples and explanations for its operation. We will start with a general overview of transformation and then examine a few practical examples to make the operation more understandable.

An overview of transformation

The `GroupBy` objects provide a `.transform()` method, which applies a function to each group and returns either `Series` or `DataFrame` that has the following parameters:

- Indexed identically to the concatenation of the indexes in all the groups
- The number of rows is equal to the sum of the number of rows in all the groups
- Consists of non-noise, nongrouped columns to which pandas has applied the given function

To start the demonstration of the use of `.transform()`, we will start with a basic example that can be used to demonstrate the characteristics just stated:

```
In [26]:
    # a DataFrame to use for examples
    df = pd.DataFrame({ 'Label': ['A', 'C', 'B', 'A', 'C'],
                        'Values': [0, 1, 2, 3, 4],
                        'Values2': [5, 6, 7, 8, 9],
                        'Noise': ['foo', 'bar', 'baz',
                                  'foobar', 'barbaz']})
    df

Out[26]:
    Label   Noise   Values   Values2
0     A      foo      0        5
1     C      bar      1        6
```

2	B	baz	2	7
3	A	foobar	3	8
4	C	barbaz	4	9

This `DataFrame` object has a default index, a `Label` column that will be used to group the data, two numerical columns (`Values` and `Values2`), and one `Noise` column that will demonstrate pandas making an automatic decision to drop columns in transformations that it considers not appropriate for the specific operation.

First, we group `DataFrame` by its `Label` column:

```
In [27]:
    # group by label
    grouped = df.groupby('Label')
    print_groups(grouped)
```

```
Out[27]:
    A
```

	Label	Noise	Values	Values2
0	A	foo	0	5
3	A	foobar	3	8

```
    B
```

	Label	Noise	Values	Values2
2	B	baz	2	7

```
    C
```

	Label	Noise	Values	Values2
1	C	bar	1	6
4	C	barbaz	4	9

Each resulting group consists of the rows that were identified with each distinct value in the `Label` column and which are using the same index and labels from the original `DataFrame`.

Now, to demonstrate a transformation in process, the following adds the numeric value of `10` to each value (the values in both the `Values` and `Values2` columns):

```
In [28]:
    # add ten to all values in all columns
    grouped.transform(lambda x: x + 10)
```

```
Out[28]:
```

	Values	Values2
0	10	15
1	11	16
2	12	17
3	13	18
4	14	19

What pandas does here is pass the columns of DataFrame one by one and with only the rows for the specific group to the function supplied to .transform(). The result, in this example, is that the Noise column has been dropped in the result, as pandas determines that + 10 is not a valid operation for that column. Then, the other columns are passed as Series objects to the method and therefore, they have 10 added to each value.

To understand what is going on more clearly, we can change the function being passed to .transform() to write some diagnostic information. The following changes the x + 10 transform to also print what the data, that is being worked upon at each step of the execution, is:

In [29]:

```
# a function to print the input before we are adding 10 to it
def xplus10(x):
    print(x)
    return x + 10
```

In [30]:

```
# transform using xplus10
grouped.transform(xplus10)
```

```
0        foo
3     foobar
Name: Noise, dtype: object
0        foo
3     foobar
Name: Noise, dtype: object
0        foo
3     foobar
Name: A, dtype: object
0     0
```

```
3    3
Name: A, dtype: int64
2    2
Name: B, dtype: int64
1    1
4    4
Name: C, dtype: int64
0    5
3    8
Name: A, dtype: int64
2    7
Name: B, dtype: int64
1    6
4    9
Name: C, dtype: int64
```

```
Out[30]:
     Values   Values2
0       10        15
1       11        16
2       12        17
3       13        18
4       14        19
```

pandas has called our transformation function nine times, one time for every column in every group (3 x 3), and passed a Series object for each combination of group / rows / column, and for each of these calls, pandas stores the results and when complete, does a merge of the results back in to DataFrame (or if the result is a single column, Series) that is indexed identically to the original data.

The function passed to .transform() must return Series with the same number of rows and the same index values. Otherwise, the result will often not be what was expected. As an example of violating this statement, the following sums each Series object in each group. The result is a DataFrame object identical to the source (and not an exception or note that you did something wrong):

```
In [31]:
    # sum returns existing as it is applied to each individual item
```

```
grouped.transform(lambda x: x.sum())
```

Out[31]:

	Noise	Values	Values2
0	foo	0	5
1	bar	1	6
2	baz	2	7
3	foobar	3	8
4	barbaz	4	9

Having examined the details of how .transform() operates, we will now examine a couple of practical examples of using .transform().

Practical examples of transformation

A common transformation in statistical analysis, with grouped data, is to replace missing data within each group with the mean of the non-NaN values in the group. The following creates DataFrame with a Label categorical variable with two values ('A' and 'B') and a Values column containing a series of integers but with one value replaced with NaN:

In [32]:

```
# data to demonstrate replacement on NaN
df = pd.DataFrame({ 'Label': list("ABABAB"),
                    'Values': [10, 20, 11, np.nan, 12, 22]},
                  index=['i1', 'i2', 'i3', 'i4', 'i5', 'i6'])
df
```

Out[32]:

	Label	Values
i1	A	10
i2	B	20
i3	A	11
i4	B	NaN
i5	A	12
i6	B	22

Now, we group the data by `Label`, resulting in the following groups:

```
In [33]:
    # show the groups in the data based upon Label
    grouped = df.groupby('Label')
    print_groups(grouped)
```

```
Out[33]:
    A
        Label   Values
    i1      A       10
    i3      A       11
    i5      A       12
    B
        Label   Values
    i2      B       20
    i4      B      NaN
    i6      B       22
```

We can calculate the mean of each group using the `GroupBy` object's `.mean()` method. We can use this result to later verify that we did this transformation correctly:

```
In [34]:
    # calculate the mean of the two groups
    grouped.mean()
```

```
Out[34]:
            Values
    Label
    A           11
    B           21
```

The default operation of .mean() skips NaN in its calculation for the B group. However, suppose that we need the B group to have all NaN values filled, as other code we use may take offense to the NaN value, so we could replace it with the mean of the group (which should not affect group level mean calculations). This can be done with the following code:

```
In [35]:
    # use transform to fill the NaNs with the mean of the group
    filled_NaNs = grouped.transform(lambda x: x.fillna(x.mean()))
    filled_NaNs
```

```
Out[35]:
        Values
    i1      10
    i2      20
    i3      11
    i4      21
    i5      12
    i6      22
```

Here is where I have had trouble with pandas and have also seen others have problems. This result appears odd at first glance because of the following reasons:

- It does not have a Label column
- It has returned the Series object when we passed DataFrame to it
- It does not provide an explicit statement of which values in which group have been filled with the mean of the group

On the first two points, our original DataFrame had two columns, one of which was used in the grouping process. This column is not passed to the .transform() method, and in this scenario, the only column processed is Values. Upon applying the .transform() method on each group, pandas merges the results, which are all Series objects, into a single Series object.

With respect to the third point, we do not know which values in which groups were changed, but we do know the index in the original data, as the index labels are preserved through the process. This allows us to go back to the original data and fill in the NaN values in the original DataFrame:

```
In [36]:
    # overwrite old values with the new ones
```

```
df.Values = filled_NaNs
df
```

Out[36]:

	Label	Values
i1	A	10
i2	B	20
i3	A	11
i4	B	21
i5	A	12
i6	B	22

The path through this example was deliberate, so that I can make a point about `.transform()`.

 The `.transform()` method does not change the original data or the data in the group that is being applied to. Index labels are preserved, so you can go back and relate the results to the original data or any of the groups. If you want to patch this data, you will need to align/merge the results with the original data or grouped data. These changes, then, do not affect already calculated groups or the results for the apply step.

Another common and practical example, is that of using `.transform()` in statistical analysis and is the process of normalizing multiple groups of data to have a mean of 0 and a standard deviation of 1, also referred to as creating a normalized z score of the data.

To demonstrate normalizing groups into z scores, we will create a series of data that does not have a mean of 0, or a standard deviation of 1. The following code creates a series of normally distributed values with a `0.5` mean and a standard deviation of `2`, is indexed by day, and calculates a rolling mean of these values across `90` periods (roughly one quarter of a year):

In [37]:

```
# generate a rolling mean time series
np.random.seed(123456)
data = pd.Series(np.random.normal(0.5, 2, 365*3),
                 pd.date_range('2011-01-01', periods=365*3))
rolling = pd.rolling_mean(data, 100, 100).dropna()
```

```
rolling
```

```
Out[37]:
    2011-04-10    0.073603
    2011-04-11    0.057313
    2011-04-12    0.089255
    ...
    2013-12-28    0.850998
    2013-12-29    0.842293
    2013-12-30    0.848419
    Freq: D, Length: 996
```

 Don't worry now if you do not understand time-series data. We will cover it in detail in the next chapter.

Taking a quick peek at the code:

```
In [38]:
    # visualize the series
    rolling.plot();
```

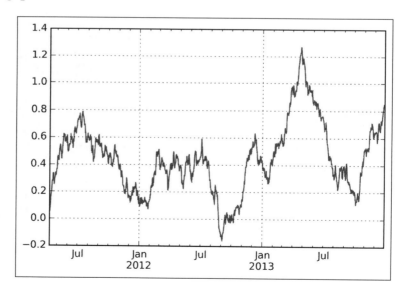

We can verify that this data is following the specified mean and standard deviation by grouping the data and looking at these values. Technically, the wider the date range of the group, the more we should expect these values to approach those specified in the normal random distribution. The following breaks things down into calendar years and calculates the mean and standard deviation:

```
In [39]:
    # calculate mean and std by year
    groupkey = lambda x: x.year
    groups = rolling.groupby(groupkey)
    groups.agg([np.mean, np.std])
```

```
Out[39]:
              mean         std
    2011   0.454233    0.171988
    2012   0.286874    0.181930
    2013   0.599933    0.276009
```

The mean is definitely not 0, nor is the standard deviation equal to 1.

To scale each group into a z score (mean = 0, std = 1), we can use the following function and apply it to each group:

```
In [40]:
    # normalize to the z-score
    zscore = lambda x: (x - x.mean()) / x.std()
    normed = rolling.groupby(groupkey).transform(zscore)
    normed.groupby(groupkey).agg([np.mean, np.std])
```

```
Out[40]:
               mean      std
    2011   -3.172066e-17    1
    2012    4.246755e-17    1
    2013   -3.388620e-16    1
```

This confirms our grouping and scaling to a standard z score.

As they say, a picture is worth a thousand words. The following code plots the original and normalized values against each other:

```
In [41]:
    # plot original vs normalize
    compared = pd.DataFrame({ 'Original': rolling,
                              'Normed': normed })
    compared.plot();
```

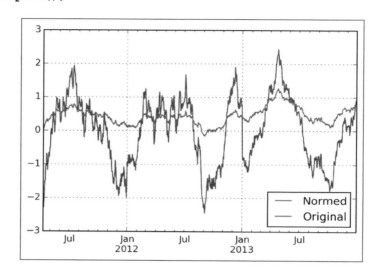

We can see that the initial data had a tighter curve and was mostly above 0 (a mean of 0.5), as we would expect from the given distribution. The normalized data has a wider range of values, as we moved the mean from 0.5 to 0.0 and also made the standard deviation larger.

We can perform one more check to see whether we did the math correctly. In a normal distribution, 64.2 percent of the data points should be within a standard deviation of 1:

```
In [42]:
    # check the distribution % within one std
    # should be roughly 64.2%
    normed_in1std = normed[np.abs(normed) <= 1.0].count()
    float(normed_in1std) / len(normed)

Out[42]:
    0.6485943775100401
```

We got 64.85 percent, which is close enough to demonstrate that we did this correctly.

Filtering groups

The pandas `GroupBy` object provides a `.filter()` method, which can be used to make group level decisions on whether or not the entire group is included in the result after the combination. The function passed to `.filter()` should return `True` if the group is to be included in the result and `False` to exclude it.

To demonstrate several scenarios, we will use the following `DataFrame`:

```
In [43]:
    # data for our examples
    df = pd.DataFrame({'Label': list('AABCCC'),
                       'Values': [1, 2, 3, 4, np.nan, 8]})
    df
```

```
Out[43]:
    Label   Values
  0    A        1
  1    A        2
  2    B        3
  3    C        4
  4    C      NaN
  5    C        8
```

The first demonstration will drop groups that do not have a minimum number of items. Specifically, if they only have one item or less, they will be omitted (therefore, only selecting groups with Label A and C):

```
In [44]:
    # drop groups with one or fewer non-NaN values
    f = lambda x: x.Values.count() > 1
    df.groupby('Label').filter(f)
```

```
Out[44]:
    Label   Values
  0    A        1
  1    A        2
```

3	C	4
4	C	NaN
5	C	8

Notice that there is a subtle difference when it comes to using `.filter()` as compared to `.translate()`. The data passed to the function specified in the call to `.filter()` is passed to the columns specified in the `.groupby()` method. Therefore, in this example, it is necessary to reference the `Values` column. This can cause some subtle bugs if you forget to take this into account.

The following will omit groups that do not have all values supplied (which is the C group):

```
In [45]:
    # drop any groups with NaN values
    f = lambda x: x.Values.isnull().sum() == 0
    df.groupby('Label').filter(f)
```

```
Out[45]:
    Label   Values
0     A        1
1     A        2
2     B        3
```

The following will select groups that have a mean that is over a particular threshold, larger than the means of all of the groups (basically, a group of data that has exceptional behavior as compared to the whole — in this case, the C group):

```
In [46]:
    # select groups with a mean of 2.0 or greater
    grouped = df.groupby('Label')
    mean = grouped.mean().mean()
    f = lambda x: abs(x.Values.mean() - mean) > 2.0
    df.groupby('Label').filter(f)
```

```
Out[46]:
    Label   Values
3     C        4
4     C       NaN
5     C        8
```

The final example demonstrates that instead of dropping a group, the use of the `dropna=False` parameter allows the return of the offending groups, but with all their values replaced with NaN. This is useful if you want to determine which items have been omitted:

```
In [47]:
    # replace values in a group where the # of items is <= 1
    f = lambda x: x.Values.count() > 1
    df.groupby('Label').filter(f, dropna=False)
```

```
Out[47]:
     Label  Values
  0     A      1
  1     A      2
  2   NaN    NaN
  3     C      4
  4     C    NaN
  5     C      8
```

Discretization and Binning

Although not directly using grouping constructs, in a chapter on grouping, it is worth explaining the process of discretization of continuous data. Discretization is a means of slicing up continuous data into a set of "bins", where each bin represents a range of the continuous sample and the items are then placed into the appropriate bin—hence the term "binning". Discretization in pandas is performed using the `pd.cut()` and `pd.qcut()` functions.

We will look at discretization by generating a large set of normally distributed random numbers and cutting these numbers into various pieces and analyzing the contents of the bins. The following generates `10000` numbers and reports the mean and standard deviation, which we expect to approach 0 and 1 as the sample size gets larger:

```
In [48]:
    # generate 10000 normal random #'s
    np.random.seed(123456)
    dist = np.random.normal(size = 10000)

    # show the mean and std
```

```
    "{0} {1}".format(dist.mean(), dist.std())
```

Out[48]:

```
    '-0.00286332404091 1.0087162032'
```

In [49]:

```
    dist
```

Out[49]:

```
    array([ 0.4691123 , -0.28286334, -1.5090585 , ...,  0.26296448,
            -0.83377412, -0.10418135])
```

The following cuts the data into five bins evenly spread across the values in the sample:

In [50]:

```
    # split the data into 5 bins
    bins = pd.cut(dist, 5)
    bins
```

Out[50]:

```
        (-0.633, 0.81]
        (-0.633, 0.81]
      (-2.0771, -0.633]
      (-2.0771, -0.633]
         (0.81, 2.254]
    ...
        (-0.633, 0.81]
      (-2.0771, -0.633]
        (-0.633, 0.81]
        (-0.633, 0.81]
      (-2.0771, -0.633]
        (-0.633, 0.81]
    Length: 10000
    Categories (5, object): [(-3.528, -2.0771] < (-2.0771, -0.633]
    < (-0.633, 0.81] < (0.81, 2.254] < (2.254, 3.698]]
```

The resulting `bins` object is a type of pandas variable known as `Categorical`. A categorical variable that is a result of `pd.cut()` consists of a set of labels and an index that describes how the data has been split.

The `.categories` property will return the index and describe the intervals that pandas decided upon:

```
In [51]:
    # show the categories in the bins
    bins.categories
```

```
Out[51]:
    Index([u'(-3.528, -2.0771]', u'(-2.0771, -0.633]', u'(-0.633, 0.81]',
    u'(0.81, 2.254]', u'(2.254, 3.698]'], dtype='object')
```

Each item in the index represents the range of values that the data has been mapped into. As previously stated, the width of the bins is determined by evenly dividing the data into five equal intervals, with the caveat that pandas automatically increases the overall range by 0.1 percent to ensure that all points are included. To exemplify, we can verify the calculated ranges as follows:

```
In [52]:
    # demonstrate the math to calculate the bins
    min = dist.min()
    max = dist.max()
    delta = max - min
    iwidth = delta/5
    extra = delta*0.001
    intervals = np.arange(min, max + extra, iwidth)
    intervals[0] -= delta*0.001
    intervals
```

```
Out[52]:
    array([-3.52809473, -2.07714421, -0.63341235,  0.81031951,
    2.25405137,  3.69778323])
```

The `.codes` property is an array that specifies which of the bins (intervals) each item has been assigned:

```
In [53]:
    # codes tells us which bin each item is in
    bins.codes
```

```
Out[53]:
    array([2, 2, 1, ..., 2, 1, 2], dtype=int8)
```

The notation for the intervals follows standard mathematical intervals where a parenthesis represents that the end is open while square brackets are closed. Closed ends include values at that exact number. By default, pandas closes the right-hand side of intervals. The closed end can be moved to the left-hand side of the interval using the `right=False` option in `pd.cut()`:

```
In [54]:
    # move the closed side of the interval to the left
    pd.cut(dist, 5, right=False).categories
```

```
Out[54]:
    Index([u'[-3.521, -2.0771)', u'[-2.0771, -0.633)', u'[-0.633, 0.81)',
    u'[0.81, 2.254)', u'[2.254, 3.705)'], dtype='object')
```

Instead of passing an integer number of bins to cut data into, you can pass an array of values that represent the bins. A common example of this scenario involves mapping ages into age range buckets. The following generates 50 ages between 6 and 45:

```
In [55]:
    # generate 50 ages between 6 and 45
    np.random.seed(123456)
    ages = np.random.randint(6, 45, 50)
    ages
```

```
Out[55]:
    array([ 7, 33, 38, 29, 42, 14, 16, 16, 18, 17, 26, 28, 44, 40, 20, 12,
    8, 10, 36, 29, 26, 26, 11, 29, 42, 17, 41, 35, 22, 40, 24, 21, 38, 33,
    26, 23, 16, 34, 26, 20, 18, 42, 27, 13, 37, 37, 10,  7, 10, 23])
```

We can specify specific ranges for the bins by passing them in an array where the extent of each bin is specified by each set of adjacent integers. The following cuts the data into the specified bins and reports the distribution of the ages to each bin using the `.describe()` method of the `pd.cut()` result:

```
In [56]:
    # cut into ranges and then get descriptive stats
    ranges = [6, 12, 18, 35, 50]
    agebins = pd.cut(ages, ranges)
    agebins.describe()
```

```
Out[56]:
                counts  freqs

    categories
    (6, 12]          8   0.16
    (12, 18]         9   0.18
    (18, 35]        21   0.42
    (35, 50]        12   0.24
```

To specify a name for each bin that is different than the standard mathematical notation, use the `labels` property:

```
In [57]:
    # add names for the bins
    ranges = [6, 12, 18, 35, 50]
    labels = ['Youth', 'Young Adult', 'Adult', 'Middle Aged']
    agebins = pd.cut(ages, ranges, labels=labels)
    agebins.describe()
```

```
Out[57]:
                counts  freqs

    categories
    Youth            8   0.16
    Young Adult      9   0.18
    Adult           21   0.42
    Middle Aged     12   0.24
```

This is not only convenient here, but also when plotting the bins, as pandas will pass the bin names to be plotted on a chart.

Data can also be sliced according to specified quantiles using pd.qcut(). This is the process of placing values into bins such that each bin has the same number of items. To do this, the ranges of the quantiles must be determined during the process, so that the distribution is even.

The following code splits the random values from earlier into 5 quantile bins, where each bin will have the same number of items allocated to it:

```
In [58]:
    # cut into quantiles
    # 5 bins with an equal quantity of items
    qbin = pd.qcut(dist, 5)
    # this will tell us the range of values in each quantile
    qbin.describe()
```

```
Out[58]:

                      counts   freqs
    categories
    [-3.521, -0.861]    2000     0.2
    (-0.861, -0.241]    2000     0.2
    (-0.241, 0.261]     2000     0.2
    (0.261, 0.866]      2000     0.2
    (0.866, 3.698]      2000     0.2
```

Instead of an integer number of bins, you can also specify your own quantile ranges. The following allocates ranges based on +/- 3, 2, and 1 standard deviations. As this is normally distributed data, we would expect 0.1 percent, 2.1 percent, 13.6 percent, and 34.1 percent of the values on each side of the mean:

```
In [59]:
    # make the quantiles at the +/- 3, 2 and 1 std deviations
    quantiles = [0,0.001,
                 0.021,
                 0.5-0.341,
                 0.5,
                 0.5+0.341,
                 1.0-0.021,
                 1.0-0.001,
                 1.0]
```

```
qbin = pd.qcut(dist, quantiles)
# this data should be a perfect normal distribution
qbin.describe()
```

Out[59]:

	counts	freqs
categories		
[-3.521, -3.131]	10	0.001
(-3.131, -2.0562]	200	0.020
(-2.0562, -1.0332]	1380	0.138
(-1.0332, -0.00363]	3410	0.341
(-0.00363, 1.0114]	3410	0.341
(1.0114, 2.0428]	1380	0.138
(2.0428, 3.0619]	200	0.020
(3.0619, 3.698]	10	0.001

These are exactly the results we expect from this distribution.

Summary

In this chapter, we examined various techniques for grouping and analyzing groups of data with pandas. An introduction to the split-apply-combine pattern for data analysis is given, along with an explanation of how this pattern is implemented in pandas. We also covered how to make transformations of grouped data and how to filter out groups of data based on results of functions that you can provide to pandas. Finally, we covered how to convert data into discrete intervals and analyze the results.

In the next chapter, we will take what you learned up to this point and get into some of the most interesting capabilities of pandas (at least in my opinion): the analysis of time-series data.

10
Time-series Data

A time series is a measurement of one or more variables over a period of time and at a specific interval. Once a time series is captured, analysis is often performed to identify patterns in the data, in essence, determining what is happening as time goes by. Being able to process time-series data is essential in the modern world, be it in order to analyze financial information or to monitor exercise on a wearable device and match your exercises to goals and diet.

pandas provides extensive support for working with time-series data. When working with time-series data, you are frequently required to perform a number of tasks, such as the following:

- Converting string-based dates and time into objects
- Standardizing date and time values to specific time zones
- Generating sequences of fixed-frequency dates and time intervals
- Efficiently reading/writing the value at a specific time in a series
- Converting an existing time series to another with a new frequency of sampling
- Computing relative dates, not only taking into account time zones, but also dealing with specific calendars based upon business days
- Identifying missing samples in a time series and determining appropriate substitute values
- Shifting dates and time forward or backward by a given amount
- Calculating aggregate summaries of values as time changes

pandas provides abilities to handle all of these tasks (and more). In this chapter, we will examine each of these scenarios and see how to use pandas to address them. We will start with looking at how pandas represents dates and times differently than Python. Next, we look at how pandas can create indexes based on dates and time. We will then look at how pandas represents durations of time with `timedelta` and `Period` objects. We will then progress to examining calendars and time zones and how they can be used to facilitate various calculations. The chapter will finish with an examination of operations on time-series data, including shifts, up and down sampling, and moving-window calculations.

Specifically, in this chapter, we will cover:

- Creating time series with specific frequencies
- Date offsets
- Representation of differences in time with `timedelta`
- Durations of time with `Period` objects
- Calendars
- Time zones
- Shifting and lagging
- Up and down sampling
- Time series moving-window operations

Setting up the IPython notebook

To utilize the examples in this chapter, we will need to include the following imports and settings:

In [1]:

```
# import pandas, numpy and datetime
import numpy as np
import pandas as pd

# needed for representing dates and times
import datetime
from datetime import datetime

# Set some pandas options for controlling output
pd.set_option('display.notebook_repr_html', False)
```

```
pd.set_option('display.max_columns', 10)
pd.set_option('display.max_rows', 10)


# matplotlib and inline graphics
import matplotlib.pyplot as plt
%matplotlib inline
```

Representation of dates, time, and intervals

pandas has extensive built-in capabilities to represent dates, time, and various intervals of time. Many of the calculations required to work with time-series data require both a richer and more accurate representation of the concepts of time than are provided in Python or NumPy.

To address this, pandas provides its own representations of dates, time, time intervals, and periods. The pandas implementations provide additional capabilities that are required to model time-series data. These include capabilities such as being able to transform data across different frequencies to change the frequency of sampled data and to apply different calendars to take into account things such as business days and holidays in financial calculations.

We will examine several of the common constructs in both Python and pandas to represent dates, time, and combinations of both, as well as intervals of time. There are many details to each of these, so here, we will focus just on the parts and patterns involved with each that are important for the understanding of the examples in the remainder of the chapter.

The datetime, day, and time objects

The datetime object is part of the datetime library and not a part of pandas. This class can be utilized to construct objects representing a fixed point in time at a specific date and time or simply a day without a time component or a time without a date component.

With respect to pandas, the datetime objects do not have the accuracy needed for much of the mathematics involved in extensive calculations on time-series data. However, they are commonly used to initialize pandas objects with pandas converting them into pandas timestamp objects behind the scenes. Therefore, they are worth a brief mention here, as they will be used frequently during initialization.

A datetime object can be initialized using a minimum of three parameters representing year, month, and day:

In [2]:
```
# datetime object for Dec 15 2014
datetime(2014, 12, 15)
```

Out[2]:
```
datetime.datetime(2014, 12, 15, 0, 0)
```

Notice that the result has defaulted two values to 0, which represents the hour and minute. The hour and minute components can also be specified with two more values to the constructor. The following creates a datetime object that also specifies 5:30 p.m.:

In [3]:
```
# specific date and also with a time of 5:30 pm
datetime(2014, 12, 15, 17, 30)
```

Out[3]:
```
datetime.datetime(2014, 12, 15, 17, 30)
```

The current date and time can be determined using the datetime.now() function, which retrieves the local date and time:

In [4]:
```
# get the local "now" (date and time)
# can take a time zone, but that's not demonstrated here
datetime.now()
```

Out[4]:
```
datetime.datetime(2015, 3, 6, 11, 7, 51, 216921)
```

A datetime.date object represents a specific day (no time). It can be created by passing a datetime object to the constructor:

In [5]:
```
# a date without time can be represented
# by creating a date using a datetime object
```

```
datetime.date(datetime(2014, 12, 15))
```

Out[5]:

```
datetime.date(2014, 12, 15)
```

To get the current local date, use the following:

In [6]:

```
# get just the current date
datetime.now().date()
```

Out[6]:

```
datetime.date(2015, 3, 6)
```

A time without a date component can be represented by creating a `datetime.time` object by passing a `datetime` object to its constructor:

In [7]:

```
# get just a time from a datetime
datetime.time(datetime(2014, 12, 15, 17, 30))
```

Out[7]:

```
datetime.time(17, 30)
```

The current local time can be retrieved using the following:

In [8]:

```
# get the current local time
datetime.now().time()
```

Out[8]:

```
datetime.time(11, 7, 51, 233760)
```

Timestamp objects

Specific dates and times in pandas are represented using the `pandas.tslib.Timestamp` class. Timestamp is based on the `datetime64` dtype and has higher precision than the Python `datetime` object. Timestamp objects are generally interchangeable with `datetime` objects, so you can typically use them wherever you may use `datetime` objects.

You can create a `Timestamp` object using `pd.Timestamp` (a shortcut for `pandas.tslib.Timestamp`) and by passing a string representing a date, time, or date and time:

```
In [9]:
    # a timestamp representing a specific date
    pd.Timestamp('2014-12-15')
```

```
Out[9]:
    Timestamp('2014-12-15 00:00:00')
```

A time element can also be specified, as shown here:

```
In [10]:
    # a timestamp with both date and time
    pd.Timestamp('2014-12-15 17:30')
```

```
Out[10]:
    Timestamp('2014-12-15 17:30:00')
```

`Timestamp` can be created using just a time, which will default to also assigning the current local date:

```
In [11]:
    # timestamp with just a time
    # which adds in the current local date
    pd.Timestamp('17:30')
```

```
Out[11]:
    Timestamp('2015-03-06 17:30:00')
```

The following demonstrates how to retrieve the current date and time using `Timestamp`:

```
In [12]:
    # get the current date and time (now)
    pd.Timestamp("now")
```

```
Out[12]:
    Timestamp('2015-03-06 11:07:51.254386')
```

Normally, as a pandas user, you will not create `Timestamp` objects directly. Many of the pandas functions that use dates and times will allow you to pass in a `datetime` object or a text representation of a date/time and the functions will perform the conversion internally.

Timedelta

A difference between two pandas `Timestamp` objects is represented by a `timedelta` object, which is a representation of an exact difference in time. These are common as results of determining the duration between two dates or to calculate the date at a specific interval of time from another date and/or time.

To demonstrate, the following uses a `timedelta` object to calculate a one-day increase in the time from the specified date:

```
In [13]:
    # what is one day from 2014-11-30?
    today = datetime(2014, 11, 30)
    tomorrow = today + pd.Timedelta(days=1)
    tomorrow


Out[13]:
    datetime.datetime(2014, 12, 1, 0, 0)
```

The following demonstrates how to calculate how many days there are between two dates:

```
In [14]:
    # how many days between these two dates?
    date1 = datetime(2014, 12, 2)
    date2 = datetime(2014, 11, 28)
    date1 - date2


Out[14]:
    datetime.timedelta(4)
```

Introducing time-series data

Due to its roots in finance, pandas excels in manipulating time-series data. Its abilities have been continuously refined over all of its versions to progressively increase its capabilities for time-series manipulation. These capabilities are the core of pandas and do not require additional libraries, unlike R, which requires the inclusion of Zoo to provide this functionality.

The core of the time-series functionality in pandas revolves around the use of specialized indexes that represent measurements of data at one or more timestamps. These indexes in pandas are referred to as DatetimeIndex objects. These are incredibly powerful objects, and their being core to pandas provides the ability to automatically align data based on dates and time, making working with sequences of data collected and time-stamped as easy as with any other type of indexes.

We will now examine how to create time-series data and DatetimeIndex objects both using explicit timestamp objects and using specific durations of time (referred to in pandas as frequencies).

DatetimeIndex

Sequences of timestamp objects are represented by pandas as DatetimeIndex, which is a type of pandas index that is optimized for indexing by date and time.

There are several ways to create DatetimeIndex objects in pandas. The following creates a DateTimeindex by passing a list of datetime objects as Series:

```
In [15]:
    # create a very simple time-series with two index labels
    # and random values
    dates = [datetime(2014, 8, 1), datetime(2014, 8, 2)]
    ts = pd.Series(np.random.randn(2), dates)
    ts

Out[15]:
    2014-08-01    1.566024
    2014-08-02    0.938517
    dtype: float64
```

Series has taken the datetime objects and constructed a DatetimeIndex from the date values, where each value of DatetimeIndex is a Timestamp object. This is one of the cases where pandas directly constructs Timestamp objects on your behalf.

The following verifies the type of the index and the types of the labels in the index:

```
In [16]:
    # what is the type of the index?
    type(ts.index)
```

```
Out[16]:
    pandas.tseries.index.DatetimeIndex
```

```
In [17]:
    # and we can see it is a collection of timestamps
    type(ts.index[0])
```

```
Out[17]:
    pandas.tslib.Timestamp
```

It is not required that you pass datetime objects in the list to create a time series. The Series object is smart enough to recognize that a string represents datetime and does the conversion for you. The following is equivalent to the previous example:

```
In [18]:
    # create from just a list of dates as strings!
    np.random.seed(123456)
    dates = ['2014-08-01', '2014-08-02']
    ts = pd.Series(np.random.randn(2), dates)
    ts
```

```
Out[18]:
    2014-08-01     0.469112
    2014-08-02    -0.282863
    dtype: float64
```

pandas provides a utility function in pd.to_datetime(). This function takes a sequence of similar- or mixed-type objects and pandas attempts to convert each into Timestamp and the collection of these timestamps into DatetimeIndex. If an object in the sequence cannot be converted, then NaT, representing not-a-time will be returned at the position in the index:

```
In [19]:
    # convert a sequence of objects to a DatetimeIndex
```

```
dti = pd.to_datetime(['Aug 1, 2014',
                       '2014-08-02',
                       '2014.8.3',
                       None])
for l in dti: print (l)


2014-08-01 00:00:00
2014-08-02 00:00:00
2014-08-03 00:00:00
NaT
```

Be careful, as the `pd.to_datetime()` function will, by default, fall back to returning a NumPy array of objects instead of `DatetimeIndex` if it cannot parse a value to `Timestamp`:

In [20]:

```
# this is a list of objects, not timestamps...
pd.to_datetime(['Aug 1, 2014', 'foo'])
```

Out[20]:

```
array(['Aug 1, 2014', 'foo'], dtype=object)
```

To force the function to convert to dates, you can use the `coerce=True` parameter. Values that cannot be converted will be assigned `NaT` in the resulting index:

In [21]:

```
# force the conversion, NaT for items that don't work
pd.to_datetime(['Aug 1, 2014', 'foo'], coerce=True)
```

Out[21]:

```
<class 'pandas.tseries.index.DatetimeIndex'>
[2014-08-01, NaT]
Length: 2, Freq: None, Timezone: None
```

A range of timestamps at a specific frequency can be easily created using the `pd.date_range()` function. The following creates a `Series` object from `DatetimeIndex` of `10` consecutive days:

In [22]:

```
# create a range of dates starting at a specific date
# and for a specific number of days, creating a Series
```

```
np.random.seed(123456)
periods = pd.date_range('8/1/2014', periods=10)
date_series = pd.Series(np.random.randn(10), index=periods)
date_series
```

Out[22]:

```
2014-08-01    0.469112
2014-08-02   -0.282863
2014-08-03   -1.509059
2014-08-04   -1.135632
2014-08-05    1.212112
2014-08-06   -0.173215
2014-08-07    0.119209
2014-08-08   -1.044236
2014-08-09   -0.861849
2014-08-10   -2.104569
Freq: D, dtype: float64
```

Like any pandas index, DatetimeIndex can be used for various index operations, such as data alignment, selection, and slicing. The following demonstrates slicing using index locations:

In [23]:

```
# slice by location
subset = date_series[3:7]
subset
```

Out[23]:

```
2014-08-04   -1.135632
2014-08-05    1.212112
2014-08-06   -0.173215
2014-08-07    0.119209
Freq: D, dtype: float64
```

To demonstrate, we will use the following Series created with the index of the subset we just created:

```
In [24]:
    # a Series to demonstrate alignment
    s2 = pd.Series([10, 100, 1000, 10000], subset.index)
    s2
```

```
Out[24]:
    2014-08-04        10
    2014-08-05       100
    2014-08-06      1000
    2014-08-07     10000
    Freq: D, dtype: int64
```

When we add s2 and date_series, alignment will be performed, returning NaN where items do not align and the sum of the two values where they align:

```
In [25]:
    # demonstrate alignment by date on a subset of items
    date_series + s2
```

```
Out[25]:
    2014-08-01              NaN
    2014-08-02              NaN
    2014-08-03              NaN
    2014-08-04         8.864368
    2014-08-05       101.212112
    2014-08-06       999.826785
    2014-08-07     10000.119209
    2014-08-08              NaN
    2014-08-09              NaN
    2014-08-10              NaN
    Freq: D, dtype: float64
```

Items in Series with DatetimeIndex can be retrieved using a string representing a date instead having to specify a datetime object:

```
In [26]:
    # lookup item by a string representing a date
```

```
date_series['2014-08-05']
```

Out[26]:

```
1.2121120250208506
```

DatetimeIndex can also be indexed and sliced using a string that represents a date or using datetime objects:

In [27]:

```
# slice between two dates specified by string representing dates
date_series['2014-08-05':'2014-08-07']
```

Out[27]:

```
2014-08-05    1.212112
2014-08-06   -0.173215
2014-08-07    0.119209
Freq: D, dtype: float64
```

Another convenient feature of pandas is that DatetimeIndex can be sliced using partial date specifications. As an example, the following code creates a Series object with dates spanning two years and then selects only those items of the year 2013:

In [28]:

```
# a two year range of daily data in a Series
# only select those in 2013
s3 = pd.Series(0, pd.date_range('2013-01-01', '2014-12-31'))
s3['2013']
```

Out[28]:

```
2013-01-01    0
2013-01-02    0
2013-01-03    0
...
2013-12-29    0
2013-12-30    0
2013-12-31    0
Freq: D, Length: 365
```

We can also select items only in a specific year and month. This is demonstrated by the following, which selects the items in August 2014:

```
In [29]:
    # 31 items for May 2014
    s3['2014-05']
```

```
Out[29]:
    2014-05-01    0
    2014-05-02    0
    2014-05-03    0
    ...
    2014-05-29    0
    2014-05-30    0
    2014-05-31    0
    Freq: D, Length: 31
```

We can slice data contained within two specified months, as demonstrated by the following, which returns items in August and September, 2014:

```
In [30]:
    # items between two months
    s3['2014-08':'2014-09']
```

```
Out[30]:
    2014-08-01    0
    2014-08-02    0
    2014-08-03    0
    ...
    2014-09-28    0
    2014-09-29    0
    2014-09-30    0
    Freq: D, Length: 61
```

Creating time-series data with specific frequencies

Time-series data in pandas can be created on intervals other than daily frequency. Different frequencies can be generated with `pd.date_range()` by utilizing the `freq` parameter. This parameter defaults to a value of `'D'`, which represents daily frequency.

To demonstrate alternative frequencies, the following creates a `DatetimeIndex` with 1-minute intervals between the two specified dates by specifying `freq='T'`:

```
In [31]:
    # generate a Series at one minute intervals
    np.random.seed(123456)
    bymin = pd.Series(np.random.randn(24*60*90),
                    pd.date_range('2014-08-01',
                                '2014-10-29 23:59',
                                freq='T'))

    bymin

    Out[31]:
    2014-08-01 00:00:00     0.469112
    2014-08-01 00:01:00    -0.282863
    2014-08-01 00:02:00    -1.509059
    ...
    2014-10-29 23:57:00     1.850604
    2014-10-29 23:58:00    -1.589660
    2014-10-29 23:59:00     0.266429
    Freq: T, Length: 129600
```

This time series allows us to slice at a finer resolution, down to the minute and smaller intervals if using finer frequencies. To demonstrate minute-level slicing, the following slices the values at 9 consecutive minutes:

```
In [32]:
    # slice down to the minute
    bymin['2014-08-01 00:02':'2014-08-01 00:10']

Out[32]:
    2014-08-01 00:02:00    -1.509059
```

```
2014-08-01 00:03:00    -1.135632
2014-08-01 00:04:00     1.212112
2014-08-01 00:05:00    -0.173215
2014-08-01 00:06:00     0.119209
2014-08-01 00:07:00    -1.044236
2014-08-01 00:08:00    -0.861849
2014-08-01 00:09:00    -2.104569
2014-08-01 00:10:00    -0.494929
Freq: T, dtype: float64
```

The following table lists the possible frequency values:

Alias	Description
B	Business day frequency
C	Custom business day frequency
D	Calendar day frequency (the default)
W	Weekly frequency
M	Month end frequency
BM	Business month end frequency
CBM	Custom business month end frequency
MS	Month start frequency
BMS	Business month start frequency
CBMS	Custom business month start frequency
Q	Quarter end frequency
BQ	Business quarter frequency
QS	Quarter start frequency
BQS	Business quarter start frequency
A	Year end frequency
BA	Business year-end frequency
AS	Year start frequency
BAS	Business year start frequency
H	Hourly frequency
T	Minute-by-minute frequency
S	Second-by-second frequency
L	Milliseconds
U	Microseconds

As an example, if you want to generate a time series that uses only business days, then use the 'B' frequency:

```
In [33]:
    # generate a series based upon business days
    days = pd.date_range('2014-08-29', '2014-09-05', freq='B')
    for d in days : print (d)


    2014-08-29 00:00:00
    2014-09-01 00:00:00
    2014-09-02 00:00:00
    2014-09-03 00:00:00
    2014-09-04 00:00:00
    2014-09-05 00:00:00
```

In this time series, we can see that two days were skipped as they were on the weekend, which would not have occurred using a calendar-day frequency.

A range can be created starting at a particular date and time with a specific frequency and for a specific number of periods using the `periods` parameter. To demonstrate, the following creates a 10-item `DatetimeIndex` starting at `2014-08-01 12:10:01` and at 1-second intervals:

```
In [34]:
    # periods will use the frequency as the increment
    pd.date_range('2014-08-01 12:10:01', freq='S', periods=10)


Out[34]:
    <class 'pandas.tseries.index.DatetimeIndex'>
    [2014-08-01 12:10:01, ..., 2014-08-01 12:10:10]
    Length: 10, Freq: S, Timezone: None
```

Calculating new dates using offsets

Frequencies in pandas are represented using date offsets. We have touched on this concept at the beginning of the chapter when discussing `Timedelta` objects. pandas extends the capabilities of these using the concept of `DateOffset` objects, which represent knowledge of how to integrate time offsets and frequencies relative to `DatetimeIndex` objects.

We will examine how pandas uses date offsetting in two different ways. The first calculates offsets of a specific duration from a given date, and the other calculates offsets based on what are referred to as anchored offsets.

Date offsets

`DatetimeIndex` objects are created at various frequencies by passing in frequency strings, such as `'M'`, `'W'`, and `'BM'` to the `freq` parameter of `pd.date_range()`. Under the hood, these frequency strings are translated into an instance of the pandas `DateOffset` object, which is associated with the frequency of the index.

`DateOffset` represents a regular frequency increment. Specific date offset logic, such as "month", "business day", or "hour", is represented in pandas with various subclasses of `DateOffset`. A `DateOffset` provides pandas with the intelligence to be able to determine how to calculate a specific interval of time from a reference date and time.

The use of `DatetimeIndex` and `DateOffset` objects provides the user of pandas great flexibility in calculating a new date/time from another using an offset other than one that represents a fixed period of time. A practical example would be to calculate the next day of business. This is not simply determined by adding one day to `datetime`. If a date represents a Friday, the next business day in the US financial market is not Saturday but Monday. In some cases, one business day from a Friday may actually be Tuesday if Monday is a holiday. pandas gives us all the tools required to handle these scenarios.

We can start to examine the use of date offsets by generating a date range using `'B'` as the frequency, which will return a sequence of dates between the specified dates—but only dates that are considered business days during that interval:

```
In [35]:
    # get all business days between and inclusive of these two dates
    dti = pd.date_range('2014-08-29', '2014-09-05', freq='B')
    dti.values

Out[35]:
    array(['2014-08-28T18:00:00.000000000-0600',
           '2014-08-31T18:00:00.000000000-0600',
           '2014-09-01T18:00:00.000000000-0600',
           '2014-09-02T18:00:00.000000000-0600',
           '2014-09-03T18:00:00.000000000-0600',
           '2014-09-04T18:00:00.000000000-0600'],
    dtype='datetime64[ns]')
```

This time series has omitted `2014-08-30` and `2014-08-30`, as they are Saturday and Sunday and not considered a business day.

`DatetimeIndex` has a `.freq` property that represents the frequency of the timestamps in the index:

```
In [36]:
    # check the frequency is BusinessDay
    dti.freq
```

```
Out[36]:
    <BusinessDay>
```

Notice that pandas has created an instance of the `BusinessDay` class to represent the `DateOffset` unit of this index. As mentioned earlier, pandas represents different date offsets with a subclass of the `DateOffset` class. The following are the various built-in date offset classes that are provided by pandas:

Class	Description
DateOffset	Generic offset defaults to one calendar day
BDay	Business day
CDay	Custom business day
Week	One week, optionally anchored on a day of the week
WeekOfMonth	The x-th day of the y-th week of each month
LastWeekOfMonth	The x-th day of the last week of each month
MonthEnd	Calendar month end
MonthBegin	Calendar month start
BMonthEnd	Business month end
BMonthBegin	Business month start
CBMonthEnd	Custom business month end
CBMonthBegin	Custom business month start
QuarterEnd	Quarter end
QuarterBegin	Quarter start
BQuarterEnd	Business quarter end
BQuarterBegin	Business quarter start
FYS253Quarter	Retail (52-53 week) quarter
YearEnd	Calendar year end
YearBegin	Calendar year start
BYearEnd	Business quarter end

Class	Description
BYearBegin	Business quarter start
FYS253	Retail (52-53 week) year
Hour	One hour
Minute	One minute
Second	One second
Milli	One millisecond
Micro	One microsecond

pandas takes this strategy of using DateOffset and its specializations to codify logic to calculate the next datetime from another datetime. This makes using these objects very flexible as well as powerful. DateOffset objects can be used in various scenarios, including the following:

- They can be added/subtracted to/from a datetime object to obtain a shifted date

- They can be multiplied by an integer (positive or negative) so that the increment will be applied multiple times

- They have rollforward and rollback methods to move a date forward or backward to the next or previous "offset date"

DateOffset objects can be created by passing them a datetime object that represents a fixed duration of time or using a number of keyword arguments. Keyword arguments fall into two general categories. The first category is keywords that represent absolute dates: year, month, day, hour, minute, second, and microsecond. The second category represents relative durations and can be negative values: years, months, weeks, day, hours, minutes, seconds, and microseconds.

The following creates a 1-day offset and adds it to datetime:

```
In [37]:
    # calculate a one day offset from 2014-8-29
    d = datetime(2014, 8, 29)
    do = pd.DateOffset(days = 1)
    d + do

Out[37]:
    Timestamp('2014-08-30 00:00:00')
```

The following calculates the next business day from a given date:

```
In [38]:
    # import the data offset types
    from pandas.tseries.offsets import *
    # calculate one business day from 2014-8-31
    d + BusinessDay()

Out[38]:
    Timestamp('2014-09-01 00:00:00')
```

Multiple units of a specific `DateOffset` can be used using multiplication:

```
In [39]:
    # determine 2 business days from 2014-8-29
    d + 2 * BusinessDay()

Out[39]:
    Timestamp('2014-09-02 00:00:00')
```

The following demonstrates using a `BMonthEnd` object to calculate the last business day of a month from a given date (in this case, `2014-09-02`):

```
In [40]:
    # what is the next business month end
    # from a specific date?
    d + BMonthEnd()

Out[40]:
    Timestamp('2014-09-30 00:00:00')
```

The following uses the `BMonthEnd` objects' `.rollforward()` method to calculate the next month end:

```
In [41]:
    # calculate the next month end by
    # rolling forward from a specific date
    BMonthEnd().rollforward(datetime(2014, 9, 15))

Out[41]:
    Timestamp('2014-09-30 00:00:00')
```

Several of the offset classes can be parameterized to provide finer control of the offset behavior. As an example, the following calculates the date of the Tuesday (`weekday` = 1) in the week prior to `2014-08-31`:

```
In [42]:
    # calculate the date of the Tuesday previous
    # to a specified date
    d - Week(weekday = 1)
```

```
Out[42]:
    Timestamp('2014-08-26 00:00:00')
```

Anchored offsets

pandas also supports the concept of anchored offsets, which are frequencies that can be specified using a specific suffix. One version of anchored offsets allows you to specify weekly intervals that fall on a specific day of the week. These aliases are of this form:

Alias	Description
W-SUN	Weekly on Sunday (same as 'W')
W-MON	Weekly on Monday
W-TUE	Weekly on Tuesday
W-WED	Weekly on Wednesday
W-THU	Weekly on Thursday
W-FRI	Weekly on Friday
W-SAT	Weekly on Saturday

As an example, the following generates an index that consists of the dates of all Wednesdays between the two specified dates:

```
In [43]:
    # calculate all Wednesdays between 2014-06-01
    # and 2014-08-31
    wednesdays = pd.date_range('2014-06-01',
                               '2014-08-31', freq="W-WED")
    wednesdays.values
```

```
Out[43]:
```

```
array(['2014-06-03T18:00:00.000000000-0600',
       '2014-06-10T18:00:00.000000000-0600',
       '2014-06-17T18:00:00.000000000-0600',
       '2014-06-24T18:00:00.000000000-0600',
       '2014-07-01T18:00:00.000000000-0600',
       '2014-07-08T18:00:00.000000000-0600',
       '2014-07-15T18:00:00.000000000-0600',
       '2014-07-22T18:00:00.000000000-0600',
       '2014-07-29T18:00:00.000000000-0600',
       '2014-08-05T18:00:00.000000000-0600',
       '2014-08-12T18:00:00.000000000-0600',
       '2014-08-19T18:00:00.000000000-0600',
       '2014-08-26T18:00:00.000000000-0600'],
    dtype='datetime64[ns]')
```

Anchored offsets can also be created using the annual and quarterly frequencies. These frequency anchors are of the general form [B] [A|Q] [S] - [MON], where B (business days) and S (start of period instead end) are optional, A is for annual or Q for quarterly, and MON is the three-digit abbreviation for the month (JAN, FEB, ...).

To demonstrate, the following generates the business dates for quarter end in the year 2014 with the year anchored at the end of June:

```
In [44]:
    # what are all of the business quarterly end
    # dates in 2014?
    qends = pd.date_range('2014-01-01', '2014-12-31',
                          freq='BQS-JUN')
    qends.values
```

```
Out[44]:
    array(['2014-03-02T17:00:00.000000000-0700',
           '2014-06-01T18:00:00.000000000-0600',
           '2014-08-31T18:00:00.000000000-0600',
           '2014-11-30T17:00:00.000000000-0700'],
        dtype='datetime64[ns]')
```

Representing durations of time using Period objects

Many useful mathematical operations on time-series data require that events within a specific time interval be analyzed. A simple example would be to determine how many financial transactions occurred in a specific period.

This can be performed using `Timestamp` and `DateOffset`, where the bounds are calculated and then items filtered based on these bounds. However, this becomes cumbersome when you need to deal with events that must be grouped into multiple periods of time as you start to need to manage sets of the `Timestamp` and `DateOffset` objects.

To facilitate these types of data organization and calculations, pandas makes intervals of time a formal construct using the `Period` class. pandas also formalizes series of `Period` objects using `PeriodIndex`, which provides capabilities of aligning data items based on the indexes' associated period objects.

We will look at the `Period` object and `PeriodIndex` in detail in the following subsections.

The Period object

pandas formalizes the concept of an interval of time using a `Period` object. `Period` allows you to specify durations based on frequencies such as daily, weekly, monthly, annually, quarterly, and so on, and it will provide a specific start and end `Timestamp` representing the specific bounded interval of time.

`Period` is created using a timestamp and a frequency (seen in the table earlier), where the timestamp represents the anchor used as a point of reference and the frequency is the duration of time.

To demonstrate, the following creates a period representing one month anchored in August 2014:

```
In [45]:
    # create a period representing a month of time
    # starting in August 2014
    aug2014 = pd.Period('2014-08', freq='M')
    aug2014

Out[45]:
    Period('2014-08', 'M')
```

`Period` has `start_time` and `end_time` properties that inform us about the derived start and end times of `Period`:

```
In [46]:
    # examine the start and end times of this period
    aug2014.start_time, aug2014.end_time
```

```
Out[46]:
    (Timestamp('2014-08-01 00:00:00'), Timestamp('2014-08-31
    23:59:59.999999999'))
```

As we specified a period that is August 2014, pandas determines the anchor (`start_time`) and then calculates `end_time` based on the specified frequency. In this case, it calculates one month from `start_time` and returns the last unit of the prior time.

Mathematical operations are overloaded on `Period` to calculate another `Period` based on the given value. The following creates a new `Period` object based on `aug2014`, which is shifted by 1 unit of its represented frequency (which is one month):

```
In [47]:
    # calculate the period that is one frequency
    # unit of the aug2014 period further along in time
    # This happens to be September 2014
    sep2014 = aug2014 + 1
    sep2014
```

```
Out[47]:
    Period('2014-09', 'M')
```

The concept of the shift is very important and powerful. The addition of 1 to this `Period` object informs it to shift in time one positive unit of whatever frequency is represented by the object. In this case, it shifts the period one month forward to September 2014.

If we examine the start and end times represented in the `sep2014` object, we see that pandas has gone through the effort of determining the correct dates representing the entirety of September 2014:

```
In [48]:
    sep2014.start_time, sep2014.end_time
```

```
Out[48]:
    (Timestamp('2014-09-01 00:00:00'), Timestamp('2014-09-30
    23:59:59.999999999'))
```

Note that `Period` had the intelligence to know that September is 30 days and not 31. This is part of the incredible intelligence behind the `Period` object that saves us a lot of coding. It is not simply adding 30 days (in this example) but one unit frequency of the period. This helps solve many difficult date management problems.

PeriodIndex

A series of `Period` objects can be combined into a special form of pandas index known as `PeriodIndex`. A `PeriodIndex` index is useful for being able to associate data to specific intervals of time and being able to slice and perform analysis on the events in each interval represented in `PeriodIndex`.

The following code creates a `PeriodIndex` consisting of 1-month intervals for the year 2013:

```
In [49]:
    # create a period index representing
    # all monthly boundaries in 2013
    mp2013 = pd.period_range('1/1/2013', '12/31/2013', freq='M')
    mp2013
```

```
Out[49]:
    <class 'pandas.tseries.period.PeriodIndex'>
    [2013-01, ..., 2013-12]
    Length: 12, Freq: M
```

PeriodIndex differs from DatetimeIndex in that the index labels are the Period objects. The following prints the start and end times for all the Period objects in the index:

```
In [50]:
    # loop through all period objects in the index
    # printing start and end time for each
    for p in mp2013:
        print ("{0} {1}".format(p.start_time, p.end_time))
```

```
Out[50]:
    2013-01-01 00:00:00 2013-01-31 23:59:59.999999999
    2013-02-01 00:00:00 2013-02-28 23:59:59.999999999
    2013-03-01 00:00:00 2013-03-31 23:59:59.999999999
    2013-04-01 00:00:00 2013-04-30 23:59:59.999999999
    2013-05-01 00:00:00 2013-05-31 23:59:59.999999999
    2013-06-01 00:00:00 2013-06-30 23:59:59.999999999
    2013-07-01 00:00:00 2013-07-31 23:59:59.999999999
    2013-08-01 00:00:00 2013-08-31 23:59:59.999999999
    2013-09-01 00:00:00 2013-09-30 23:59:59.999999999
    2013-10-01 00:00:00 2013-10-31 23:59:59.999999999
    2013-11-01 00:00:00 2013-11-30 23:59:59.999999999
    2013-12-01 00:00:00 2013-12-31 23:59:59.999999999
```

pandas has conveniently determined the start and end of each month, taking into account the actual number of days in each specific month.

Using PeriodIndex, we can construct a Series object using it as the index and associate a value to each Period in the index:

```
In [51]:
    # create a Series with a PeriodIndex
    np.random.seed(123456)
    ps = pd.Series(np.random.randn(12), mp2013)
    ps
```

```
Out[51]:
    2013-01    0.469112
    2013-02   -0.282863
```

```
2013-03    -1.509059
...
2013-10    -2.104569
2013-11    -0.494929
2013-12     1.071804
Freq: M, Length: 12
```

We now have a time series where the value at a specific index label represents a measurement that spans a period of time, such as the average value of a security in a given month instead of at a specific time. This becomes very useful when we perform the resampling of the time series to another frequency.

Like `DatetimeIndex`, `PeriodIndex` can be used to index values using `Period`, a string representing a period or partial period specification. To demonstrate, we will create another series similar to the previous one but spanning two years, 2013 and 2014:

```
In [52]:
    # create a Series with a PeriodIndex and which
    # represents all calendar month periods in 2013 and 2014
    np.random.seed(123456)
    ps = pd.Series(np.random.randn(24),
                   pd.period_range('1/1/2013',
                                   '12/31/2014', freq='M'))
    ps

Out[52]:
    2013-01     0.469112
    2013-02    -0.282863
    2013-03    -1.509059
    ...
    2014-10     0.113648
    2014-11    -1.478427
    2014-12     0.524988
    Freq: M, Length: 24
```

Individual values can be selected using the specific index label using either a `Period` object or a string representing a period. The following demonstrates how to use a string representation:

```
In [53]:
    # get value for period represented by 2014-06
```

```
ps['2014-06']
```

Out[53]:

```
0.567020349793672
```

Partial specifications can also be used, such as the following, which retrieves all values just for periods in 2014:

In [54]:

```
# get values for all periods in 2014
ps['2014']
```

Out[54]:

```
2014-01     0.721555
2014-02    -0.706771
2014-03    -1.039575
...
2014-10     0.113648
2014-11    -1.478427
2014-12     0.524988
Freq: M, Length: 12
```

Like any index in pandas, PeriodIndex can also be sliced. The following retrieves all values for periods between (and inclusive of) March and June 2014:

In [55]:

```
# all values between (and including) March and June 2014
ps['2014-03':'2014-06']
```

Out[55]:

```
2014-03    -1.039575
2014-04     0.271860
2014-05    -0.424972
2014-06     0.567020
Freq: M, dtype: float64
```

Handling holidays using calendars

Earlier, when we calculated the next business day from August 29, 2014, we were told by pandas that this date is September 1, 2014. This is actually not correct in the United States: September 1, 2014 is a US federal holiday and banks and exchanges are closed on this day. The reason for this is that pandas uses a specific default calendar when calculating the next business day, and this default pandas calendar does not include September 1, 2014 as a holiday.

The solution to this is to either create a custom calendar (which we will not get into the details of), or use the one custom calendar provided by pandas for just this situation, USFederalHolidayCalendar. This custom calendar can then be passed to a CustomBusinessDay object that will be used instead of a BusinessDay object. This calculation using this CustomBusinessDay object will then use the new calendar and take into account the US federal holidays.

The following demonstrates the creation of a USFederalCalendar object and how to use it to report the days that it considers holidays:

```
In [56]:
    # demonstrate using the US federal holiday calendar
    # first need to import it
    from pandas.tseries.holiday import *
    # create it and show what it considers holidays
    cal = USFederalHolidayCalendar()
    for d in cal.holidays(start='2014-01-01', end='2014-12-31'):
        print (d)
    2014-01-01 00:00:00
    2014-01-20 00:00:00
    2014-02-17 00:00:00
    2014-05-26 00:00:00
    2014-07-04 00:00:00
    2014-09-01 00:00:00
    2014-10-13 00:00:00
    2014-11-11 00:00:00
    2014-11-27 00:00:00
    2014-12-25 00:00:00
```

We can now use this calendar object to calculate the next business day from August 29, 2014:

```
In [57]:
    # create CustomBusinessDay object based on the federal calendar
    cbd = CustomBusinessDay(holidays=cal.holidays())

    # now calc next business day from 2014-8-29
    datetime(2014, 8, 29) + cbd
```

```
Out[57]:
    Timestamp('2014-09-02 00:00:00')
```

Note that instead of using a `BusinessDay` object, we used an instance of `CustomBusinessDay` and specified the holidays using `USFederalHolidayCalendar`. The resulting calculation now takes into account Labor Day not being a business day and returns the correct date of `2014-09-02`.

Normalizing timestamps using time zones

Time zone management can be one of the most complicated issues to deal with when working with time-series data. Data is often collected in different systems across the globe using local time, and at some point, it will require coordination with data collected in other time zones.

Fortunately, pandas provides rich support for working with timestamps in different time zones. Under the covers, pandas utilizes the `pytz` and `dateutil` libraries to manage the time zone operations. The `dateutil` support is new as of pandas 0.14.1 and currently only supported for fixed offset and tzfile zones. The default library used by pandas is `pytz`, with support for `dateutil` provided for compatibility with other applications.

pandas objects that are time zone-aware support a `.tz` property. By default, pandas objects that are time zone-aware do not utilize a `timezone` object for purposes of efficiency. The following gets the current time and demonstrates that there is no time zone information by default:

```
In [58]:
    # get the current local time and demonstrate there is no
    # timezone info by default
```

```
now = pd.Timestamp('now')
now, now.tz is None
```

Out[58]:

```
(Timestamp('2015-03-06 11:07:51.687326'), True)
```

 This demonstrates that pandas treats `Timestamp("now")` as UTC by default but without time zone data. This is a good default, but be aware of this. In general, I find that if you are ever collecting data based on the time that will be stored for later access, or collected from multiple data sources, it is best to always localize to UTC.

Likewise, `DatetimeIndex` and its `Timestamp` objects will not have associated time zone information by default:

In [59]:

```
# default DatetimeIndex and its Timestamps do not have
# time zone information
rng = pd.date_range('3/6/2012 00:00', periods=15, freq='D')
rng.tz is None, rng[0].tz is None
```

Out[59]:

```
(True, True)
```

A list of common time zone names can be retrieved as shown in the following example. If you do a lot with time zone data, these will become very familiar:

In [60]:

```
# import common timezones from pytz
from pytz import common_timezones
# report the first 5
common_timezones[:5]
```

Out[60]:

```
['Africa/Abidjan',
 'Africa/Accra',
 'Africa/Addis_Ababa',
 'Africa/Algiers',
 'Africa/Asmara']
```

The local UTC time can be found using the following, which utilizes the
`.tz_localize()` method of `Timestamp` passing the `'UTC'` method:

```
In [61]:
    # get now, and now localized to UTC
    now = Timestamp("now")
    local_now = now.tz_localize('UTC')
    now, local_now
```

```
Out[61]:
    (Timestamp('2015-03-06 11:07:51.750893'),
     Timestamp('2015-03-06 11:07:51.750893+0000', tz='UTC'))
```

Any `Timestamp` can be localized to a specific time zone by passing the time zone
name to `.tz_localize()`:

```
In [62]:
    # localize a timestamp to US/Mountain time zone
    tstamp = Timestamp('2014-08-01 12:00:00', tz='US/Mountain')
    tstamp
```

```
Out[62]:
    Timestamp('2014-08-01 12:00:00-0600', tz='US/Mountain')
```

`DatetimeIndex` can be created with a specific time zone using the `tz` parameter of
the `pd.date_range()` method:

```
In [63]:
    # create a DatetimeIndex using a time zone
    rng = pd.date_range('3/6/2012 00:00:00',
                        periods=10, freq='D', tz='US/Mountain')
    rng.tz, rng[0].tz
```

```
Out[63]:
    (<DstTzInfo 'US/Mountain' LMT-1 day, 17:00:00 STD>,
     <DstTzInfo 'US/Mountain' MST-1 day, 17:00:00 STD>)
```

It is also possible to construct other time zones explicitly. This model can give you more control over which time zone is used in .tz_localize(). The following creates two different timezone objects and localizes a Timestamp to each:

```
In [64]:
    # show use of time zone objects
    # need to reference pytz
    import pytz
    # create an object for two different time zones
    mountain_tz = pytz.timezone("US/Mountain")
    eastern_tz = pytz.timezone("US/Eastern")
    # apply each to 'now'
    mountain_tz.localize(now), eastern_tz.localize(now)
```

```
Out[64]:
    (Timestamp('2015-03-06 11:07:51.750893-0700', tz='US/Mountain'),
     Timestamp('2015-03-06 11:07:51.750893-0500', tz='US/Eastern'))
```

Operations on multiple time-series objects will be aligned by Timestamp in their index by taking into account the time zone information. To demonstrate, we will use the following, which creates two Series objects using the two DatetimeIndex objects, each with the same start, periods, and frequency but using different time zones:

```
In [65]:
    # create two Series, same start, same periods, same frequencies,
    # each with a different time zone
    s_mountain = Series(np.arange(0, 5),
                        index=pd.date_range('2014-08-01',
                                            periods=5, freq="H",
                                            tz='US/Mountain'))
    s_eastern = Series(np.arange(0, 5),
                       index=pd.date_range('2014-08-01',
                                           periods=5, freq="H",
                                           tz='US/Eastern'))
    s_mountain
```

```
Out[65]:
    2014-08-01 00:00:00-06:00    0
    2014-08-01 01:00:00-06:00    1
```

```
    2014-08-01 02:00:00-06:00      2
    2014-08-01 03:00:00-06:00      3
    2014-08-01 04:00:00-06:00      4
    Freq: H, dtype: int64
```

In [66]:

```
    s_eastern
```

Out[66]:

```
    2014-08-01 00:00:00-04:00      0
    2014-08-01 01:00:00-04:00      1
    2014-08-01 02:00:00-04:00      2
    2014-08-01 03:00:00-04:00      3
    2014-08-01 04:00:00-04:00      4
    Freq: H, dtype: int64
```

The following demonstrates the alignment of these two Series objects by time zone by adding the two together:

In [67]:

```
    # add the two Series
    # This only results in three items being aligned
    s_eastern + s_mountain
```

Out[67]:

```
    2014-08-01 04:00:00+00:00      NaN
    2014-08-01 05:00:00+00:00      NaN
    2014-08-01 06:00:00+00:00        2
    2014-08-01 07:00:00+00:00        4
    2014-08-01 08:00:00+00:00        6
    2014-08-01 09:00:00+00:00      NaN
    2014-08-01 10:00:00+00:00      NaN
    Freq: H, dtype: float64
```

Once a time zone is assigned to an object, that object can be converted to another time zone using the `tz.convert()` method:

```
In [68]:
    # convert s1 from US/Eastern to US/Pacific
    s_pacific = s_eastern.tz_convert("US/Pacific")
    s_pacific
```

```
Out[68]:
    2014-07-31 21:00:00-07:00    0
    2014-07-31 22:00:00-07:00    1
    2014-07-31 23:00:00-07:00    2
    2014-08-01 00:00:00-07:00    3
    2014-08-01 01:00:00-07:00    4
    Freq: H, dtype: int64
```

Now if we add `s_pacific` to `s_mountain`, the alignment will force the same result:

```
In [69]:
    # this will be the same result as s_eastern + s_mountain
    # as the time zones still get aligned to be the same
    s_mountain + s_pacific
```

```
Out[69]:
    2014-08-01 04:00:00+00:00    NaN
    2014-08-01 05:00:00+00:00    NaN
    2014-08-01 06:00:00+00:00    2
    2014-08-01 07:00:00+00:00    4
    2014-08-01 08:00:00+00:00    6
    2014-08-01 09:00:00+00:00    NaN
    2014-08-01 10:00:00+00:00    NaN
    Freq: H, dtype: float64
```

Manipulating time-series data

We will now examine several common operations that are performed on time-series data. These operations entail realigning data, changing the frequency of the samples and their values, and calculating aggregate results on continuously moving subsets of the data to determine the behavior of the values in the data as time changes. We will examine each of the following:

- Shifting and lagging values to calculate percentage changes
- Changing the frequency of the data in the time series
- Up and down sampling of the intervals and values in the time series
- Performing rolling-window calculations

Shifting and lagging

A common operation on time-series data is to shift the values backward and forward in time. The pandas method for this is `.shift()`, which will shift values in `Series` or `DataFrame` a specified number of units of the index's frequency.

To demonstrate shifting, we will use the following `Series`. This `Series` has five values, is indexed by date starting at `2014-08-01`, and uses a daily frequency:

```
In [70]:
    # create a Series to work with
    np.random.seed(123456)
    ts = Series([1, 2, 2.5, 1.5, 0.5],
                pd.date_range('2014-08-01', periods=5))
    ts


Out[70]:
    2014-08-01    1.0
    2014-08-02    2.0
    2014-08-03    2.5
    2014-08-04    1.5
    2014-08-05    0.5
    Freq: D, dtype: float64
```

The following shifts the values forward by 1 day:

```
In [71]:
    # shift forward one day
    ts.shift(1)
```

```
Out[71]:
    2014-08-01    NaN
    2014-08-02    1.0
    2014-08-03    2.0
    2014-08-04    2.5
    2014-08-05    1.5
    Freq: D, dtype: float64
```

pandas has moved the values forward one unit of the index's frequency, which is one day. The index remains unchanged. There was no replacement data for 2014-08-01, so it is filled with NaN.

A lag is a shift in a negative direction. The following lags the Series by 2 days:

```
In [72]:
    # lag two days
    ts.shift(-2)
```

```
Out[72]:
    2014-08-01    2.5
    2014-08-02    1.5
    2014-08-03    0.5
    2014-08-04    NaN
    2014-08-05    NaN
    Freq: D, dtype: float64
```

Index labels 2014-08-04 and 2014-08-03 now have NaN values as there were no items to replace.

A common calculation that is performed using a shift is to calculate the percentage daily change in values. This can be performed by dividing a `Series` object by its values shifted by 1:

```
In [73]:
    # calculate daily percentage change
    ts / ts.shift(1)
```

```
Out[73]:
    2014-08-01          NaN
    2014-08-02     2.000000
    2014-08-03     1.250000
    2014-08-04     0.600000
    2014-08-05     0.333333
    Freq: D, dtype: float64
```

Shifts can be performed on different frequencies than that in the index. When this is performed, the index will be modified and the values remain the same. As an example, the following shifts the `Series` forward by one business day:

```
In [74]:
    # shift forward one business day
    ts.shift(1, freq="B")
```

```
Out[74]:
    2014-08-04     1.0
    2014-08-04     2.0
    2014-08-04     2.5
    2014-08-05     1.5
    2014-08-06     0.5
    dtype: float64
```

As another example, the following shifts forward by 5 hours:

```
In [75]:
    # shift forward five hours
    ts.tshift(5, freq="H")
```

```
Out[75]:
    2014-08-01 05:00:00     1.0
```

```
2014-08-02 05:00:00    2.0
2014-08-03 05:00:00    2.5
2014-08-04 05:00:00    1.5
2014-08-05 05:00:00    0.5
dtype: float64
```

A time series can also be shifted using `DateOffset`. The following code shifts the time series forward by 0.5 minutes:

```
In [76]:
    # shift using a DateOffset
    ts.shift(1, DateOffset(minutes=0.5))
```

```
Out[76]:
    2014-08-01 00:00:30    1.0
    2014-08-02 00:00:30    2.0
    2014-08-03 00:00:30    2.5
    2014-08-04 00:00:30    1.5
    2014-08-05 00:00:30    0.5
    dtype: float64
```

There is an alternative form of shifting provided by the `.tshift()` method. This method shifts the index labels by the specified units and a frequency specified by the `freq` parameter (which is required). The following code demonstrates this approach by adjusting the index by `-1` hour:

```
In [77]:
    # shift just the index values
    ts.tshift(-1, freq='H')
```

```
Out[77]:
    2014-07-31 23:00:00    1.0
    2014-08-01 23:00:00    2.0
    2014-08-02 23:00:00    2.5
    2014-08-03 23:00:00    1.5
    2014-08-04 23:00:00    0.5
    dtype: float64
```

Frequency conversion

Frequency data can be converted in pandas using the `.asfreq()` method of a time-series object, such as `Series` or `DataFrame`. When converting frequency, a new `Series` object with a new `DatatimeIndex` object will be created. The `DatetimeIndex` of the new `Series` object starts at the first `Timestamp` of the original and progresses at the given frequency until the last `Timestamp` of the original. Values will then be aligned into the new `Series`.

To demonstrate, we will use the following time series of consecutive incremental integers mapped into each hour of each day for August 2014:

```
In [78]:
    # create a Series of incremental values
    # index by hour through all of August 2014
    periods = 31 * 24
    hourly = Series(np.arange(0, periods),
                    pd.date_range('08-01-2014', freq="2H",
                                  periods = periods))

    hourly
```

```
Out[78]:
    2014-08-01 00:00:00    0
    2014-08-01 02:00:00    1
    2014-08-01 04:00:00    2
    ...
    2014-10-01 18:00:00    741
    2014-10-01 20:00:00    742
    2014-10-01 22:00:00    743
    Freq: 2H, Length: 744
```

As an example, the following converts this time series to a daily frequency using `.asfreq('D')`:

```
In [79]:
    # convert to daily frequency
    # many items will be dropped due to alignment
    daily = hourly.asfreq('D')
```

```
    daily
```

Out[79]:

```
    2014-08-01      0
    2014-08-02     12
    2014-08-03     24
    ...
    2014-09-29    708
    2014-09-30    720
    2014-10-01    732
    Freq: D, Length: 62
```

As data was aligned to the new daily time series from the hourly time series, only values matching the exact days were copied.

If we convert this result back to an hourly frequency, we will see that many of the values are NaN:

In [80]:

```
    # convert back to hourly.  Results in many NaNs
    # as the new index has many labels that do not
    # align with the source
    daily.asfreq('H')
```

Out[80]:

```
    2014-08-01 00:00:00      0
    2014-08-01 01:00:00    NaN
    2014-08-01 02:00:00    NaN
    ...
    2014-09-30 22:00:00    NaN
    2014-09-30 23:00:00    NaN
    2014-10-01 00:00:00    732
    Freq: H, Length: 1465
```

The new index has Timestamp objects at hourly intervals, so only the timestamps at exact days align with the daily time series, resulting in 670 NaN values.

This default behavior can be changed using the method parameter of the .asfreq() method. This value can be used for forward fill, reverse fill, or to pad the NaN values.

The ffill method will forward fill the last known value (pad also does the same):

```
In [81]:
    # forward fill values
    daily.asfreq('H', method='ffill')
```

```
Out[81]:
    2014-08-01 00:00:00    0
    2014-08-01 01:00:00    0
    2014-08-01 02:00:00    0

    ...

    2014-09-30 22:00:00    720
    2014-09-30 23:00:00    720
    2014-10-01 00:00:00    732
    Freq: H, Length: 1465
```

The bfill method will back fill values from the next known value:

```
In [82]:
    daily.asfreq('H', method='bfill')
```

```
Out[82]:
    2014-08-01 00:00:00    0
    2014-08-01 01:00:00    12
    2014-08-01 02:00:00    12

    ...

    2014-09-30 22:00:00    732
    2014-09-30 23:00:00    732
    2014-10-01 00:00:00    732
    Freq: H, Length: 1465
```

Up and down resampling

Frequency conversion provides a basic way to convert the index in a time series to another frequency. Data in the new time series is aligned with the old data and can result in many NaN values. This can be partially solved using a fill method, but that is limited in its capabilities to fill with appropriate information.

Resampling differs in that it does not perform a pure alignment. The values placed in the new series can use the same forward and reverse fill options, but they can also be specified using other pandas-provided algorithms or with your own functions.

To demonstrate resampling, we will use the following time series, which represents a random walk of values over a 5-day period:

```
In [83]:
    # calculate a random walk five days long at one second intervals
    # these many items will be needed
    count = 24 * 60 * 60 * 5
    # create a series of values
    np.random.seed(123456)
    values = np.random.randn(count)
    ws = pd.Series(values)
    # calculate the walk
    walk = ws.cumsum()
    # patch the index
    walk.index = pd.date_range('2014-08-01', periods=count, freq="S")
    walk
```

```
Out[83]:
    2014-08-01 00:00:00      0.469112
    2014-08-01 00:00:01      0.186249
    2014-08-01 00:00:02     -1.322810
    ...
    2014-08-05 23:59:57    455.202981
    2014-08-05 23:59:58    454.947362
    2014-08-05 23:59:59    456.191430
    Freq: S, Length: 432000
```

Resampling in pandas is accomplished using the `.resample()` method, by passing it a new frequency. To demonstrate this the following resamples our by-the-second data to by-the-minute. This is a downsampling as the result has a lower frequency and results in less values:

```
In [84]:
    # resample to minute intervals
    walk.resample("1Min")
```

```
Out[84]:
    2014-08-01 00:00:00     -8.718220
    2014-08-01 00:01:00    -15.239213
    2014-08-01 00:02:00     -9.179315
    ...
    2014-08-05 23:57:00    450.078149
    2014-08-05 23:58:00    444.637806
    2014-08-05 23:59:00    453.837417
    Freq: T, Length: 7200
```

Notice that the first value is -8.718220 whereas the original data had a value of 0.469112. A frequency conversion would have left this value at -8.718220. This is because a resampling does not copy data through alignment. A resampling will actually split the data into buckets of data based on new periods and then apply a particular operation to the data in each bucket. The default scenario is to calculate the mean of each bucket. This can be verified with the following, which slices the first minute of data from the walk and calculates its mean:

```
In [85]:
    # calculate the mean of the first minute of the walk
    walk['2014-08-01 00:00'].mean()
```

```
Out[85]:
    -8.7182200528326437
```

In downsampling, as the existing data is put into buckets based on the new intervals, there can often be a question of what values are on each end of the bucket. As an example, should the first interval in the previous resampling be from 2014-08-01 00:00:00 through 2014-08-01 23:59:59, or should it end at 2014-08-04 00:00:00 but start at 2014-08-03 23:59:59?

The default is the former, and it is referred to as a left close. To other scenario that excludes the left value and includes the right is a right close and can be performed by using the `close='right'` parameter. The following demonstrates this; notice the slight difference in the intervals and values:

```
In [86]:
    # use a right close
    walk.resample("1Min", closed='right')
```

```
Out[86]:
    2014-07-31 23:59:00      0.469112
    2014-08-01 00:00:00     -8.907477
    2014-08-01 00:01:00    -15.280685
    ...
    2014-08-05 23:57:00    450.039159
    2014-08-05 23:58:00    444.631719
    2014-08-05 23:59:00    453.955377
    Freq: T, Length: 7201
```

The decision about whether to use a right or left close is really up to you and your data modeling, but pandas gives you the option.

The specific method that is applied to each group of samples can be specified using the how parameter. As an example, the following takes the first value of each bucket:

```
In [87]:
    # take the first value of each bucket
    walk.resample("1Min", how='first')
```

```
Out[87]:
    2014-08-01 00:00:00      0.469112
    2014-08-01 00:01:00    -10.886314
    2014-08-01 00:02:00    -13.374656
    ...
    2014-08-05 23:57:00    449.582419
    2014-08-05 23:58:00    447.243014
    2014-08-05 23:59:00    446.877810
    Freq: T, Length: 7200
```

The how parameter can be supplied the name of any NumPy array function that takes an array and produces aggregated values as well as any function you create on your own.

To demonstrate upsampling, we will resample the walk to minutes and then back to seconds:

```
In [88]:
    # resample to 1 minute intervals, then back to 1 sec
    bymin = walk.resample("1Min")
    bymin.resample('S')

Out[88]:
    2014-08-01 00:00:00    -8.71822
    2014-08-01 00:00:01          NaN
    2014-08-01 00:00:02          NaN
    ...
    2014-08-05 23:58:58          NaN
    2014-08-05 23:58:59          NaN
    2014-08-05 23:59:00    453.837417
    Freq: S, Length: 431941
```

The upsampling created the index values for the second-by-second data but inserted NaN values by default. This default behavior can be modified using the fill_method parameter. We saw this when changing frequency with the options of forward and backward filling. These are also available with resampling. The following demonstrates how to use the forward fill:

```
In [89]:
    # resample to 1 second intervals using forward fill
    bymin.resample("S", fill_method="bfill")

Out[89]:
    2014-08-01 00:00:00     -8.718220
    2014-08-01 00:00:01    -15.239213
    2014-08-01 00:00:02    -15.239213
    ...
    2014-08-05 23:58:58    453.837417
    2014-08-05 23:58:59    453.837417
    2014-08-05 23:59:00    453.837417
    Freq: S, Length: 431941
```

It is also possible to interpolate the missing values using the `.interpolate()` method on the result. This will calculate a linear interpolation between the values existing in the result for all of the NaN values created during the resampling:

```
In [90]:
    # demonstrate interpolating the NaN values
    interpolated = bymin.resample("S").interpolate()
    interpolated
```

```
Out[90]:
    2014-08-01 00:00:00    -8.718220
    2014-08-01 00:00:01    -8.826903
    2014-08-01 00:00:02    -8.935586
    ...
    2014-08-05 23:58:58    453.530764
    2014-08-05 23:58:59    453.684090
    2014-08-05 23:59:00    453.837417
    Freq: S, Length: 431941
```

pandas provides a very convenient resampling method referred to as open, high, low, and close, which is specified by the `how='ohlc'` parameter. The following example takes our second-by-second data and calculates hour-by-hour `ohlc` values:

```
In [91]:
    # show ohlc resampling
    ohlc = walk.resample("H", how="ohlc")
    ohlc
```

```
Out[91]:
                              open         high         low         close
    2014-08-01 00:00:00     0.469112     0.469112   -67.873166    -2.922520
    2014-08-01 01:00:00    -3.374321    23.793007   -56.585154   -55.101543
    2014-08-01 02:00:00   -54.276885     5.232441   -87.809456     1.913276
    2014-08-01 03:00:00     0.260576    17.124638   -65.820652   -38.530620
    2014-08-01 04:00:00   -38.436581     3.537231  -109.805294   -61.014553
    ...                        ...          ...          ...          ...
    2014-08-05 19:00:00   437.652077   550.408942   430.549178   494.471788
    2014-08-05 20:00:00   496.539759   510.371745   456.365565   476.505765
```

```
2014-08-05 21:00:00   476.025498   506.952877   425.472410   498.547578
2014-08-05 22:00:00   497.941355   506.599652   411.119919   443.925832
2014-08-05 23:00:00   443.017962   489.083657   426.062444   456.191430


[120 rows x 4 columns]
```

Time-series moving-window operations

pandas provides a number of functions to compute moving (also known as rolling) statistics. In a rolling window, pandas computes the statistic on a window of data represented by a particular period of time. The window is then rolled along a certain interval, and the statistic is continually calculated on each window as long as the window fits within the dates of the time series.

pandas provides direct support for rolling windows with the following functions:

Function	Description
rolling_mean	The mean of values in the window
rolling_std	The standard deviation of values in the window
rolling_var	The variance of values
rolling_min	The minimum of values in the window
rolling_max	The maximum of values in the window
rolling_cov	The covariance of values
rolling_quantile	Moving window score at percentile/sample quantile
rolling_corr	The correlation of values in the window
rolling_median	The median of values in the window
rolling_sum	The sum of values in the window
rolling_apply	The application of a user function to values in the window
rolling_count	The number of non-NaN values in a window
rolling_skew	The skewedness of the values in the window
rolling_kurt	The kurtosis of values in the window

As a practical example, a rolling mean is commonly used to smooth out short-term fluctuations and highlight longer-term trends in data and is used quite commonly in financial time-series analysis.

To demonstrate, we will calculate a rolling mean with a window of 5 on the first minute of the random walk created earlier in the chapter. The following calculates this and then plots the result against the raw data to demonstrate the smoothing created by the rolling mean:

```
In [92]:
    first_minute = walk['2014-08-01 00:00']
    # calculate a rolling mean window of 5 periods
    pd.rolling_mean(first_minute, 5).plot()
    # plot it against the raw data
    first_minute.plot()
    # add a legend
    plt.legend(labels=['Rolling Mean', 'Raw']);
```

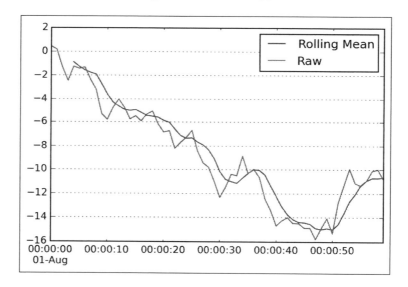

 The generation of charts will be covered in more detail in *Chapter 11, Visualization*.

It can be seen how `rolling_mean` provides a smoother representation of the underlying data. A larger window will create less variance, and smaller windows will create more (until the window size is 1, which will be identical to the original series).

The following demonstrates the rolling mean with windows of 2, 5, and 10 plotted against the original series:

```
In [93]:
    # demonstrate the difference between 2, 5 and
    # 10 interval rolling windows
    h1w = walk['2014-08-01 00:00']
    h1w.plot()
    pd.rolling_mean(h1w, 2).plot()
    pd.rolling_mean(h1w, 5).plot()
    pd.rolling_mean(h1w, 10).plot()
    plt.legend(labels=['Raw', '2-interval RM',
                       '5-interval RM',
                       '10-interval RM']);
```

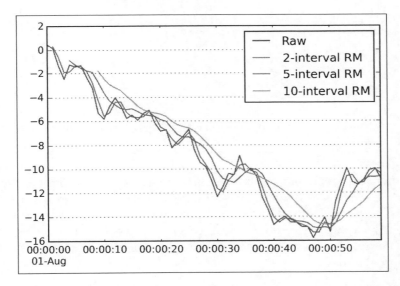

Note that the larger the window, the more data is missing at the beginning of the curve. A window of size n requires n data points before the measure can be calculated and hence the gap in the beginning of the plot.

Any function can be applied via a rolling window using the pd.rolling_apply function. The supplied function will be passed an array of values in the window and should return a single value, which pandas will aggregate with these results into a time series.

To demonstrate, the following code calculates the mean average deviation, which gives you a feel of how far all values in the sample are from the overall mean on an average:

```
In [94]:
    # calculate mean average deviation with window of 5 intervals
    mean_abs_dev = lambda x: np.fabs(x - x.mean()).mean()
    pd.rolling_apply(h1w, 5, mean_abs_dev).plot();
```

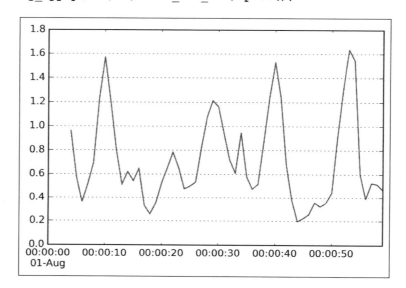

An expanding window mean can be calculated using a slight variant of the use of the `pd.rolling_mean` function that repeatedly calculates the mean by always starting with the first value in the time series and for each iteration increases the window size by one. An expanding window mean will be more stable (less responsive) than a rolling window, because as the size of the window increases, the less the impact of the next value will be:

```
In [95]:
    # calculate an expanding rolling mean
    expanding_mean = lambda x: pd.rolling_mean(x, len(x),
                                                min_periods=1)
    h1w.plot()
    pd.expanding_mean(h1w).plot()
    plt.legend(labels=['Expanding mean', 'Raw']);
```

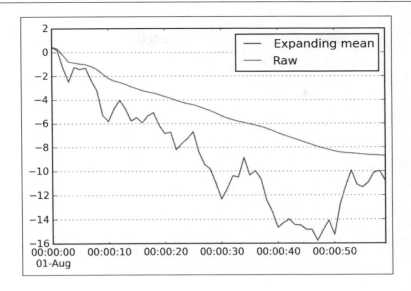

Summary

In this chapter, we examined many of the ways to represent dates and times and also saw how to represent time-series data and perform various analyses upon these series. There is actually quite a bit of detail in these tasks and the capabilities that are provided by pandas, and it is almost impossible to summarize it in one simple chapter. This chapter provided a core set of examples that can get you working quickly with these concepts.

In the remaining two chapters of this book, we will look more into both visualization of data and working with real examples of data that also take a look at analysis of time-series data from a different perspective by demonstrating how it can be applied to analyzing financial information.

11
Visualization

Humans are visual creatures and have evolved to be able to quickly notice the meaning when information is presented in certain ways that cause the wiring in our brains to have the light bulb of insight turn on. This "aha" can often be performed very quickly, given the correct tools, instead of through tedious numerical analysis.

Tools for data analysis, such as pandas, take advantage of being able to quickly and iteratively provide the user to take data, process it, and quickly visualize the meaning. Often, much of what you will do with pandas is massaging your data to be able to visualize it in one or more visual patterns, in an attempt to get to "aha" by simply glancing at the visual representation of the information.

This chapter will cover common patterns in visualizing data with pandas. It is not meant to be exhaustive in coverage. The goal is to give you the required knowledge to create beautiful data visualizations on pandas data quickly and with very few lines of code.

This chapter is presented in three sections. The first introduces you to the general concepts of programming visualizations with pandas, emphasizing the process of creating time-series charts. We will also dive into techniques to label axes and create legends, colors, line styles, and markets.

The second part of the chapter will then focus on the many types of data visualizations commonly used in pandas programs and data sciences, including:

- Bar plots
- Histograms
- Box and whisker charts
- Area plots
- Scatter plots
- Density plots
- Scatter plot matrixes
- Heatmaps

The final section will briefly look at creating composite plots by dividing plots into subparts and drawing multiple plots within a single graphical canvas.

Setting up the IPython notebook

The first step to plot with pandas data, is to first include the appropriate libraries, primarily, matplotlib. The examples in this chapter will all be based on the following imports, where the plotting capabilities are from matplotlib, which will be aliased with `plt`:

In [1]:

```
# import pandas, numpy and datetime
import numpy as np
import pandas as pd

# needed for representing dates and times
import datetime
from datetime import datetime

# Set some pandas options for controlling output
pd.set_option('display.notebook_repr_html', False)
pd.set_option('display.max_columns', 10)
pd.set_option('display.max_rows', 10)

# used for seeding random number sequences
```

```
seedval = 111111

# matplotlib
import matplotlib as mpl
# matplotlib plotting functions
import matplotlib.pyplot as plt
# we want our plots inline
%matplotlib inline
```

The `%matplotlib inline` line is the statement that tells matplotlib to produce inline graphics. This will make the resulting graphs appear either inside your IPython notebook or IPython session.

All examples will seed the random number generator with `111111`, so that the graphs remain the same every time they run, and so that the reader can reproduce the same charts as in the book.

Plotting basics with pandas

The pandas library itself performs data manipulation. It does not provide data visualization capabilities itself. The visualization of data in pandas data structures is handed off by pandas to other robust visualization libraries that are part of the Python ecosystem, most commonly, matplotlib, which is what we will use in this chapter.

All of the visualizations and techniques covered in this chapter can be performed without pandas. These techniques are all available independently in matplotlib. pandas tightly integrates with matplotlib, and by doing this, it is very simple to go directly from pandas data to a matplotlib visualization without having to work with intermediate forms of data.

pandas does not draw the graphs, but it will tell matplotlib how to draw graphs using pandas data, taking care of many details on your behalf, such as automatically selecting `Series` for plots, labeling axes, creating legends, and defaulting color. Therefore, you often have to write very little code to create stunning visualizations.

Creating time-series charts with .plot()

One of the most common data visualizations created, is of the time-series data. Visualizing a time series in pandas is as simple as calling `.plot()` on a `DataFrame` or `Series` object. To demonstrate, the following creates a time series representing a random walk of values over time, akin to the movements in the price of a stock:

```
In [2]:
    # generate a random walk time-series
    np.random.seed(seedval)
    s = pd.Series(np.random.randn(1096),
                index=pd.date_range('2012-01-01',
                                    '2014-12-31'))
    walk_ts = s.cumsum()
    # this plots the walk - just that easy :)
    walk_ts.plot();
```

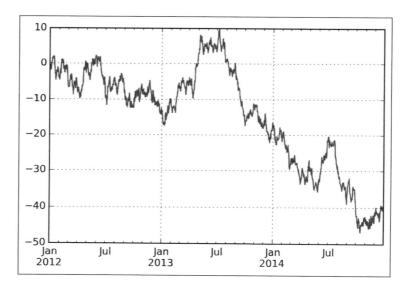

 The ; character at the end suppresses the generation of an IPython out tag, as well as the trace information.

It is a common practice to execute the following statement to produce plots that have a richer visual style. This sets a pandas option that makes resulting plots have a shaded background and what is considered a slightly more pleasing style:

```
In [3]:
    # tells pandas plots to use a default style
    # which has a background fill
    pd.options.display.mpl_style = 'default'
    walk_ts.plot();
```

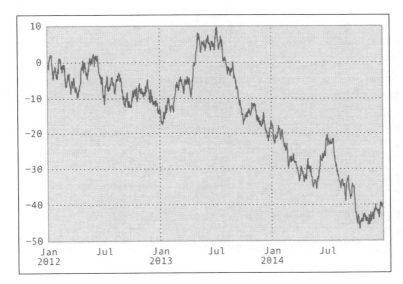

The .plot() method on pandas objects is a wrapper function around the matplotlib libraries' plot() function. It makes plots of pandas data very easy to create. It is coded to know how to use the data in the pandas objects to create the appropriate plots for the data, handling many of the details of plot generation, such as selecting series, labeling, and axes generation. In this situation, the .plot() method determines that as Series contains dates for its index that the *x* axis should be formatted as dates and it selects a default color for the data.

This example used a single series and the result would be the same using DataFrame with a single column. As an example, the following produces the same graph with one small difference. It has added a legend to the graph, which charts by default, generated from a DataFrame object, will have a legend even if there is only one series of data:

```
In [4]:
    # a DataFrame with a single column will produce
```

```
# the same plot as plotting the Series it is created from
walk_df = pd.DataFrame(walk_ts)
walk_df.plot();
```

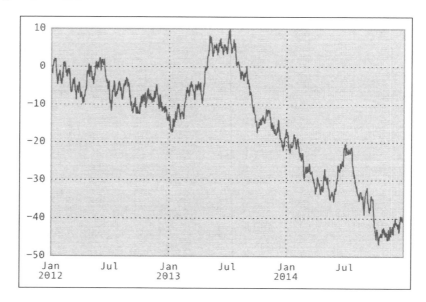

The `.plot()` function is smart enough to know whether `DataFrame` has multiple columns, and it should create multiple lines/series in the plot and include a key for each, and also select a distinct color for each line. This is demonstrated with the following example:

```
In [5]:
    # generate two random walks, one in each of
    # two columns in a DataFrame
    np.random.seed(seedval)
    df = pd.DataFrame(np.random.randn(1096, 2),
                      index=walk_ts.index, columns=list('AB'))
    walk_df = df.cumsum()
    walk_df.head()

Out [5]:
                    A          B
    2012-01-01  -1.878324   1.362367
```

```
2012-01-02  -2.804186   1.427261
2012-01-03  -3.241758   3.165368
2012-01-04  -2.750550   3.332685
2012-01-05  -1.620667   2.930017
```

In [6]:

```
# plot the DataFrame, which will plot a line
# for each column, with a legend
walk_df.plot();
```

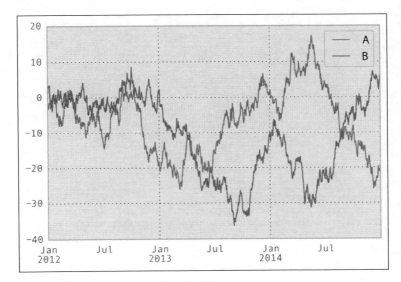

If you want to use one column of DataFrame as the labels on the *x* axis of the plot instead of the index labels, you can use the *x* and *y* parameters to the .plot() method, giving the *x* parameter the name of the column to use as the *x* axis and *y* parameter the names of the columns to be used as data in the plot. The following recreates the random walks as columns 'A' and 'B', creates a column 'C' with sequential values starting with 0, and uses these values as the *x* axis labels and the 'A' and 'B' columns values as the two plotted lines:

In [7]:

```
# copy the walk
df2 = walk_df.copy()
# add a column C which is 0 .. 1096
```

```
df2['C'] = pd.Series(np.arange(0, len(df2)), index=df2.index)
# instead of dates on the x axis, use the 'C' column,
# which will label the axis with 0..1000
df2.plot(x='C', y=['A', 'B']);
```

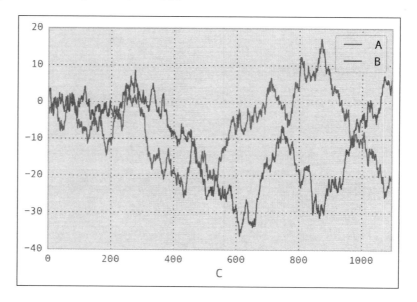

 The .plot() functions, provided by pandas for the Series and DataFrame objects, take care of most of the details of generating plots. However, if you want to modify characteristics of the generated plots beyond their capabilities, you can directly use the matplotlib functions or one of more of the many optional parameters of the .plot() method.

Adorning and styling your time-series plot

The built-in .plot() method has many options that you can use to change the content in the plot. We will cover several of the common options used in most plots.

Adding a title and changing axes labels

The title of the chart can be set using the title parameter of the .plot() method. Axes labels are not set with .plot(), but by directly using the plt.ylabel() and plt.xlabel() functions after calling .plot():

In [8]:

```
# create a time-series chart with a title and specific
```

```
# x and y axes labels

# the title is set in the .plot() method as a parameter
walk_df.plot(title='Title of the Chart')
# explicitly set the x and y axes labels after the .plot()
plt.xlabel('Time')
plt.ylabel('Money');
```

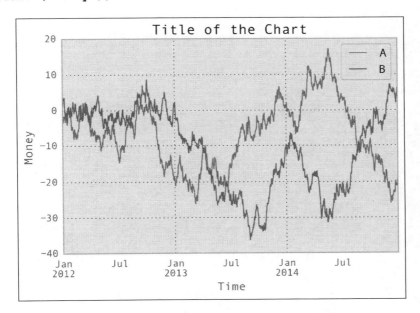

The labels in this plot were added after the call to .plot(). A question that may be asked, is that if the plot is generated in the call to .plot(), then how are they changed on the plot?

The answer, is that plots in matplotlib are not displayed until either .show() is called on the plot or the code reaches the end of the execution and returns to the interactive prompt. At either of these points, any plot generated by plot commands will be flushed out to the display. In this example, although .plot() is called, the plot is not generated until the IPython notebook code section finishes completion, so the changes for labels and title are added to the plot.

Specifying the legend content and position

To change the text used in the legend (the default is the column name from
DataFrame), you can use the ax object returned from the .plot() method to modify
the text using its .legend() method. The ax object is an AxesSubplot object, which
is a representation of the elements of the plot, that can be used to change various
aspects of the plot before it is generated:

```
In [9]:
    # change the legend items to be different
    # from the names of the columns in the DataFrame
    ax = walk_df.plot(title='Title of the Chart')
    # this sets the legend labels
    ax.legend(['1', '2']);
```

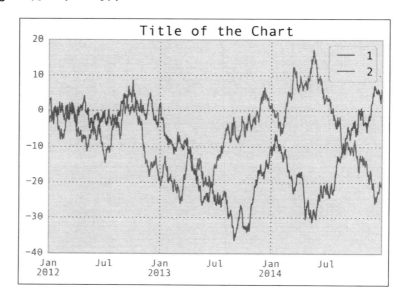

The location of the legend can be set using the loc parameter of the .legend()
method. By default, pandas sets the location to 'best', which tells matplotlib to
examine the data and determine the best place to put the legend. However, you can
also specify any of the following to position the legend more specifically (you can use
either the string or the numeric code):

Text	Code
'best'	0
'upper right'	1

Text	Code
'upper left'	2
'lower left'	3
'lower right'	4
'right'	5
'center left'	6
'center right'	7
'lower center'	8
'upper center'	9
'center'	10

In our last chart, the 'best' option actually had the legend overlap the line from one of the series. We can reposition the legend in the upper center of the chart, which will prevent this and create a better chart of this data:

In [10]:

```
# change the position of the legend
ax = walk_df.plot(title='Title of the Chart')
# put the legend in the upper center of the chart
ax.legend(['1', '2'], loc='upper center');
```

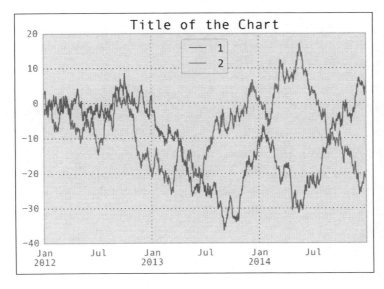

Legends can also be turned off with the `legend` parameter:

```
In [11]:
    # omit the legend by using legend=False
    walk_df.plot(title='Title of the Chart', legend=False);
```

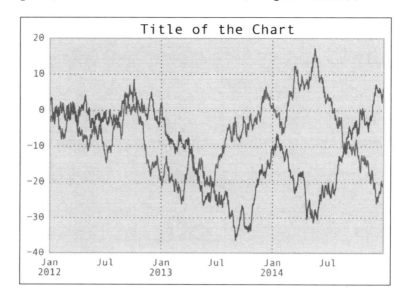

 There are more possibilities for locating and actually controlling the content of the legend, but we leave that for you to do some more experimentation.

Specifying line colors, styles, thickness, and markers

pandas automatically sets the colors of each series on any chart. If you would like to specify your own color, you can do so by supplying style code to the style parameter of the plot function. pandas has a number of built-in single character code for colors, several of which are listed here:

- `b`: Blue
- `g`: Green
- `r`: Red
- `c`: Cyan
- `m`: Magenta

- y: Yellow
- k: Black
- w: White

It is also possible to specify the color using a hexadecimal RGB code of the `#RRGGBB` format. To demonstrate both options, the following example sets the color of the first series to green using a single digit code and the second series to red using the hexadecimal code:

```
In [12]:
    # change the line colors on the plot
    # use character code for the first line,
    # hex RGB for the second
    walk_df.plot(style=['g', '#FF0000']);
```

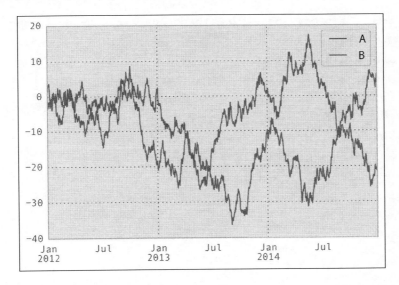

Line styles can be specified using a line style code. These can be used in combination with the color style codes, following the color code. The following are examples of several useful line style codes:

- `'-'` = solid
- `'--'` = dashed
- `':'` = dotted
- `'-.'` = dot-dashed
- `'.'` = points

The following plot demonstrates these five line styles by drawing five data series, each with one of these styles. Notice how each style item now consists of a color symbol and a line style code:

```
In [13]:
    # show off different line styles
    t = np.arange(0., 5., 0.2)
    legend_labels = ['Solid', 'Dashed', 'Dotted',
                    'Dot-dashed', 'Points']
    line_style = pd.DataFrame({0 : t,
                                1 : t**1.5,
                                2 : t**2.0,
                                3 : t**2.5,
                                4 : t**3.0})
    # generate the plot, specifying color and line style for each line
    ax = line_style.plot(style=['r-', 'g--', 'b:', 'm-.', 'k:'])
    # set the legend
    ax.legend(legend_labels, loc='upper left');
```

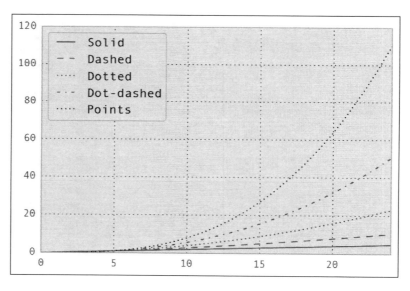

The thickness of lines can be specified using the `lw` parameter of `.plot()`. This can be passed a thickness for multiple lines, by passing a list of widths, or a single width that is applied to all lines. The following redraws the graph with a line width of `3`, making the lines a little more pronounced:

```
In [14]:
    # regenerate the plot, specifying color and line style
    # for each line and a line width of 3 for all lines
    ax = line_style.plot(style=['r-', 'g--', 'b:', 'm-.', 'k:'], lw=3)
    ax.legend(legend_labels, loc='upper left');
```

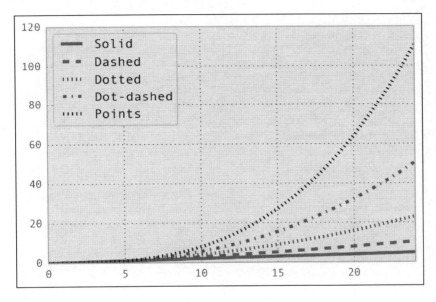

Markers on a line can also be specified using abbreviations in the style code. There are quite a few marker types provided and you can see them all at http://matplotlib. org/api/markers_api.html. We will examine five of them in the following chart by having each series use a different marker from the following: circles, stars, triangles, diamonds, and points. The type of marker is also specified using a code at the end of the style:

```
In [15]:
    # redraw, adding markers to the lines
    ax = line_style.plot(style=['r-o', 'g--^', 'b:*',
                                'm-.D', 'k:o'], lw=3)
    ax.legend(legend_labels, loc='upper left');
```

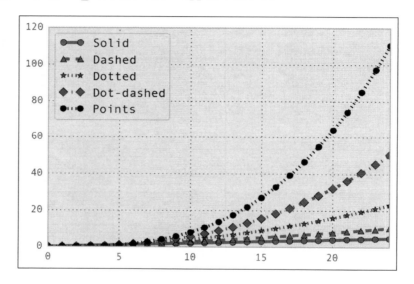

Specifying tick mark locations and tick labels

Every plot we have seen to this point, has used the default tick marks and labels on the ticks that pandas decides are appropriate for the plot. These can also be customized using various matplotlib functions.

We will demonstrate how ticks are handled by first examining a simple `DataFrame`. We can retrieve the locations of the ticks that were generated on the *x* axis using the `plt.xticks()` method. This method returns two values, the location, and the actual labels:

```
In [16]:
    # a simple plot to use to examine ticks
    ticks_data = pd.DataFrame(np.arange(0,5))
    ticks_data.plot()
    ticks, labels = plt.xticks()
    ticks
```

```
Out [16]:
    array([ 0. ,   0.5,   1. ,   1.5,   2. ,   2.5,   3. ,   3.5,   4. ])
```

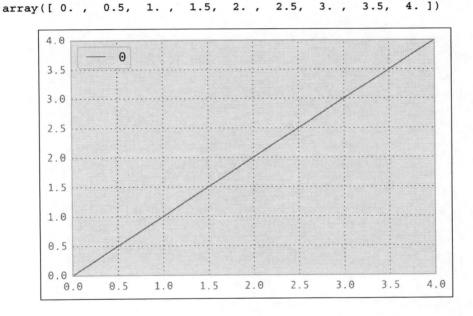

This array contains the locations of the ticks in units of the values along the *x* axis. pandas has decided that a range of 0 through 4 (the min and max) and an interval of 0.5 is appropriate. If we want to use other locations, we can provide these by passing them to `plt.xticks()` as a list. The following demonstrates these using even integers from `-1` to `5`, which will both change the extents of the axis, as well as remove non integral labels:

```
In [17]:
    # resize x axis to (-1, 5), and draw ticks
    # only at integer values
    ticks_data = pd.DataFrame(np.arange(0,5))
    ticks_data.plot()
    plt.xticks(np.arange(-1, 6));
```

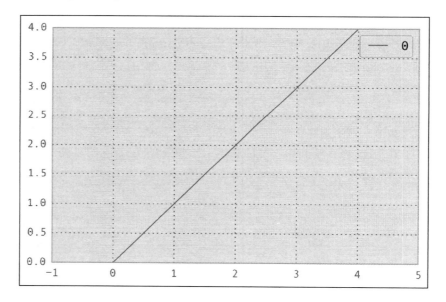

Also, we can specify new labels at these locations by passing them as the second parameter. Just as an example, we can change the *y* axis ticks and labels to integral values and consecutive alpha characters using the following:

```
In [18]:
    # rename y axis tick labels to A, B, C, D, and E
    ticks_data = pd.DataFrame(np.arange(0,5))
    ticks_data.plot()
    plt.yticks(np.arange(0, 5), list("ABCDE"));
```

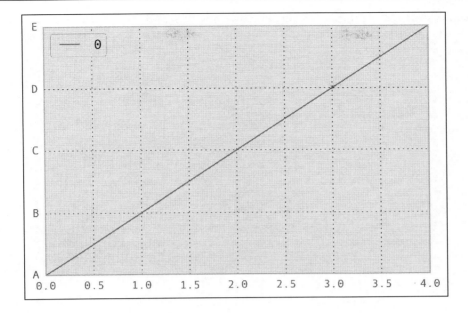

Formatting axes tick date labels using formatters

The formatting of axes labels whose underlying data types is datetime is performed using locators and formatters. Locators control the position of the ticks, and the formatters control the formatting of the labels.

To facilitate locating ticks and formatting labels based on dates, matplotlib provides several classes in maptplotlib.dates to help facilitate the process:

- MinuteLocator, HourLocator, DayLocator, WeekdayLocator, MonthLocator, and YearLocator: These are specific locators coded to determine where ticks for each type of date field will be found on the axis

- DateFormatter: This is a class that can be used to format date objects into labels on the axis

By default, the default locator and formatter are AutoDateLocator and AutoDateFormatter, respectively. You can change these by providing different objects to use the appropriate methods on the specific axis object.

To demonstrate, we will use a subset of the random walk data from earlier, which represents just the data from January through February of 2014. Plotting this gives us the following output:

```
In [19]:
    # plot January-February 2014 from the random walk
    walk_df.loc['2014-01':'2014-02'].plot();
```

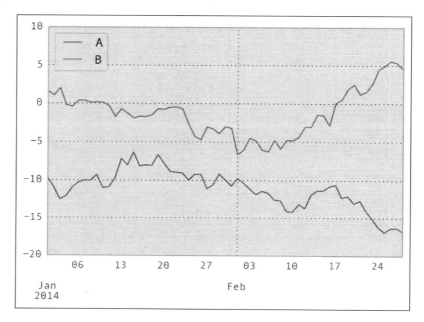

The labels on the *x* axis of this plot have two series of labels, the minor and the major. The minor labels in this plot contain the day of the month, and the major contains the year and month (the year only for the first month). We can set locators and formatters for each of the minor and major levels.

This will be demonstrated by changing the minor labels to be located at the Monday of each week and to contain the date and day of the week (right now, the chart uses weekly and only Friday's date—without the day name). On the major labels, we will use the monthly location and always include both the month name and the year:

```
In [20]:
    # this import styles helps us type less
```

```
from matplotlib.dates import WeekdayLocator, \
DateFormatter, MonthLocator

# plot Jan-Feb 2014
ax = walk_df.loc['2014-01':'2014-02'].plot()

# do the minor labels
weekday_locator = WeekdayLocator(byweekday=(0), interval=1)
ax.xaxis.set_minor_locator(weekday_locator)
ax.xaxis.set_minor_formatter(DateFormatter("%d\n%a"))

# do the major labels
ax.xaxis.set_major_locator(MonthLocator())
ax.xaxis.set_major_formatter(DateFormatter('\n\n\n%b\n%Y'));
```

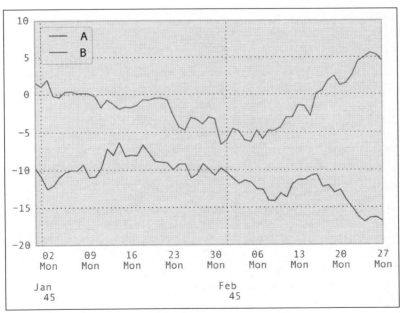

This is almost what we wanted. However, note that the year is being reported as **45**. This, unfortunately, seems to be an issue between pandas and the matplotlib representation of values for the year. The best reference I have on this is this following link from Stack Overflow (http://stackoverflow.com/ questions/12945971/pandas-timeseries-plot-setting-x-axis-major-and-minor-ticks-and-labels).

So, it appears to create a plot with custom-date-based labels, we need to avoid the pandas .plot() and need to kick all the way down to using matplotlib. Fortunately, this is not too hard. The following changes the code slightly and renders what we wanted:

In [21]:

```
# this gets around the pandas / matplotlib year issue
# need to reference the subset twice, so let's make a variable
walk_subset = walk_df['2014-01':'2014-02']

# this gets the plot so we can use it, we can ignore fig
fig, ax = plt.subplots()

# inform matplotlib that we will use the following as dates
# note we need to convert the index to a pydatetime series
ax.plot_date(walk_subset.index.to_pydatetime(), walk_subset, '-')

# do the minor labels
weekday_locator = WeekdayLocator(byweekday=(0), interval=1)
ax.xaxis.set_minor_locator(weekday_locator)
ax.xaxis.set_minor_formatter(DateFormatter('%d\n%a'))

# do the major labels
ax.xaxis.set_major_locator(MonthLocator())
ax.xaxis.set_major_formatter(DateFormatter('\n\n\n%b\n%Y'));
ax.xaxis.set_major_formatter(DateFormatter('\n\n\n%b\n%Y'));
```

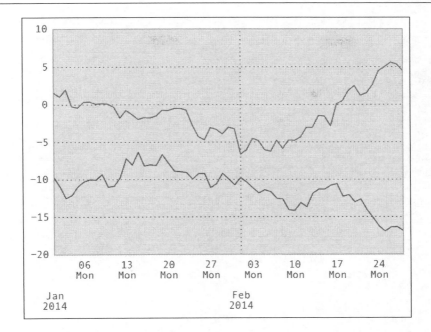

To add grid lines for the minor axes ticks, you can use the `.grid()` method of the x axis object of the plot, the first parameter specifying the lines to use and the second parameter specifying the minor or major set of ticks. The following replots this graph without the major grid line and with the minor grid lines:

```
In [22]:
    # this gets the plot so we can use it, we can ignore fig
    fig, ax = plt.subplots()

    # inform matplotlib that we will use the following as dates
    # note we need to convert the index to a pydatetime series
    ax.plot_date(walk_subset.index.to_pydatetime(), walk_subset, '-')

    # do the minor labels
    weekday_locator = WeekdayLocator(byweekday=(0), interval=1)
    ax.xaxis.set_minor_locator(weekday_locator)
    ax.xaxis.set_minor_formatter(DateFormatter('%d\n%a'))
    ax.xaxis.grid(True, "minor") # turn on minor tick grid lines
```

```
ax.xaxis.grid(False, "major") # turn off major tick grid lines

# do the major labels
ax.xaxis.set_major_locator(MonthLocator())
ax.xaxis.set_major_formatter(DateFormatter('\n\n\n%b\n%Y'));
```

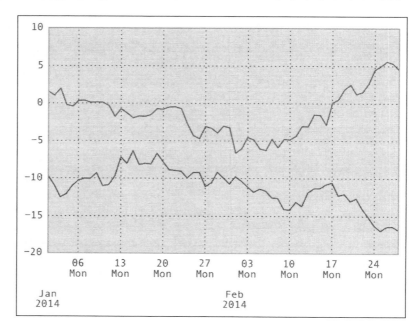

The last demonstration of formatting will use only the major labels but on a weekly basis and using a YYYY-MM-DD format. However, because these would overlap, we will specify that they should be rotated to prevent the overlap. This is done using the fig.autofmt_xdate() function:

In [23]:

```
# this gets the plot so we can use it, we can ignore fig
fig, ax = plt.subplots()

# inform matplotlib that we will use the following as dates
# note we need to convert the index to a pydatetime series
```

```
ax.plot_date(walk_subset.index.to_pydatetime(), walk_subset, '-')

ax.xaxis.grid(True, "major") # turn off major tick grid lines

# do the major labels
ax.xaxis.set_major_locator(weekday_locator)
ax.xaxis.set_major_formatter(DateFormatter('%Y-%m-%d'));

# informs to rotate date labels
fig.autofmt_xdate();
```

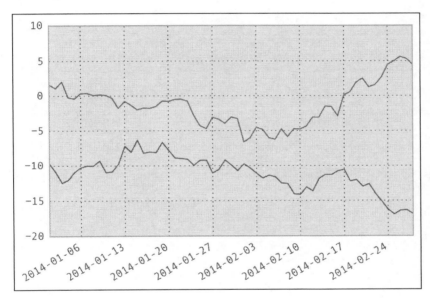

Common plots used in statistical analyses

Having seen how to create, lay out, and annotate time-series charts, we will now look at creating a number of charts, other than time series that are commonplace in presenting statistical information.

Bar plots

Bar plots are useful in order to visualize the relative differences in values of non time-series data. Bar plots can be created using the kind='bar' parameter of the .plot() method:

```
In [24]:
    # make a bar plot
    # create a small series of 10 random values centered at 0.0
    np.random.seed(seedval)
    s = pd.Series(np.random.rand(10) - 0.5)
    # plot the bar chart
    s.plot(kind='bar');
```

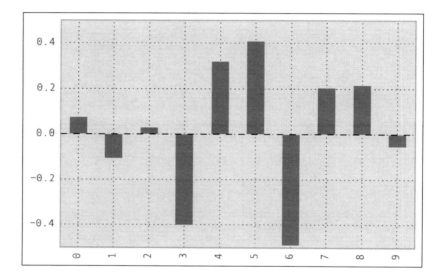

If the data being plotted consists of multiple columns, a multiple series bar plot will be created:

```
In [25]:
    # draw a multiple series bar chart
    # generate 4 columns of 10 random values
    np.random.seed(seedval)
    df2 = pd.DataFrame(np.random.rand(10, 4),
                       columns=['a', 'b', 'c', 'd'])
    # draw the multi-series bar chart
    df2.plot(kind='bar');
```

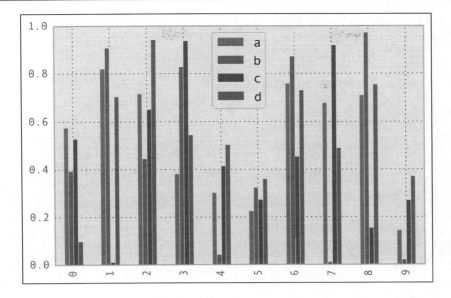

If you would prefer stacked bars, you can use the stacked parameter, setting it to True:

In [26]:

```
# horizontal stacked bar chart
df2.plot(kind='bar', stacked=True);
```

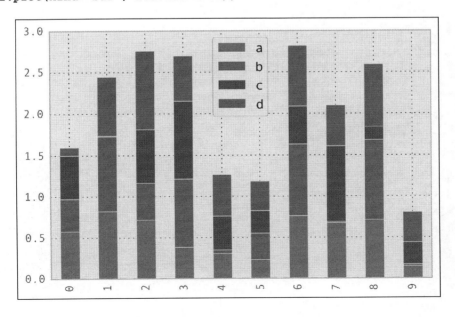

If you want the bars to be horizontally aligned, you can use `kind='barh'`:

In [27]:

```
# horizontal stacked bar chart
df2.plot(kind='barh', stacked=True);
```

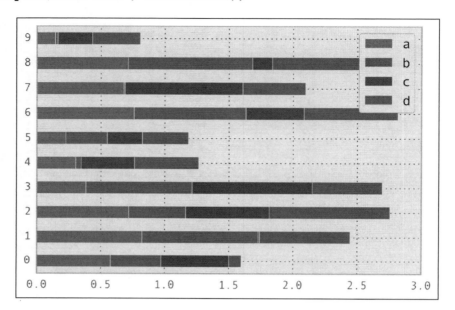

Histograms

Histograms are useful for visualizing distributions of data. The following shows you a histogram of generating 1000 values from the normal distribution:

In [28]:

```
# create a histogram
np.random.seed(seedval)
# 1000 random numbers
dfh = pd.DataFrame(np.random.randn(1000))
# draw the histogram
dfh.hist();
```

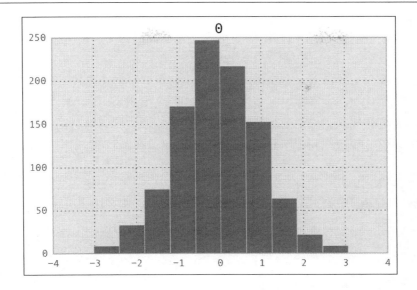

The resolution of a histogram can be controlled by specifying the number of bins to allocate to the graph. The default is 10, and increasing the number of bins gives finer detail to the histogram. The following increases the number of bins to `100`:

In [29]:

```
# histogram again, but with more bins
dfh.hist(bins = 100);
```

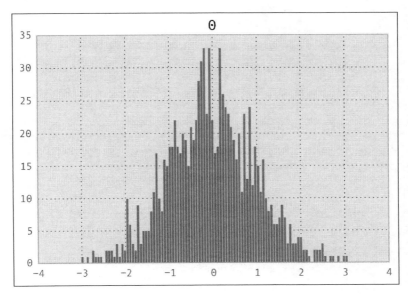

If the data has multiple series, the histogram function will automatically generate multiple histograms, one for each series:

```
In [30]:
    # generate a multiple histogram plot
    # create DataFrame with 4 columns of 1000 random values
    np.random.seed(seedval)
    dfh = pd.DataFrame(np.random.randn(1000, 4),
                       columns=['a', 'b', 'c', 'd'])
    # draw the chart.  There are four columns so pandas draws
    # four historgrams
    dfh.hist();
```

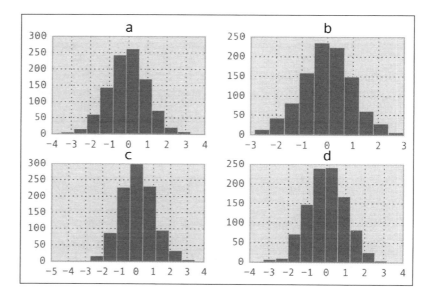

If you want to overlay multiple histograms on the same graph (to give a quick visual difference of distribution), you can call the `pyplot.hist()` function multiple times before `.show()` is called to render the chart:

```
In [31]:
    # directly use pyplot to overlay multiple histograms
    # generate two distributions, each with a different
    # mean and standard deviation
    np.random.seed(seedval)
```

```
x = [np.random.normal(3,1) for _ in range(400)]
y = [np.random.normal(4,2) for _ in range(400)]

# specify the bins (-10 to 10 with 100 bins)
bins = np.linspace(-10, 10, 100)

# generate plot x using plt.hist, 50% transparent
plt.hist(x, bins, alpha=0.5, label='x')
# generate plot y using plt.hist, 50% transparent
plt.hist(y, bins, alpha=0.5, label='y')
plt.legend(loc='upper right');
```

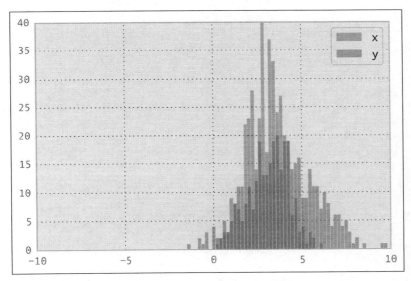

Box and whisker charts

Box plots come from descriptive statistics and are a useful way of graphically depicting the distributions of categorical data using quartiles. Each box represents the values between the first and third quartiles of the data with a line across the box at the median. Each whisker reaches out to demonstrate the extent to five interquartile ranges below and above the first and third quartiles:

```
In [32]:
    # create a box plot
```

```
# generate the series
np.random.seed(seedval)
dfb = pd.DataFrame(np.random.randn(10,5))
# generate the plot
dfb.boxplot(return_type='axes');
```

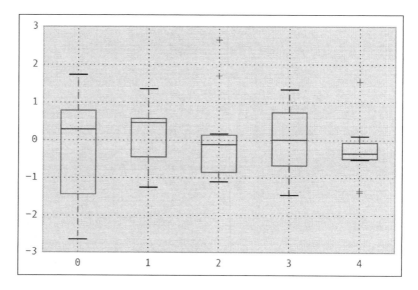

 There are ways to overlay dots and show outliers, but for
brevity, they will not be covered in this text.

Area plots

Area plots are used to represent cumulative totals over time, to demonstrate the
change in trends over time among related attributes. They can also be "stacked"
to demonstrate representative totals across all variables.

Area plots are generated by specifying `kind='area'`. A stacked area chart is
the default:

```
In [33]:
    # create a stacked area plot
    # generate a 4-column data frame of random data
    np.random.seed(seedval)
    dfa = pd.DataFrame(np.random.rand(10, 4),
```

```
                    columns=['a', 'b', 'c', 'd'])

# create the area plot
dfa.plot(kind='area');
```

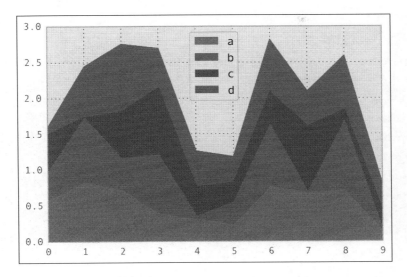

To produce an unstacked plot, specify `stacked=False`:

In [34]:

```
    # do not stack the area plot
    dfa.plot(kind='area', stacked=False);
```

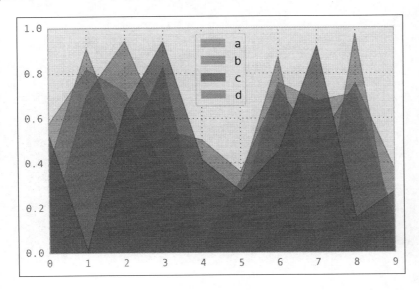

By default, unstacked plots have an alpha value of 0.5, so that it is possible to see how the data series overlaps.

Scatter plots

A scatter plot displays the correlation between a pair of variables. A scatter plot can be created from `DataFrame` using `.plot()` and specifying `kind='scatter'`, as well as specifying the x and y columns from the `DataFrame` source:

```
In [35]:
    # generate a scatter plot of two series of normally
    # distributed random values
    # we would expect this to cluster around 0,0
    np.random.seed(111111)
    sp_df = pd.DataFrame(np.random.randn(10000, 2),
                    columns=['a', 'b'])
    sp_df.plot(kind='scatter', x='a', y='b')
```

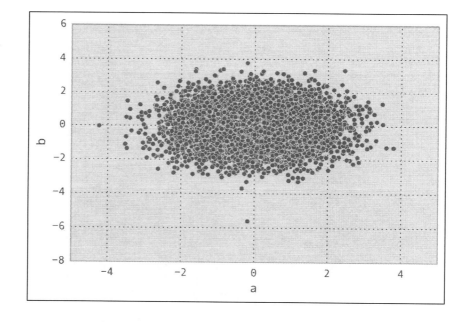

We can easily create more elaborate scatter plots by dropping down a little lower into matplotlib. The following code gets Google stock data for the year of 2011 and calculates delta in the closing price per day, and renders close versus volume as bubbles of different sizes, derived on the size of the values in the data:

```
In [36]:
    # get Google stock data from 1/1/2011 to 12/31/2011
    from pandas.io.data import DataReader
    stock_data = DataReader("GOOGL", "yahoo",
                            datetime(2011, 1, 1),
                            datetime(2011, 12, 31))

    # % change per day
    delta = np.diff(stock_data["Adj Close"])/stock_data["Adj Close"][:-1]

    # this calculates size of markers
    volume = (15 * stock_data.Volume[:-2] / stock_data.Volume[0])**2
    close = 0.003 * stock_data.Close[:-2] / 0.003 * stock_data.Open[:-2]

    # generate scatter plot
    fig, ax = plt.subplots()
    ax.scatter(delta[:-1], delta[1:], c=close, s=volume, alpha=0.5)

    # add some labels and style
    ax.set_xlabel(r'$\Delta_i$', fontsize=20)
    ax.set_ylabel(r'$\Delta_{i+1}$', fontsize=20)
    ax.set_title('Volume and percent change')
    ax.grid(True);
```

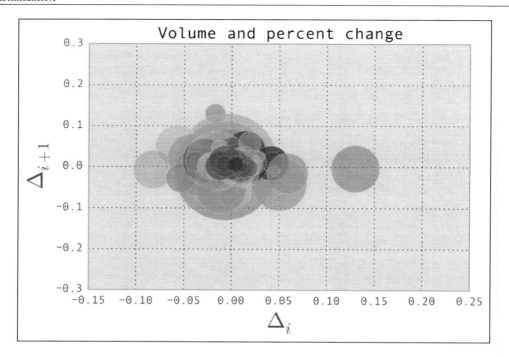

 Note the nomenclature for the x and y axes labels, which creates a nice mathematical style for the labels.

Density plot

You can create kernel density estimation plots using the `.plot()` method and setting the `kind='kde'` parameter. A kernel density estimate plot, instead of being a pure empirical representation of the data, makes an attempt and estimates the true distribution of the data, and hence smoothes it into a continuous plot. The following generates a normal distributed set of numbers, displays it as a histogram, and overlays the `kde` plot:

```
In [37]:
    # create a kde density plot
    # generate a series of 1000 random numbers
    np.random.seed(seedval)
    s = pd.Series(np.random.randn(1000))
```

```
# generate the plot
s.hist(normed=True) # shows the bars
s.plot(kind='kde');
```

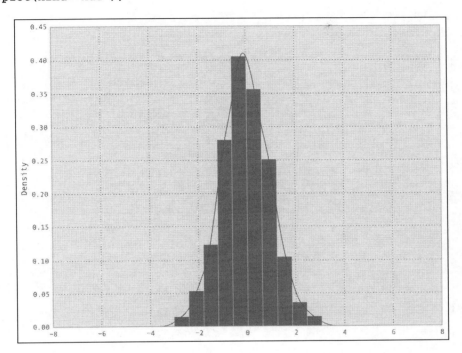

The scatter plot matrix

The final composite graph we'll look at in this chapter, is one that is provided by pandas in its plotting tools subcomponent: the scatter plot matrix. A scatter plot matrix is a popular way of determining whether there is a linear correlation between multiple variables. The following creates a scatter plot matrix with random values, which then shows a scatter plot for each combination, as well as a kde graph for each variable:

```
In [38]:
    # create a scatter plot matrix
    # import this class
    from pandas.tools.plotting import scatter_matrix

    # generate DataFrame with 4 columns of 1000 random numbers
```

```
np.random.seed(111111)

df_spm = pd.DataFrame(np.random.randn(1000, 4),
                      columns=['a', 'b', 'c', 'd'])
# create the scatter matrix
scatter_matrix(df_spm, alpha=0.2, figsize=(6, 6), diagonal='kde');
```

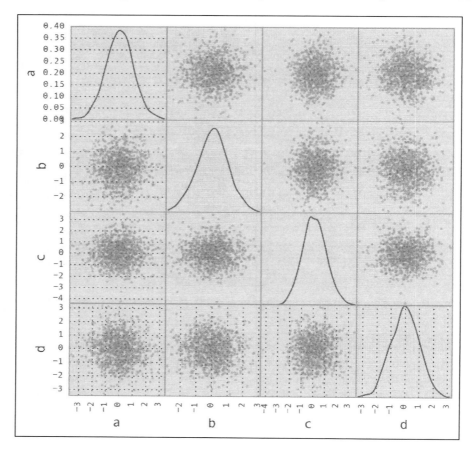

 We will see this plot again, as it is applied to finance in the next chapter, where we look at correlations of various stocks.

Heatmaps

A heatmap is a graphical representation of data, where values within a matrix are represented by colors. This is an effective means to show relationships of values that are measured at the intersection of two variables, at each intersection of the rows and the columns of the matrix. A common scenario, is to have the values in the matrix normalized to 0.0 through 1.0 and have the intersections between a row and column represent the correlation between the two variables. Values with less correlation (0.0) are the darkest, and those with the highest correlation (1.0) are white.

Heatmaps are easily created with pandas and matplotlib using the `.imshow()` function:

```
In [39]:
    # create a heatmap
    # start with data for the heatmap
    s = pd.Series([0.0, 0.1, 0.2, 0.3, 0.4],
                  ['V', 'W', 'X', 'Y', 'Z'])
    heatmap_data = pd.DataFrame({'A' : s + 0.0,
                                 'B' : s + 0.1,
                                 'C' : s + 0.2,
                                 'D' : s + 0.3,
                                 'E' : s + 0.4,
                                 'F' : s + 0.5,
                                 'G' : s + 0.6
                                })
    heatmap_data
```

```
Out [39]:
       A     B     C     D     E     F     G
    V  0.0   0.1   0.2   0.3   0.4   0.5   0.6
    W  0.1   0.2   0.3   0.4   0.5   0.6   0.7
    X  0.2   0.3   0.4   0.5   0.6   0.7   0.8
    Y  0.3   0.4   0.5   0.6   0.7   0.8   0.9
    Z  0.4   0.5   0.6   0.7   0.8   0.9   1.0
```

```
In [40]:
    # generate the heatmap
    plt.imshow(heatmap_data, cmap='hot', interpolation='none')
```

```
plt.colorbar()  # add the scale of colors bar
# set the labels
plt.xticks(range(len(heatmap_data.columns)), heatmap_data.columns)
plt.yticks(range(len(heatmap_data)), heatmap_data.index);
```

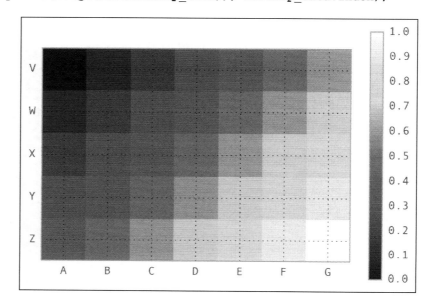

 We will see an example of heatmaps to show correlations in the next chapter.

Multiple plots in a single chart

It is often useful to contrast data by displaying multiple plots next to each other. This is actually quite easy to when using matplotlib.

To draw multiple subplots on a grid, we can make multiple calls to `plt.subplot2grid()`, each time passing the size of the grid the subplot is to be located on (`shape=(height, width)`) and the location on the grid of the upper-left section of the subplot (`loc=(row, column)`). Each call to `plt.subplot2grid()` returns a different `AxesSubplot` object that can be used to reference the specific subplot and direct the rendering into.

The following demonstrates this, by creating a plot with two subplots based on a two row by one column grid (`shape=(2,1)`). The first subplot, referred to by `ax1`, is located in the first row (`loc=(0,0)`), and the second, referred to as `ax2`, is in the second row (`loc=(1,0)`):

```
In [41]:
    # create two sub plots on the new plot using a 2x1 grid
    # ax1 is the upper row
    ax1 = plt.subplot2grid(shape=(2,1), loc=(0,0))
    # and ax2 is in the lower row
    ax2 = plt.subplot2grid(shape=(2,1), loc=(1,0))
```

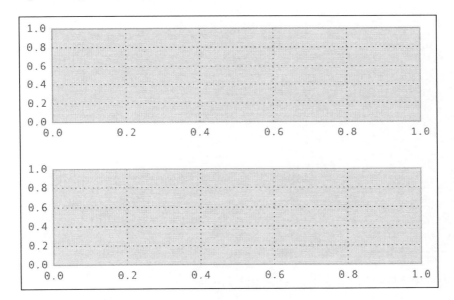

The subplots have been created, but we have not drawn into either yet.

The size of any subplot can be specified using the `rowspan` and `colspan` parameters in each call to `plt.subplot2grid()`. This actually feels a lot like placing content in HTML tables.

The following demonstrates a more complicated layout of five plots, specifying different row and column spans for each:

```
In [42]:
    # layout sub plots on a 4x4 grid
    # ax1 on top row, 4 columns wide
    ax1 = plt.subplot2grid((4,4), (0,0), colspan=4)
```

```
# ax2 is row 2, leftmost and 2 columns wide
ax2 = plt.subplot2grid((4,4), (1,0), colspan=2)
# ax3 is 2 cols wide and 2 rows high, starting
# on second row and the third column
ax3 = plt.subplot2grid((4,4), (1,2), colspan=2, rowspan=2)
# ax4 1 high 1 wide, in row 4 column 0
ax4 = plt.subplot2grid((4,4), (2,0))
# ax4 1 high 1 wide, in row 4 column 1
ax5 = plt.subplot2grid((4,4), (2,1));
```

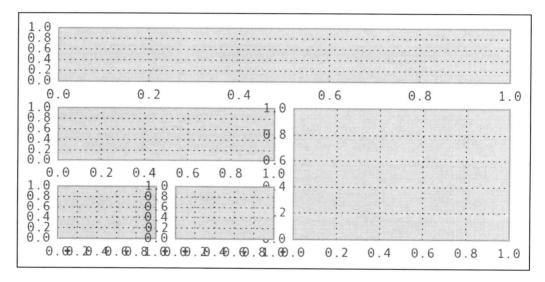

To draw into a specific subplot using the pandas .plot() method, you can pass the specific axes into the plot function via the ax parameter. The following demonstrates this by extracting each series from the random walk we created at the beginning of the chapter, and drawing each into different subplots:

```
In [43]:
    # demonstrating drawing into specific sub-plots
    # generate a layout of 2 rows 1 column
    # create the subplots, one on each row
    ax5 = plt.subplot2grid((2,1), (0,0))
    ax6 = plt.subplot2grid((2,1), (1,0))
```

```
# plot column 0 of walk_df into top row of the grid
walk_df[[0]].plot(ax = ax5)
# and column 1 of walk_df into bottom row
walk_df[[1]].plot(ax = ax6);
```

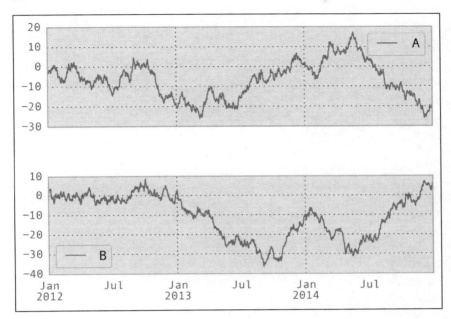

Using this technique, we can perform combinations of different series of data, such as a stock close versus volume graph. Given the data we read during a previous example for Google, the following will plot the volume versus the closing price:

```
In [44]:
    # draw the close on the top chart
    top = plt.subplot2grid((4,4), (0, 0), rowspan=3, colspan=4)
    top.plot(stock_data.index, stock_data['Close'], label='Close')
    plt.title('Google Opening Stock Price 2001')

    # draw the volume chart on the bottom
    bottom = plt.subplot2grid((4,4), (3,0), rowspan=1, colspan=4)
    bottom.bar(stock_data.index, stock_data['Volume'])
```

```
plt.title('Google Trading Volume')

# set the size of the plot
plt.gcf().set_size_inches(15,8)
```

Summary

Visualizing your data is one of the best ways to quickly understand the story that is being told with the data. Python, pandas, and matplotlib (and a few other libraries) provide a means of very quickly, and with a few lines of code, getting the gist of what you are trying to discover, as well as the underlying message (and displaying it beautifully too).

In this chapter, we examined many of the most common means of visualizing data from pandas. There are also a lot of interesting visualizations that were not covered, and indeed, the concept of data visualization with pandas and/or Python is the subject of entire texts, but I believe this chapter provides a much-needed reference to get up and going with the visualizations that provide most of what is needed.

In the next and final chapter of the book, we will look at a few applied applications of pandas, which also demonstrates visualizing real-world information.

12

Applications to Finance

Throughout the first 11 chapters of this book, we looked at pandas and how you perform various tasks with the library. We focused mostly on how to work with pandas, often using made-up data created to demonstrate the feature but with an occasional diversion now and then into some more real-world examples.

In this final chapter, we will use pandas to perform a number of different financial analyses of stock data obtained from Yahoo! Finance. We will briefly cover a number of topics in financial analysis. The focus will be on using pandas to derive results from the domain of finance, specifically, time-series stock data, and not on details of the financial theory.

Specifically, in this chapter, we will progress through the following tasks:

- Fetching and organizing stock data from Yahoo!
- Plotting time-series prices
- Plotting volume-series data
- Calculating simple daily percentage change
- Calculating simple daily cumulative returns
- Resampling data from daily to monthly returns
- Analyzing distribution of returns
- Performing a moving-average calculation
- Comparing average daily returns across stocks
- Correlating stocks based on the daily percentage change of closing price
- Volatility calculation
- Determining risk relative to expected returns

Setting up the IPython notebook

The first step is to make sure that we have included all of the necessary Python libraries for all of the tasks that will be performed. This includes matplotlib for graphs, `datetime` to manage various dates and time in the data, a few methods from NumPy, and random number capabilities from the random library:

```
In [1]:
    # necessary imports for the workbook
    import pandas as pd
    import pandas.io.data
    import numpy as np
    import datetime
    import matplotlib.pyplot as plt


    # Set some pandas options
    pd.set_option('display.notebook_repr_html', False)
    pd.set_option('display.max_columns', 6)
    pd.set_option('display.max_rows', 10)
    pd.set_option('display.width', 78)
    pd.set_option('precision', 4)


    # do all our graphics inline
    %matplotlib inline
```

Obtaining and organizing stock data from Yahoo!

The first step we will take is to write a couple of functions that help us with retrieving stock data from Yahoo! Finance. We have already seen that this data can be read using a pandas `DataReader` object, but we will need to organize the data a little differently than how it is provided by Yahoo! as we are going to perform various pivots of this information later.

To facilitate this, we will start with the following function to get all the Yahoo! data for a specific stock between the two specified dates and also add the stock's symbol in a column for each entry. This will be needed later for pivots:

In [2]:

```
# read data from Yahoo! Finance for a specific
# stock specified by ticker and between the start and end dates
def getStockData(ticker, start, end):
    # read the data
    data = pd.io.data.DataReader(ticker, "yahoo", start, end)
    # rename this column
    data.rename(columns={'Adj Close': 'AdjClose'}, inplace=True)
    # insert in the ticker as a column
    data.insert(0, "Ticker", ticker)
    return data
```

For consistency and reproducibility by the reader, examples in this chapter will use a fixed 3-year window spanning the years of 2012 through 2014. The following reads data for that 3-year period for the MSFT ticker and prints the first 5 rows:

In [3]:

```
# request the three years of data for MSFT
start = datetime.datetime(2012, 1, 1)
end = datetime.datetime(2014, 12, 31)
getStockData("MSFT", start, end).head()
```

Out [3]:

	Ticker	Open	High	...	Close	Volume	AdjClose
Date				...			
2012-01-03	MSFT	26.55	26.96	...	26.77	64731500	24.42
2012-01-04	MSFT	26.82	27.47	...	27.40	80516100	25.00
2012-01-05	MSFT	27.38	27.73	...	27.68	56081400	25.25
2012-01-06	MSFT	27.53	28.19	...	28.11	99455500	25.64
2012-01-09	MSFT	28.05	28.10	...	27.74	59706800	25.31

```
[5 rows x 7 columns]
```

Now that we have a function that can get data for a single ticker, it will be convenient to have a function that can read the data for multiple tickers and return them all in a single data structure. The following code performs this task:

```
In [4]:
    # gets data for multiple stocks
    # tickers: a list of stock symbols to fetch
    # start and end are the start and end dates
    def getDataForMultipleStocks(tickers, start, end):
        # we return a dictionary
        stocks = dict()
        # loop through all the tickers
        for ticker in tickers:
            # get the data for the specific ticker
            s = getStockData(ticker, start, end)
            # add it to the dictionary
            stocks[ticker] = s
        # return the dictionary
        return stocks
```

The examples in this chapter will use historical quotes for **Apple (AAPL)**, **Microsoft (MSFT)**, **General Electric (GE)**, **IBM (IBM)**, **American Airlines (AA)**, **Delta Airlines (DAL)**, **United Airlines (UAL)**, **Pepsi (PEP)**, and **Coca Cola (KO)**.

These stocks were chosen deliberately to have a sample of multiple stocks in each of three different sectors: technology, airlines, and soft drinks. The purpose of this is to demonstrate how to derive correlations in various stock price measurements over the selected time period among the stocks in similar sectors and to also demonstrate the difference in stocks between sectors.

We can read all of these with the following code, which uses the function we just created:

```
In [5]:
    # get the data for all the stocks that we want
    raw = getDataForMultipleStocks(
        ["MSFT", "AAPL", "GE", "IBM", "AA", "DAL",
         "UAL", "PEP", "KO"],
```

```
      start, end)
```

```
In [6]:
```

```
   # take a peek at the data for MSFT
   raw['MSFT'][:5]
```

```
Out [6]:
```

	Ticker	Open	High	...	Close	Volume	AdjClose
Date				...			
2012-01-03	MSFT	26.55	26.96	...	26.77	64731500	24.42
2012-01-04	MSFT	26.82	27.47	...	27.40	80516100	25.00
2012-01-05	MSFT	27.38	27.73	...	27.68	56081400	25.25
2012-01-06	MSFT	27.53	28.19	...	28.11	99455500	25.64
2012-01-09	MSFT	28.05	28.10	...	27.74	59706800	25.31

```
   [5 rows x 7 columns]
```

We will be particularly interested in the adjusted close values in the `AdjClose` column. However, it would be most convenient for us if we had a `DataFrame` object indexed by date but where each column is the stock ticker for one stock and the values in each column are the adjusted close value for that ticker at that date. We can have this format if we pivot the data around. The following function will do this for us:

```
In [7]:
```

```
   # given the dictionary of data frames,
   # pivots a given column into values with column
   # names being the stock symbols
   def pivotTickersToColumns(raw, column):
       items = []
       # loop through all dictionary keys
       for key in raw:
           # get the data for the key
           data = raw[key]
           # extract just the column specified
           subset = data[["Ticker", column]]
           # add to items
```

```
        items.append(subset)


    # concatenate all the items
    combined = pd.concat(items)
    # reset the index
    ri = combined.reset_index()
    # return the pivot
    return ri.pivot("Date", "Ticker", column)
```

We can now use this to pivot the data to the new organization:

```
In [8]:
    # do the pivot
    close_px = pivotTickersToColumns(raw, "AdjClose")
    # peek at the result
    close_px[:5]


Out [8]:
    Ticker          AA    AAPL    DAL    ...      MSFT     PEP    UAL
    Date                                 ...
    2012-01-03    8.89   55.41   7.92    ...     24.42   60.44  18.90
    2012-01-04    9.10   55.71   7.89    ...     25.00   60.75  18.52
    2012-01-05    9.02   56.33   8.20    ...     25.25   60.28  18.39
    2012-01-06    8.83   56.92   8.19    ...     25.64   59.52  18.21
    2012-01-09    9.09   56.83   8.15    ...     25.31   59.83  17.93


    [5 rows x 9 columns]
```

We now have the adjusted close values for all stocks as values in a column for each respective stock. In this format, we will be able to very easily compare closing price values of each stock against the others.

Plotting time-series prices

We will perform a graphical comparison of the closing values for AAPL and MSFT. Using the closing prices DataFrame, it is simple to plot the values for a specific stock using the .plot() method of Series. The following plots the adjusted closing price for AAPL:

```
In [9]:
    # plot the closing prices of AAPL
    close_px['AAPL'].plot();
```

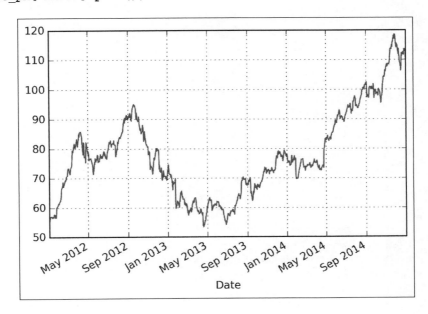

The following code plots the adjusted closing price for MSFT:

```
In [10]:
    # plot the closing prices of MSFT
    close_px['MSFT'].plot();
```

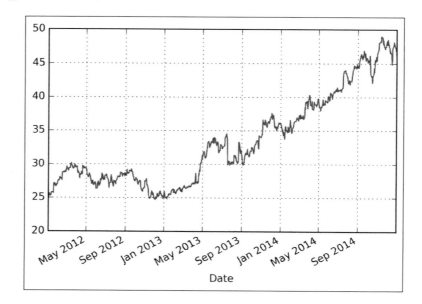

Both sets of closing values can easily be displayed on a single chart in order to give a side-by-side comparison:

```
In [11]:
    # plot MSFT vs AAPL on the same chart
    close_px[['MSFT', 'AAPL']].plot();
```

The output is seen in the following screenshot:

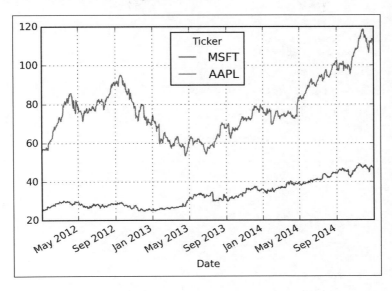

Plotting volume-series data

Volume data can be plotted using bar charts. We first need to get the volume data, which can be done using the `pivotTickersToColumns()` function created earlier:

```
In [12]:
    # pivot the volume data into columns
    volumes = pivotTickersToColumns(raw, "Volume")
    volumes.tail()


Out [12]:
    Ticker           AA      AAPL      DAL ...      MSFT      PEP      UAL
    Date                                   ...
    2014-12-24 4944200 14479600  4296200 ... 11437800 1604100  2714300
    2014-12-26 6355200 33721000  5303100 ... 13197800 1492700  3062200
    2014-12-29 7087800 27598900  6656700 ... 14439500 2453800  2874300
    2014-12-30 9262100 29881500  7318900 ... 16384700 2134400  2644600
    2014-12-31 8842400 41403400  7801700 ... 21552500 3727400  4451200


    [5 rows x 9 columns]
```

We can now use this `DataFrame` to plot a bar chart. The following plots the volume for MSFT:

```
In [13]:
    # plot the volume for MSFT
    msftV = volumes[["MSFT"]]
    plt.bar(msftV.index, msftV["MSFT"])
    plt.gcf().set_size_inches(15,8)
```

The output is seen in the following screenshot:

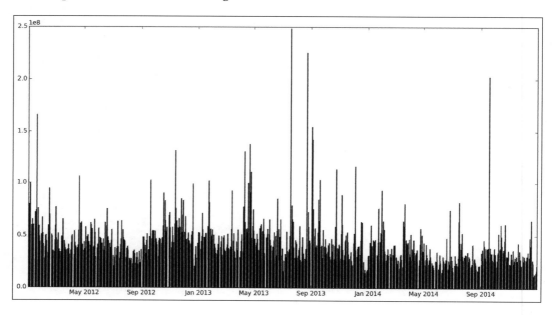

A common type of financial graph plots a stock volume relative to its closing price:

```
In [14]:
    # draw the price history on the top
    top = plt.subplot2grid((4,4), (0, 0), rowspan=3, colspan=4)
    top.plot(close_px['MSFT'].index, close_px['MSFT'], label='MSFT\
    Adjusted Close')
    plt.title('Microsoft Adjusted Close Price 2012 - 2014')
    plt.legend(loc=2)

    # and the volume along the bottom
    bottom = plt.subplot2grid((4,4), (3,0), rowspan=1, colspan=4)
```

```
bottom.bar(msftV.index, msftV['MSFT'])
plt.title('Microsoft Trading Volume 2012 - 2014')
plt.subplots_adjust(hspace=0.75)
plt.gcf().set_size_inches(15,8)
```

The output is seen in the following screenshot:

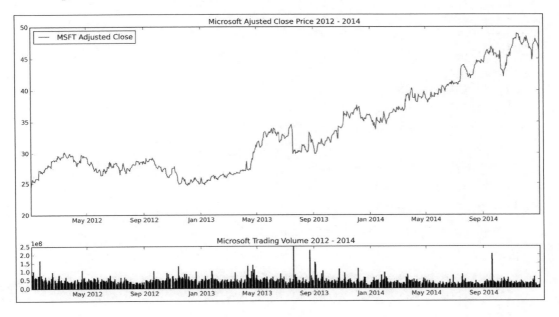

Calculating the simple daily percentage change

The simple daily percentage change (without dividends and other factors) is the percentage change in value of a stock over a single day of trading. It is defined by the following formula:

$$r_t = \frac{p_t}{p_{t-1}} - 1$$

This can be easily calculated in pandas using `.shift()`:

```
In [15]:
    # calculate daily percentage change
    daily_pc = close_px / close_px.shift(1) - 1
    daily_pc[:5]
```

```
Out [15]:
    Ticker          AA     AAPL     DAL   ...      MSFT     PEP     UAL
    Date                                  ...
    2012-01-03     NaN      NaN     NaN   ...       NaN     NaN     NaN
    2012-01-04   0.024    0.005  -0.004   ...     0.024   0.005  -0.020
    2012-01-05  -0.009    0.011   0.039   ...     0.010  -0.008  -0.007
    2012-01-06  -0.021    0.010  -0.001   ...     0.015  -0.013  -0.010
    2012-01-09   0.029   -0.002  -0.005   ...    -0.013   0.005  -0.015

    [5 rows x 9 columns]
```

A quick check shows you that the return for AAPL on 2011-09-08 is correct:

```
In [16]:
    # check the percentage on 2012-01-05
    close_px.ix['2012-01-05']['AAPL'] / close_px.ix['2012-01-04']\
    ['AAPL'] -1
```

```
Out [16]:
    0.011129061209836699
```

Plotting the daily percentage change yields the following plot:

```
In [17]:
    # plot daily percentage change for AAPL
    daily_pc["AAPL"].plot();
```

The output is seen in the following screenshot:

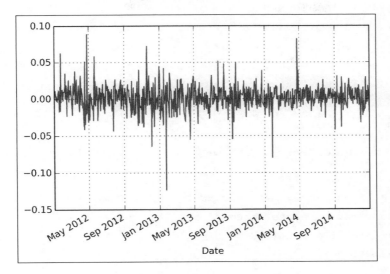

A plot of daily percentage change will tend to look like noise, as shown in the preceding chart. However, when we use the cumulative product of these values, known as the daily cumulative return, then we can see how the value changes over time.

Calculating simple daily cumulative returns

We can calculate the cumulative daily return by taking the cumulative product of the daily percentage change. This calculation is represented by the following equation:

$$i_t = \left(1 + r_t\right) \cdot i_{t-1}, \quad i_0 = 1$$

This is actually calculated very succinctly using the following code, which utilizes the .cumprod() method:

```
In [18]:
    # calculate daily cumulative return
    daily_cr = (1 + daily_pc).cumprod()
    daily_cr[:5]

Out [18]:
    Ticker          AA    AAPL    DAL    ...    MSFT    PEP    UAL
```

```
Date                            ...
2012-01-03   NaN   NaN   NaN   ...    NaN   NaN   NaN
2012-01-04   1.024  1.005  0.996  ...   1.024  1.005  0.980
2012-01-05   1.015  1.017  1.035  ...   1.034  0.997  0.973
2012-01-06   0.993  1.027  1.034  ...   1.050  0.985  0.963
2012-01-09   1.022  1.026  1.029  ...   1.036  0.990  0.949

[5 rows x 9 columns]
```

We can plot the cumulative returns to see how the different stocks compare:

```
In [19]:
    # plot all the cumulative returns to get an idea
    # of the relative performance of all the stocks
    daily_cr.plot(figsize=(8,6))
    plt.legend(loc=2);
```

The output is seen in the following screenshot:

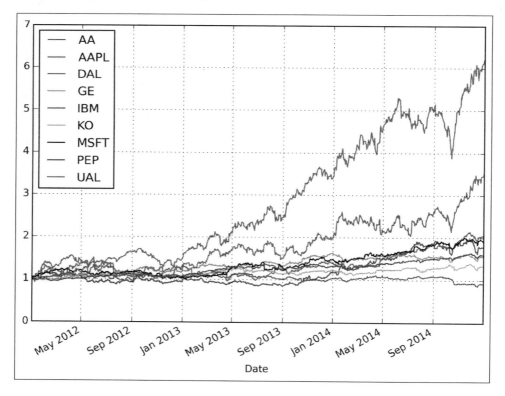

Resampling data from daily to monthly returns

To calculate the monthly rate of return, we can use a little pandas magic and resample the original daily dates to throw out the days that are not an end of month value as well as forward filling anywhere there are missing values. This can be done using the `ffill` method to replace any `NaN` values from missing data with the previous value:

```
In [20]:
    # resample to end of month and forward fill values
    monthly = close_px.asfreq('EOM', method="ffill")
    monthly[:5]
```

```
Out [20]:
    Ticker          AA    AAPL    DAL   ...      MSFT     PEP    UAL
    2012-01-31    9.79   61.51  10.39   ...     26.94   59.78  23.10
    2012-02-29    9.83   73.09   9.66   ...     29.15   57.76  20.65
    2012-03-30    9.68   80.79   9.77   ...     29.62   60.89  21.50
    2012-04-30    9.40   78.69  10.79   ...     29.40   60.57  21.92
    2012-05-31    8.29   77.85  11.92   ...     26.98   62.76  25.17

    [5 rows x 9 columns]
```

Note the date of the entries and how they are now only month-end dates. Values have not changed as the resample only selects the dates at the end of the month or fills the value with the value prior to that date if it did not exist in the source.

Now we can use this to calculate the monthly percentage changes:

```
In [21]:
    # calculate the monthly percentage changes
    monthly_pc = monthly / monthly.shift(1) - 1
    monthly_pc[:5]
```

```
Out [21]:
    Ticker          AA     AAPL    DAL    ...     MSFT     PEP     UAL
    2012-01-31     NaN      NaN    NaN    ...      NaN     NaN     NaN
    2012-02-29   0.004    0.188 -0.070    ...    0.082  -0.034  -0.106
```

```
2012-03-30  -0.015   0.105   0.011   ...    0.016   0.054   0.041
2012-04-30  -0.029  -0.026   0.104   ...   -0.007  -0.005   0.020
2012-05-31  -0.118  -0.011   0.105   ...   -0.082   0.036   0.148
```

```
[5 rows x 9 columns]
```

From that result, calculate the monthly cumulative returns and plot the results:

```
In [22]:
    # calculate monthly cumulative return
    monthly_cr = (1 + monthly_pc).cumprod()
    monthly_cr[:5]
```

```
Out [22]:
    Ticker         AA    AAPL    DAL   ...    MSFT    PEP    UAL
    2012-01-31    NaN     NaN    NaN   ...     NaN    NaN    NaN
    2012-02-29  1.004   1.188  0.930   ...   1.082  0.966  0.894
    2012-03-30  0.989   1.313  0.940   ...   1.099  1.019  0.931
    2012-04-30  0.960   1.279  1.038   ...   1.091  1.013  0.949
    2012-05-31  0.847   1.266  1.147   ...   1.001  1.050  1.090
```

```
[5 rows x 9 columns]
```

```
In [23]:
    # plot the monthly cumulative returns
    monthly_cr.plot(figsize=(12,6))
    plt.legend(loc=2);
```

The output is seen in the following screenshot:

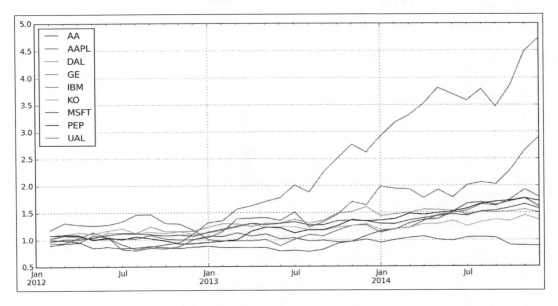

This looks very similar to the daily returns, but overall, it is not as smooth. This is because it uses roughly a 30th of the data and is tied to the end of month.

Analyzing distribution of returns

You can get a feel for the difference in distribution of the daily percentage changes for a particular stock by plotting that data in a histogram. A trick with generating histograms for data such as daily returns is to select the number of bins to lump values into. We will use 50 bins, which gives you a good feel for the distribution of daily changes across three years of data.

To demonstrate, the following shows you the distribution of the daily percentage change for AAPL:

```
In [24]:
    # histogram of the daily percentage change for AAPL
    aapl = daily_pc['AAPL']
    aapl.hist(bins=50);
```

The output is seen in the following screenshot:

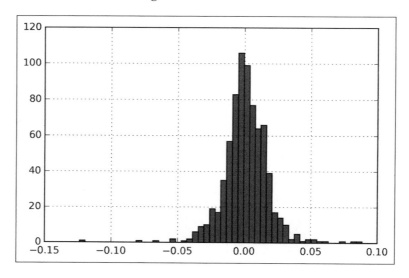

This chart tells us several things. First, most of the daily movements center around 0.0, and there is a small amount of skew to the left, but the data appears fairly symmetric. If we use the .describe() method on this data, we will very quickly get some useful analysis to describe the histogram:

```
In [25]:
    # descriptive statistics of the percentage changes
    aapl.describe()


Out [25]:
    count      753.000
    mean         0.001
    std          0.017
    min         -0.124
    25%         -0.007
    50%          0.001
    75%          0.011
    max          0.089
    Name: AAPL, dtype: float64
```

A valuable conclusion to be drawn from this is the 95 percent coverage interval, which varies from -0.007476 to 0.010893. This states that over this 3-year period, the daily percent of change fit between these two percentages 95 percent of the time. This gives us a sense of the overall volatility in the stock. Technically, the closer these values, the less volatile the stock over that time.

We can plot the histograms of the daily percentage change for all the stocks in a single histogram matrix plot. This gives us a means to quickly determine the differences in stock behavior over these 3 years:

In [26]:

```
# matrix of all stocks daily percentage changes histograms
daily_pc.hist(bins=50, figsize=(8,6));
```

The output is seen in the following screenshot:

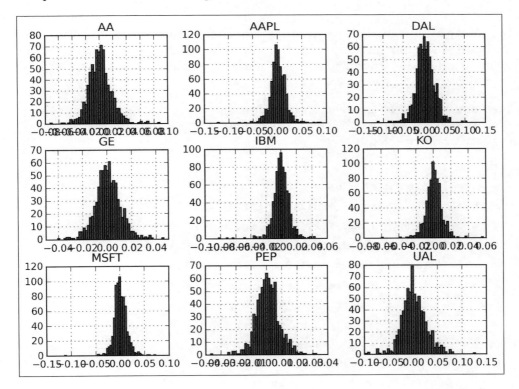

 The labels on the axis are a bit squished together, but it's the histogram shape that is the most important.

From this chart, we can very easily see the difference in performance of these nine stocks during this time, particularly, the skewedness (more exceptional values on one side of the mean) as well as easily being able to easily see the difference in the overall distribution at various confidence levels, thereby giving a quick view of which stocks have been more or less volatile.

This is an excellent demonstration of the value of a picture versus using raw data items. Exploratory analysis like this is made very simple by the pandas ecosystem and allows you to more agilely analyze information.

Performing a moving-average calculation

The moving average of a stock can be calculated using the pandas statistical package that is a part of pandas and is in the `pd.stats` namespace, specifically, the `.rolling_mean()` function.

The moving average will give you a sense of the performance of a stock over a given time period by eliminating "noise" in the performance of the stock. The larger the moving window, the smoother and less random the graph will be — at the expense of accuracy.

To demonstrate, the following calculates the moving average for MSFT on 30 and 90 day periods using the daily close. The difference in the reduction of noise can be easily determined from the visual:

```
In [27]:
    # extract just MSFT close
    msft_close = close_px[['MSFT']]['MSFT']
    # calculate the 30 and 90 day rolling means
    ma_30 = pd.stats.moments.rolling_mean(msft_close, 30)
    ma_90 = pd.stats.moments.rolling_mean(msft_close, 90)
    # compose into a DataFrame that can be plotted
    result = pd.DataFrame({'Close': msft_close,
                           '30_MA_Close': ma_30,
                           '90_MA_Close': ma_90})
    # plot all the series against each other
    result.plot(title="MSFT Close Price")
    plt.gcf().set_size_inches(12,8)
```

The output is seen in the following screenshot:

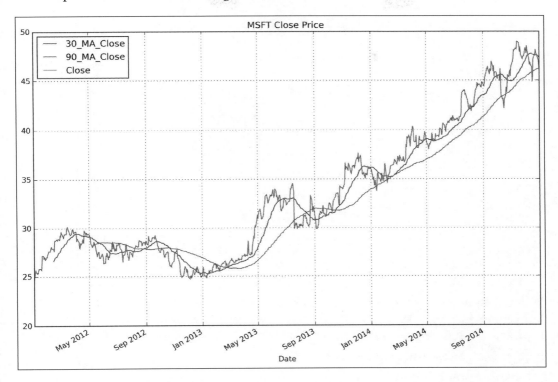

The comparison of average daily returns across stocks

A scatter plot is a very effective means of being able to visually determine the relationship between the rates of change in stock prices between two stocks. The following graphs the relationship of the daily percentage change in the closing price between MSFT and AAPL:

```
In [28]:
    # plot the daily percentage change of MSFT versus AAPL
    plt.scatter(daily_pc['MSFT'], daily_pc['AAPL'])
    plt.xlabel('MSFT')
    plt.ylabel('AAPL');
```

The output is seen in the following screenshot:

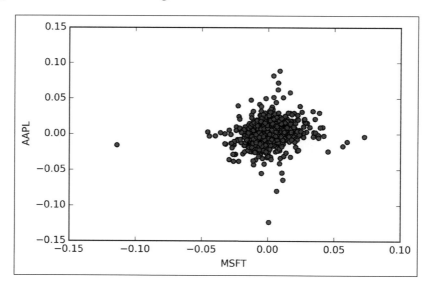

What this gives us is a very quick view of the overall correlation of the daily returns between the two stocks. Each dot represents a single day for both stocks. Each dot is plotted along the vertical based on the percentage change for AAPL and along the horizontal for MSFT.

If for every amount that AAPL changed in value, MSFT also changed an identically proportional amount each day, then all the dots would fall along a perfect vertical diagonal from the lower-left to upper-right section. In this case, the two variables would be perfectly correlated with a correlation value of 1.0. If the two variables were perfectly uncorrelated, the correlation and hence the slope of the line would be 0, which is perfectly horizontal.

To demonstrate what a perfect correlation would look like, we can plot MSFT versus MSFT. Any such series when correlated with itself will always be 1.0:

In [29]:

```
# demonstrate perfect correlation
plt.scatter(daily_pc['MSFT'], daily_pc['MSFT']);
```

The output is seen in the following screenshot:

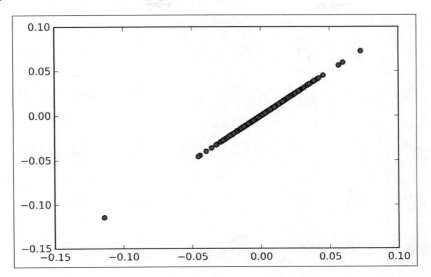

Getting back to the plot of AAPL versus MSFT, excluding several outliers, this cluster appears to demonstrate a moderate correlation between the two stocks.

An actual regression actually shows the correlation to be 0.213 (the slope of the regression line). The regression line would be more toward horizontal than diagonal. This means that for any specific change in the price of AAPL, statistically, we would, more times than not, not be able to predict the change in price of MSFT on the given day from the price change in AAPL.

To facilitate the bulk analysis of multiple correlations, pandas provides the very useful scatter matrix graph, which will plot the scatters for all combinations of stocks. This plot gives a very easy means of eyeballing correlations between all of the combinations:

In [30]:

```
# plot the scatter of daily price changes for ALL stocks
pd.scatter_matrix(daily_pc, diagonal='kde', figsize=(12,12));
```

The output is seen in the following screenshot:

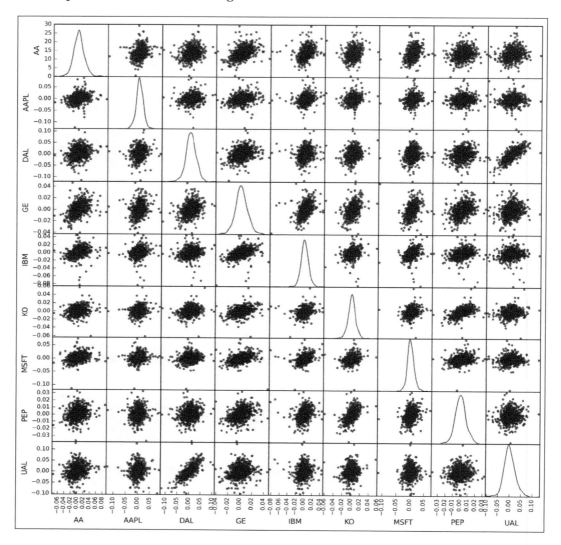

The diagonal in this plot is a kernel density estimation graph. If you refer to the section on using histograms to show the distribution of daily percentage changes for a single stock, this plot is essentially the same information, giving you a quick overview of how volatile the different stocks are relative to each other. The narrower curves are less volatile than those that are wider, with the skew representing a tendency for greater returns or losses.

The correlation of stocks based on the daily percentage change of the closing price

The previous section mentioned briefly the concept of correlation. Correlation is a measure of the strength of the association between two variables. A correlation coefficient of 1.0 means that every change in value in one set of data has a proportionate change in value to the other set of data. A 0.0 correlation means that the data sets have no relationship. The higher the correlation, the more ability there is to predict a change in the other based on a change in the first.

The correlation between columns of data in `DataFrame` can be calculated very easily by simply calling its `.corr()` method. This will produce a matrix of all possible correlations between the variables represented by the values in all columns. To demonstrate, the following calculates the correlation in the daily percentage change in the close price for all of these stocks over the 3 years of the sample:

```
In [31]:
    # calculate the correlation between all the stocks relative
    # to daily percentage change
    corrs = daily_pc.corr()
    corrs
```

```
Out [31]:
    Ticker    AA     AAPL   DAL    ...    MSFT   PEP    UAL

    Ticker                         ...

    AA        1.000  0.236  0.251  ...    0.310  0.227  0.223

    AAPL      0.236  1.000  0.135  ...    0.187  0.092  0.062

    DAL       0.251  0.135  1.000  ...    0.149  0.174  0.761

    GE        0.458  0.239  0.317  ...    0.341  0.381  0.237

    IBM       0.311  0.212  0.168  ...    0.356  0.258  0.124

    KO        0.228  0.161  0.187  ...    0.271  0.557  0.139

    MSFT      0.310  0.187  0.149  ...    1.000  0.284  0.127

    PEP       0.227  0.092  0.174  ...    0.284  1.000  0.130

    UAL       0.223  0.062  0.761  ...    0.127  0.130  1.000


    [9 rows x 9 columns]
```

The diagonal is 1.0, as a series is always perfectly correlated with itself. This correlation matrix can be visualized using a heat map with the following code:

```
In [32]:
    # plot a heatmap of the correlations
    plt.imshow(corrs, cmap='hot', interpolation='none')
    plt.colorbar()
    plt.xticks(range(len(corrs)), corrs.columns)
    plt.yticks(range(len(corrs)), corrs.columns)
    plt.gcf().set_size_inches(8,8)
```

The output is seen in the following screenshot:

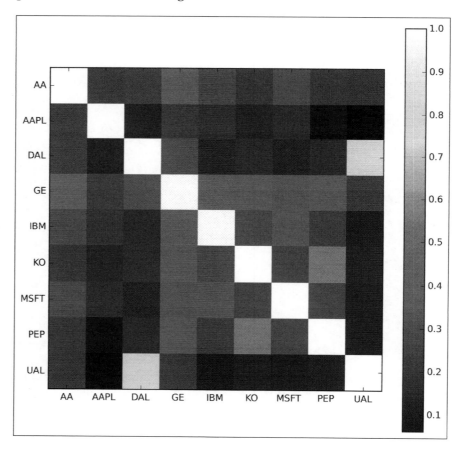

The idea with this diagram is that you can see the level of correlation via color by finding the intersection of vertical and horizontal variables. The darker the color, the less the correlation; the lighter the color, the greater the correlation. The diagonal is necessarily white (1.0), as it is each stock compared to itself.

Volatility calculation

The volatility of a stock is a measurement of the amount change of variance in the price of a stock over a specific period of time. It is common to compare the volatility to another stock to get a feel for which may have less risk or to a market index to compare the stock's volatility to the overall market. Generally, the higher the volatility, the riskier the investment in that stock.

Volatility is calculated by taking a rolling-window standard deviation on percentage change in a stock (and scaling it relative to the size of the window). The size of the window affects the overall result. The wider a window, the less representative the measurement will become. As the window narrows, the result approaches the standard deviation. So, it is a bit of an art to pick the proper window size based on the data sampling frequency. Fortunately, pandas makes this very easy to modify interactively.

As a demonstration, the following calculates the volatility of the stocks in our sample given a window of 75 periods:

```
In [33]:
    # 75 period minimum
    min_periods = 75
    # calculate the volatility
    vol = pd.stats.moments.rolling_std(daily_pc, min_periods) * \
            np.sqrt(min_periods)
    # plot it
    vol.plot(figsize=(10, 8));
```

The output is seen in the following screenshot:

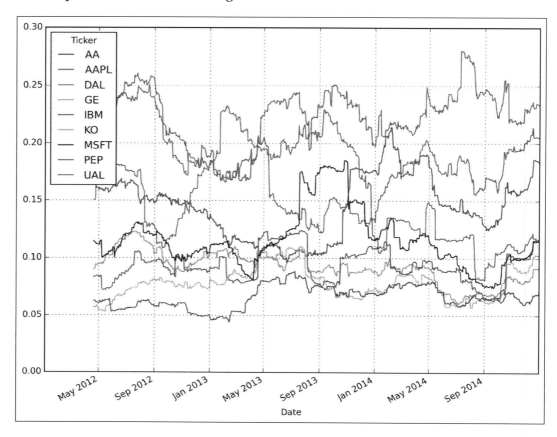

Lines higher on the chart represent overall higher volatility, and the change of volatility over time is shown.

Determining risk relative to expected returns

A useful analysis is to relate the volatility of a stock's daily percentage change to its expected return. This gives a feel for the risk/return ratio of the investment. This can be performed by mapping the mean of the daily percentage change relative to the standard deviation of the same values.

To demonstrate, the following code will create a scatter plot that relates the risk and return of our sample set of stocks:

```
In [34]:
    # generate a scatter of the mean versus std of daily % change
    plt.scatter(daily_pc.mean(), daily_pc.std())
    plt.xlabel('Expected returns')
    plt.ylabel('Risk')

    # this adds fancy labels to each dot, with an arrow too
    for label, x, y in zip(daily_pc.columns,
                           daily_pc.mean(),
                           daily_pc.std()):
        plt.annotate(
            label,
            xy = (x, y), xytext = (30, -30),
            textcoords = 'offset points', ha = 'right', va = 'bottom',
            bbox = dict(boxstyle = 'round,pad=0.5',
                        fc = 'yellow',
                        alpha = 0.5),
            arrowprops = dict(arrowstyle = '->',
                              connectionstyle = 'arc3,rad=0'))

    # set ranges and scales for good presentation
    plt.xlim(-0.001, 0.003)
    plt.ylim(0.005, 0.0275)

    # set size
    plt.gcf().set_size_inches(8,8)
```

The output is seen in the following screenshot:

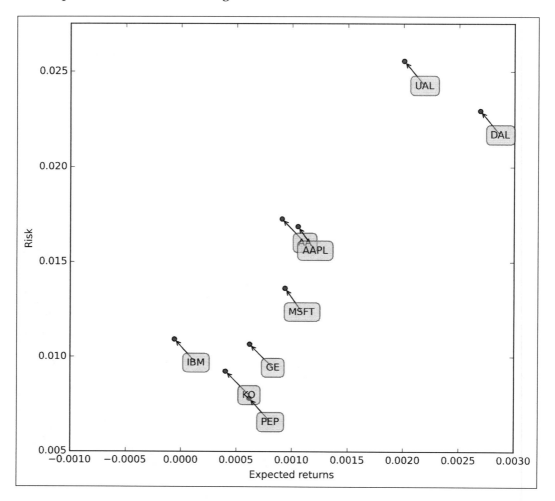

The results of this immediately jump out from the visualization and may have been more difficult to see by just looking at tables of numbers:

- Airline stocks (AA, DAL, and UAL) have the highest risk but also have the highest returns (Isn't that the general rule of investing?)
- Our tech stocks are of medium risk but also have medium return.
- Among the tech stocks, IBM and GE are the most conservative of the four.
- The cola stocks have the lowest risk but are also among the lowest returns as a group. This makes sense for a high-volume commodity.

Summary

We have reached the end of our journey in learning about pandas and the features it offers for data manipulation. Prior to this chapter, we spent our time mostly learning the features, most of the time using data designed to demonstrate the concepts instead of using real-world data.

In this chapter, we used everything that we learned up to this point to demonstrate how easy it is to use pandas to analyze real-world data—specifically, stock data—and derive results from the data, and in many cases, make quick conclusions through visualizations designed to make the patterns in the data apparent.

This chapter also introduced a number of financial concepts, such as the daily percentage change, calculating returns, and the correlation of time-series data, among several others. The focus was not on financial theory but to demonstrate how easy it is to use pandas to manage and derive meaning from what was otherwise just lists and lists of numbers.

In closing, it is worth noting that although pandas was created by financial analysts—hence its ability to provide simple solutions in the financial domain—pandas is in no way limited to just finance. It is a very robust tool for data science and can be applied just as effectively to many other domains. Several of these are emerging markets with significant opportunity, such as social network analysis or applications of wearable computing, such as fitness data collected continuously and used to make people healthier. Whatever your domain of use for pandas, I hope you find using pandas as fascinating as I do.

Index

Symbols

A

B

C

K

Kenneth French data
  accessing 225, 226
  URL 225

L

Linux
  Anaconda, installing 30, 31
logical operation
  on NumPy arrays 59-61

M

Mac OS X
  Anaconda, installing 32, 33
markers
  reference link 412
mathematical operations
  NaN values, handling 246, 247
matplotlib 3
melting 298, 299
missing data
  backward filling 250, 251
  DataFrame objects, determining 239-241
  dropping 241-245
  filling in 248, 249
  forward filling 250, 251
  index labels, used for filling 251
  missing values, interpolation 252-255
  NaN values in Series, determining 239, 241
  selecting out 241-245
  working with 237-239
moving average calculation
  average daily returns, comparing against
      stocks 461-464
  performing 460
multiple plots, in single charts 436-439

N

NaN values
  determining, in DataFrame objects 239-241
  determining, in Series 239, 240
  in mathematical operations 246

nbviewer
  URL 45
noise rows
  in field-delimited data, handling 201-203
nonhierarchical indexes
  used, for stacking 291-293
Not-A-Number (NaN) 106, 107
Numerical Python (NumPy)
  about 3, 49
  importing 50
  installing 50
  sliceability 52
NumPy arrays
  advantages 50, 51
  combining 70-73
  creating 52-57
  elements, selecting 58
  logical operations 59-61
  numerical methods 79-82
  operations, performing 52-57
  reshaping 65-69
  slicing 61-64
  splitting 73-78
NumPy ndarray 100, 101

O

objects, DataFrame
  concatenating, pd.concat() used 159-164
offsets
  anchored offsets 364-366
  date offsets 360-363
  PeriodIndex 368-370
  period object 366-368
  used, for calculating new dates 359

P

pandas
  about 1, 2, 83
  Anaconda, installing 27
  data 271
  features 2, 3
  importing 85
  IPython Notebooks 3-5

Thank you for buying
Learning pandas

About Packt Publishing

Packt, pronounced 'packed', published its first book, *Mastering phpMyAdmin for Effective MySQL Management*, in April 2004, and subsequently continued to specialize in publishing highly focused books on specific technologies and solutions.

Our books and publications share the experiences of your fellow IT professionals in adapting and customizing today's systems, applications, and frameworks. Our solution-based books give you the knowledge and power to customize the software and technologies you're using to get the job done. Packt books are more specific and less general than the IT books you have seen in the past. Our unique business model allows us to bring you more focused information, giving you more of what you need to know, and less of what you don't.

Packt is a modern yet unique publishing company that focuses on producing quality, cutting-edge books for communities of developers, administrators, and newbies alike. For more information, please visit our website at www.packtpub.com.

About Packt Open Source

In 2010, Packt launched two new brands, Packt Open Source and Packt Enterprise, in order to continue its focus on specialization. This book is part of the Packt Open Source brand, home to books published on software built around open source licenses, and offering information to anybody from advanced developers to budding web designers. The Open Source brand also runs Packt's Open Source Royalty Scheme, by which Packt gives a royalty to each open source project about whose software a book is sold.

Writing for Packt

We welcome all inquiries from people who are interested in authoring. Book proposals should be sent to author@packtpub.com. If your book idea is still at an early stage and you would like to discuss it first before writing a formal book proposal, then please contact us; one of our commissioning editors will get in touch with you.

We're not just looking for published authors; if you have strong technical skills but no writing experience, our experienced editors can help you develop a writing career, or simply get some additional reward for your expertise.

Python Data Analysis

ISBN: 978-1-78355-335-8   Paperback: 348 pages

Learn how to apply powerful data analysis techniques with popular open source Python modules

1. Learn how to find, manipulate, and analyze data using Python.

2. Perform advanced, high performance linear algebra and mathematical calculations with clean and efficient Python code.

3. An easy-to-follow guide with realistic examples that are frequently used in real-world data analysis projects.

IPython Interactive Computing and Visualization Cookbook

ISBN: 978-1-78328-481-8   Paperback: 512 pages

Over 100 hands-on recipes to sharpen your skills in high-performance numerical computing and data science with Python

1. Leverage the new features of the IPython notebook for interactive web-based big data analysis and visualization.

2. Become an expert in high-performance computing and visualization for data analysis and scientific modeling.

3. A comprehensive coverage of scientific computing through many hands-on, example-driven recipes with detailed, step-by-step explanations.

Please check **www.PacktPub.com** for information on our titles